Desert Places

ROBYN DAVIDSON

Desert Places

VIKING

VIKING
Published by the Penguin Group
Penguin Books USA Inc., 375 Hudson Street, New York, New York 10014, U.S.A.
Penguin Books Ltd, 27 Wrights Lane, London W8 5TZ, England
Penguin Books Australia Ltd, Ringwood, Victoria, Australia
Penguin Books Canada Ltd, 10 Alcorn Avenue, Toronto, Ontario, Canada M4V 3B2
Penguin Books (N.Z.) Ltd, 182–190 Wairau Road, Auckland 10, New Zealand

Penguin Books Ltd, Registered Offices:
Harmondsworth, Middlesex, England

First American edition
Published in 1996 by Viking Penguin,
a division of Penguin Books USA Inc.

1 3 5 7 9 10 8 6 4 2

Photograph credits
Dilip Mehta/Contact/Colorific: 1, 2, 3, 5, 9, 10, 11, 17, 19, 20, 21, 22
Robyn Davidson: 4, 6, 7, 8, 12, 13, 14, 15, 16, 18

LIBRARY OF CONGRESS CATALOGING IN PUBLICATION DATA
Davidson, Robyn, 1950–
Desert places / Robyn Davidson.
p. cm.
ISBN 0-670-84077-7
1. Rabaris—Social life and customs. 2. Nomads—Thar Desert (India and Pakistan)
3. Thar Desert (India and Pakistan)—Description and travel. 4. Thar Desert (India
and Pakistan)—Social life and customs. I. Title.
DS432.R13D38 1996
954´.4—dc20 96-21394

This book is printed on acid-free paper.
∞

Printed in the United States of America
Set in Monotype Bembo

They cannot scare me with their empty spaces
Between stars — on stars where no human race is.
I have it in me so much nearer home
To scare myself with my own desert places.

Robert Frost, 'Desert Places'

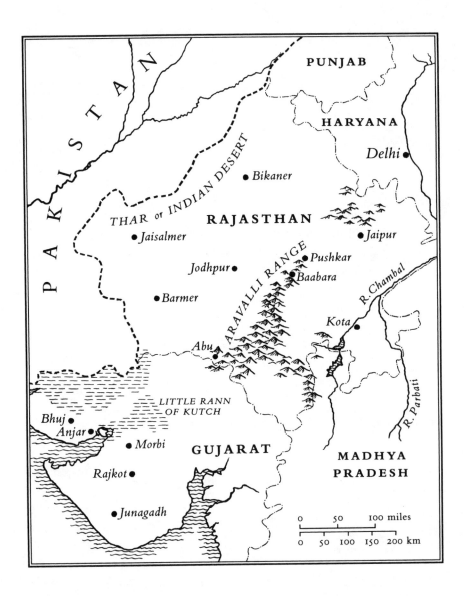

PAKISTAN

PUNJAB

HARYANA

Delhi

Bikaner

THAR or INDIAN DESERT

RAJASTHAN

Jaisalmer

Jaipur

Jodhpur

Pushkar

Baabara

Barmer

ARAVALLI RANGE

R. Chambal

Kota

Abu

R. Parbati

LITTLE RANN
OF KUTCH

Bhuj

Anjar

Morbi

GUJARAT

MADHYA
PRADESH

Rajkot

Junagadh

0   50   100 miles

0   50   100 150 200 km

Prelude

Memory is a capricious thing. The India I visited in 1978 consists of images of doubtful authenticity held together in a ground of forgetfulness. I don't know how or why I ended up in the medieval lanes of Pushkar, in Rajasthan, during one of the most important festivals in the Hindu calendar. But I'm almost sure I was the only European around.

The crowd was a deluge drowning individual will. It unmoored things from their meanings. Turbans and tinsel, cow horns lyre-shaped and painted blue, the fangs of a monkey, eyes thumbed with kohl looking into my own before bobbing under the torrent, a corner of something carved in stone, hands clutching a red veil, a dacoit playing an Arabian scale on his flute, his yards of moustache coiled in concentric circles on his cheeks – all these elements sinking and reappearing, breaking and recombining, borne along by the will of the crowd in which a whirlpool was forming, sucking me to its centre.

A beggar was lying on his back. His legs were broken and folded, permanently, into his groin. He moved sideways along the lane, using the articulations of his spine, through garbage and faeces, drawing his flotsam along with him, rolling his eyes backwards in his head and muttering mantras, or perhaps nonsense. He wore a white dhoti and his body was whitened with ash. His turban was parrot green and I think I remember make-up on his face, though I may have painted it on afterwards. A parrot took coins from the tentacles of arms swirling above it and placed them in a bowl on its master's stomach. I breasted through the crowd, past the limbs of street sleepers jumbled in shadows, hindered by hands and imprecations, out at last to air.

You can walk for months in Australia without meeting a single human. Thousands of miles empty of footprints, unburdened by history's mistakes. Through an association with the original inhabitants I had learnt to see that wilderness as a garden – man's primordial home before the plough. The tracks of the ancestors mapped it and gave it meaning so that however far an individual might travel from the place of origin, in the deepest possible sense he or she was forever at home in the world. In Aboriginal society everyone received a share of goods and the only hierarchy was one based on accumulated knowledge to which everyone could aspire. The Australian desert and the hunter-gatherers who translated it had so informed my spirit that the crowds of Pushkar were unnatural and frightening to me – evidence that agriculture had been my species' greatest blunder.

Thousands of camels were tethered on hills surrounding the town. Nomads had come here from all over north India to buy and sell their animals. I climbed up to their encampments, away from the river of souls. When I reached the crest of the hill I turned to look back. A full moon had risen. The rumble of the crowd was muffled under a layer of pink dust. There was a sensation of suspension. All around me camels sat peacefully chewing the cud. Groups of men lounged back on the sand sharing chillums. A woman called me over to her fire. Her dress was a sunset of reds, pinks and silver. When she moved, ornaments rattled. A veil was draped over a contraption in her hair so that it peaked like a pixie's hat. Had she pulled out a wand and offered me three wishes, I would not have found her more fantastic. She flung down a camel-hair mat, tugged me on to it and seemed to be asking if I would swap my necklace for her silver one. I tried to explain that hers would be more valuable than mine and, despite her entreaty to stay longer, wandered away.

But a wish was forming. It took the shape of an image. I was building a little cooking fire in the shelter of soft, pink dunes, far away from anything but a world of sand. It was twilight, the lyrical hour. The nomads were gathering beside me by the fire. There was fluency and lightness between us. We had walked a long way together. The image exalted the spirit with its spareness and its repose. My only excuse for having it is that I was young, and youth is vulnerable to Romantic sentiment.

I made some inquiries. The nomads were called Raika or Rabari and they herded camels and sometimes sheep. There was a folklorist in Jodhpur who knew everything about them and would be happy to answer my queries but was busy entertaining a French journalist that week. I had eight days left in India. French journalist notwithstanding, I had to try my luck.

The only other European on the plane was a French woman. So when she went to shake hands with a personification of elegance dressed in black jodhpurs, black kurta, black sunglasses and black moustache – who, minus the sunglasses, might have stepped out of a Persian miniature on to the tarmac – I buried my reticence, followed her and said, 'Excuse me. You are the folklorist, Mr Gomal Khotari?'

'No, but I know Khotari Sahib very well.' There was a pause, then, 'Haven't we met somewhere before?'

Sometimes it seems as if a larger power gives a damn what you do with your life. One minute you are meandering along the road you have chosen, then suddenly you are shoved up a side street where small enticements, like crumbs laid down for a bird, encourage you to believe that you are meant to travel in this direction though you can see nothing familiar up ahead. I glanced at the surrounding strangeness, at this least forgettable of creatures and said, 'I shouldn't think so.'

'But of course, you are the woman who walked across Australia with some camels. I've just been reading about you. You must come and stay in my home. My father will be delighted to meet you. How odd that you should arrive here just as I was thinking of writing to you.'

You don't have to believe in omens to be seduced by them.

He was some sort of nobleman and some sort of politician but he might have been from Sirius, so impenetrably Other did he seem to me then. I perched in the back of his World War Two jeep which bumped through the dust to a large, red-stone house with dark rooms and servants who brought tea at the clap of hands.

The Narendra I know now would not have clapped hands for a

servant. Yet I see us sitting in the paradigm of rooms from which all other, inferior rooms derive – a high-ceilinged room containing a punkah, a black telephone and a wall-to-wall mattress covered in embroidered bolsters and cushions. Narendra is half reclined on the bolsters and clapping his hands like something out of *The Arabian Nights*. Tea does appear and is placed on squat, octagonal tables, one each. The tables are edged in silver. And there is Narendra's father, the Colonel, dressed in a riding outfit, with an English cap on his shaven head, boasting about what his chest measurement had been when he was young and giving me the secret of his phenomenal health – a cup of hot ghee at four in the morning followed by push-ups and a ten-mile run.

'I will introduce you to a Raika who can train a camel to bring breakfast in the mornings. We will employ that man and you must come here to live with us and learn everything there is to know about camels. I will be interested to learn also, though I am more fond of horses. But tomorrow you and I will take the jeep to Jaisalmer.' Another person comes into the room – Narendra's sister, Minu. She is wrapped in a cocoon of blue silk; there is gold in her nose, on her arms, on her toes. She is one of the most beautiful women I have ever seen. She has spent her married life locked in purdah in a castle. She has been allowed out now to visit her family because she has just married off her only daughter.

The Colonel did drive me to Jaisalmer, a city of carved golden stone set at the edge of the Thar. I was not feeling well – the third world's revenge on the colonizer's stomach. But it would not do to admit to any kind of weakness when in the company of the Colonel. Tales of his bravery could be heard in every village from Bikaner to Kota. He was illiterate, wildly eccentric, capable of guiltless cruelty, and the embodiment of the virtues of an ancient warrior class. We stopped that night in a tiny village in the desert. My bones were unhinged by the drive, my ears and nose clogged with grit, my stomach behaving only by an effort of will. The Colonel was as crisp as a spring day. In a dark one-roomed tavern he ordered food.

'Colonel, I don't think I could . . .'

'Nonsense. It will do you good.'

Two bowls were placed by the candle on a wooden table. One

vegetable curry, one meat. My spoon knocked against something in the bowl. I pulled the candle towards it. It was an unclipped goat's hoof. This is what I remember but I do not know how much truth there is in it. I have never since seen a goat's hoof in a curry. And no Indian eating-houses I've been in since have been lit by so soft a light or been as still as a painting. And Jaisalmer, seen several times since then was, that first time, a vision. Later the Colonel bought me a bottle of bootleg liquor from some gypsies. The sediment in the bottom of the bottle, he said, was crushed pearls.

Back in Jodhpur, we all agreed that I would return the following year to travel with and write about the Raika. And a visiting astrologer studied my stars and confirmed that I would arrive in August.

He was wrong.

Years passed and, with them, any desire to live with nomads. But the images of the crippled beggar and the Raika woman by her fire remained juxtaposed in memory because they were illustrations of persistent preoccupations – freedom and restriction, wandering and sedentariness.

This century has witnessed the greatest upheavals of population in man's history. Yet it is also witnessing the end of traditional nomadism, a description of reality that has been with us since our beginnings – our oldest memory of being. And there are new kinds of nomads, not people who are at home everywhere, but who are at home nowhere. I was one of them.

After the first abandonment of the place of my birth I had lived in England, in America, lost count of the countries I had visited and had several times returned to Australia only to leave again. Somewhere in the midst of that tremendous restlessness I had lost the sense of a gravitational centre, a place with which to compare elsewhere. I now felt as much an anthropologist (mystified, alien, lonely) at a dinner party with my peers, as I did with a family of Aborigines eating witchetty grubs in a creek bed. By 1989 the feeling of being cut off at the source was becoming difficult to tolerate. I made a decision to settle in London and to try to learn to belong.

But when a friend invited me to dinner saying that he had a

surprise, and when the surprise turned out to be Narendra who was six inches shorter than I remembered him and not nearly so awesome and who, having greeted me as if we had seen each other just a month ago rather than the eleven years that had passed, reminded me of my promise to write about the Rabari and invited me to India as if it were the most unexceptional thing in the world, what could I do but agree? So it was that serendipity beckoned me again up that side alley of life and doesn't it restore faith to think that improbable meetings can set a new course, just when you think there is nothing around you but stones?

Narendra assured me that living with the nomads would be easy enough to organize. I could meet a group at the Pushkar festival and complete a year's migratory cycle with them. Easy perhaps, but it would require money and that would mean getting the sponsorship of a magazine and putting up with a photographer occasionally. If a small voice warned against eating one's words (I had sworn never to do such a thing again) it was drowned out by a chorus of pragmatisms.

I wrote a proposal; suborned editors with that twilight-and-dune picture that had been mouldering in my mental attic; signed contracts.

PART ONE

False Starts

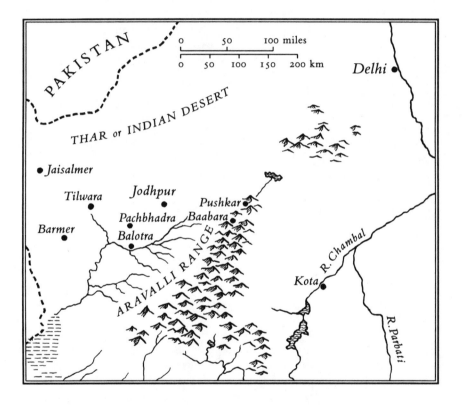

1

And arrived in India on the day of the worst communal violence since Independence.

The images I retained from the previous visit were tourist images: festivals, chiffon-clad women, decaying castles, peacocks settling in dusty trees. Or they were of 'old friends', stuck in improbable settings like those cardboard carnival cartoons behind which you place your face for the photograph: Narendra being lathered and shaved as he sits on a chair on his lawn; Minu covering her face with blue silk while she talks about the rights of women. The India I had constructed from books was tolerant and rational – a country where algebra, geometry and astronomy had been studied while Europe sank into its Dark Ages, where chess and the decimal system were invented, where great men and women had sacrificed themselves to an ideal and built a functioning democracy on the ruins of colonialism, where different intellectual opinions and religious beliefs could co-exist in peace – an India that bore little relation to what was going on outside this room.

The hotel television showed angry crowds running through streets, lathi-charging policemen, religious fanatics shouting at the camera.

As part of its effort to garner a vote bank, a right-wing Hindu chauvinist party, the Bharatiya Janata Party (BJP), had organized a march across India to Ayodhya, a small northern town revered by Hindus as the legendary birthplace of Lord Ram. There they intended to build a temple on the exact spot where there happened to be a fifteenth-century mosque – the Babri Masjid. The BJP leader Advani, who headed the ten-thousand-kilometre procession, disported himself in a giant saffron-coloured vehicle designed to look like Ram's chariot. Huge crowds of Hindu devotees had gathered, often attacking Muslim neighbourhoods along the way. Advani was arrested before he arrived at the site where a hundred thousand kar sevaks (Hindu holy volunteers) were waiting. Some of them attempted to storm the mosque. Police opened fire. The country erupted.

Pushkar festival was a fortnight away but people were being advised not to attend populous events and anyway, there was a public transport strike. It was impossible to buy a jeep in Delhi as they had all been requisitioned by the army. I paced the hotel room, devouring newspapers and television reports, until Narendra rang. He had to return to his farm in Jodhpur, two days' drive west into Rajasthan. He could drop me off in Pushkar on the way. We arrived there just in time to see herds of camels and their Raika owners dispersing in small groups, as ordered by batteries of armed police.

As for the Land of Enchantment . . . Where once little markets had cobbled together, selling everything from inlaid camel saddles to cantilevered bras, there were now rows of portable western latrines done up to look like maharajahs' tents and shops selling I'VE BEEN TO PUSHKAR T-shirts. Foreign tourists appeared to outnumber locals, most of whom had to depend on public transport which was still strike-bound. The Agriculture Ministry and the Tourism Ministry had set different dates for the fair. The nomads came early and the pilgrims came late. Any hope of heading off with the Raika was defunct.

Narendra went on to Jodhpur. I waited to meet the photographer Dilip Mehta who had been commissioned by the magazine to illustrate the Raika story. I already knew him and liked him. I also knew that writers and photographers belonged to different species and when push came to shove, which it inevitably did, relations between them could get a little strained. Therefore it was important to establish a rapport with Dilip as soon as possible. I did not have the mentality of a journalist. I liked to take my time, muse, dream – a way of absorbing information that drove real journalists crazy. Dilip had flown in the night before from Hong Kong, or Lapland, or somewhere, and driven straight here, only to find that there was nothing to photograph. Nevertheless he set off with his Nikons, looking like thunder and got into an altercation with some pilgrims who accused him of taking pictures of women bathing in the sacred tank. He returned to Delhi. I fled to Jodhpur in a taxi. There were larger things to worry about than rapport.

The night I arrived eight people were murdered in communal riots and curfew was imposed for the first time in Jodhpur's history. I wanted to stay in a hotel. The Colonel wanted me to stay with him in the town-house. Minu sent word that I should stay with her in Ghanerao. And Narendra insisted that I stay on his farm where there was a one-room cottage, just for me. I caved in to a hospitality unique to India and chose the farm for its quiet.

Narendra's house consisted of two round, red-stone jhumpas (vernacular Rajasthan architecture) with two smaller ones off each side, all roofed with conical thatch and joined by stone passages. Inside the cool white rooms a few handsome objects were distributed, simple and lovely. Shuttered windows opened on to views of chilli fields skirting castles or were covered by sticks dripping water – traditional air-conditioning. Surrounding the buildings was a raised mud and dung stoep where squirrels, birds, cobras and stoats came to sun themselves. My own little room, a hundred yards from the house, had for its roof a water tank.

On that first morning I woke to the sound of water plunging down into irrigation ditches and to peacocks, richly dressed and vacuous as maharajahs, howling like cats in the tree outside my window. From my door stretched blue-green fields dotted with trees and the coloured saris of women going to work. Grey cranes lifted their trousers and stalked about in the water like English academics on some esoteric field-trip.

My first task was trying to acquire some reliable information about the nomads. According to a census report from the nineteenth century they were camel thieves, cactus-eaters and stealers of wheat. And a Mr Dutt wrote in 1871 of the glories of Pushkar: 'We saw camels starting from this place to cross the desert, carrying men and women with their packages and supplies of food and water.' These, plus a small mention in *Annals of Rajasthan* by Colonel Todd, were the only references to Rabaris or Raikas I had been able to find in all the libraries of England.

From what I could make out, Rabari was the more generic term, while Raika designated a specific camel-breeding subcaste. But this was not a fixed rule and only later was the significance of naming made clearer to me. In any case, the nomads' origin outside India was lost in time. They were certainly Indo-European, light-skinned and often green- or blue-eyed. In the annals of the Indus Valley civilizations there was no mention of sheep or camels. Presumably the nomads brought them with them when they came. They had two main divisions, the Maru and Chalkia. Maru traditionally dealt only in camels, the animal with which all Rabari felt most strongly associated, believing its creation to be coeval with their own, whereas the Chalkia kept herds of sheep and goat. Their history began in Jaisalmer in the Thar Desert, from which over the centuries they had spread with their animals into other states, integrating themselves into Hindu cosmology as they went, splintering into sub-castes but retaining, always, their 'Rabariness', their otherness.

Everyone I met had something to say about them but whatever one person stated as fact another refuted. Similarly everyone agreed that travelling with them on migration would be very easy to organize but no one suggested exactly how it could be done.

Oh, those hesitant first steps across alien terrain when you don't know the rules. You curb your spontaneity in an effort to behave in an acceptable fashion. You do away with any critical faculty which might block absorption. You do not know which advice to take, what information is true. How unstable you feel. To blunder and be forgiven, that is to allow yourself to be what you are, may be a better way of proceeding but that brand of courage was not in my nature. I crept cautiously where others may have bounded.

My plan was to purchase a jeep and drive around the desert areas by myself until I found just that group of Rabari with whom there was a strong rapport. Then, in a few months' time, I would buy myself some camels at Chaitri livestock fair near Barmer. After which I would continue to live in whatever village had been chosen until it was time to take off on migration.

Buying a jeep took more than a week. Day after day Narendra's number one servant Khan ji, ever-smiling, ever calm, shepherded me along gullies and streets, from bank to office to bank again, organized the papers, led me to other mysterious buildings, answered questions on my behalf, indicated where I should sit, sign, wait and sign again. But at last the papers were in order and there is something empowering about sitting behind the wheel of your very own jeep, banging your fist on the horn and finding your way home through lanes hardly wider than the car – lanes which, minus scooter-rickshaws, diesel fumes, synthetic saris and plastic goods dangling from the roofs of minute shops, would have looked just like this centuries ago.

'You must have a driver.'

'Narendra, I have been travelling alone for years. I assure you I do not need a driver.'

My host pondered a moment. 'But now you are in India, and in India you *must* have a driver.' Fantasies of throwing myself at the mercy of the open road, alone and unencumbered, vanished, never to be revived. From that moment on, no matter where I went or what I did, I was to be surrounded either by a phalanx of helpers or, more often, an audience of thousands.

Having accepted the need for a driver it was but a small step to accepting that I needed several other companions (Narendra's friends and servants) and a great deal of luggage for my first trip into the desert and my first meeting with the nomads. Bedding with crisp sheets, for example, and abundant tiffins (multi-tiered metal lunch-boxes containing at least half a dozen curries of the palate-scorching kind).

My companions were as follows: Khan ji, driver, a Rajput who had come from a village at the age of fourteen to work for Narendra, been taught to read and write and who then studied a correspondence course at night until BA level. His passion for self-improvement bordered on the pathological and, being a genius, he was somewhat daunting to be around. Takat Singh ji, an officer in the Border Security Forces and retired head of the Camel Corps. I had seen a photograph of him leading the camel parade on Independence Day through Delhi. Takat was six foot tall, had a proportionately large moustache and a laugh that could seed clouds. Mohan Singh ji, a union boss, incorruptible and deeply committed to political reform. He could speak a few words of English and was, therefore, to be my interpreter. Last on board was Mornat, king of the Rajasthan Jogis. Mornat's people were tribals, that is, outside, or rather below, the caste system. They were gypsies who traditionally hunted with dogs. But these days there was little left to hunt and little free country left to do it in. Narendra had invited Mornat and his extended family to live on his farm, setting a precedent for other Jogis who would eventually have little choice but to settle. In return Mornat, or one of his brothers, tended the log fire at night or brought the family to the house to sing and dance on special occasions, or graced the table with game.

I was somehow to lead this posse of four men without knowing any of the languages they spoke, without understanding anything of the culture in which I found myself, without the slightest clue as to where we were heading or what, really, we were looking for. My own background had fostered a deep independence in me, so that when my team inspected every movement closely or grabbed things from my hand in fits of gallantry, I got performance anxiety and felt inadequate. Perhaps I should have been firmer from the beginning and refused the solicitude of Narendra and his associates. But in India to be alone is to be a freak; to be a woman alone, an insult to chivalry; and to be a European woman alone, an invitation to misunderstanding. Narendra was right. I was in India and I should do things the Indian way, which meant employing as many people as possible to work for you and giving up any hope of ever being solitary.

The jeep was filled with grins, suitcases, arms and legs. All Narendra's staff lined up at the farm gate and bowed deeply with folded hands. Spiritual insurance in the form of yogurt and jaggery (raw sugar) was consumed, hands were brought together invoking Devi to watch out for us. Khan ji tooted the horn several times and everyone laughed and talked above everyone else. Everyone except Memsahib who smiled in a strained sort of way.

'No need to call me Memsahib. Call me Robyn.'

'Yes, Memsahib.'

So unlikely was it that Memsahib could handle a jeep that when I suggested I drive Khan ji merely smiled. We were to meet an important man in Cherai, a village sixty kilometres north of

Jodhpur along the Jaisalmer road. That important man would introduce us to an important man who would introduce us to the most
important man of a Raika village. Or perhaps I'd got it all wrong. I
would simply have to wait and see. After forty kilometres I indicated in as commanding a way as I could muster 'I will now
drive'.

Memsahib sat nervously behind the wheel. Khan ji had been
performing high speed wheelies through the dunes and she wasn't
sure that she could match his style. All went well until we reached a
dry river-bed with two tyre tracks across it. I changed into four-
wheel and slowly negotiated the rocks. There was a bump. A stone
had been dislodged by the front wheel and had punctured our
diesel tank. We were stranded in the desert, surrounded by empty
dunes.

Most men when faced with a calamity such as this would at the
very least kick a tyre and say something unpleasant. Not so these
Rajasthanis. They laughed, they told jokes, they brought out a
tiffin, they spread mats in the miserly shade of an acra bush, they
took turns in sliding under the car and getting covered in grease
and diesel, they went to inspect the guilty rock in order to assure
Memsahib that it wasn't her fault. However, all their assurances
could not save my face and the leadership role was tacitly handed
back to Khan ji who now, having emptied what remained of our
diesel into a container, took the milk of an acra leaf, some soap
and a rag with which to try to fix the hole.

A man on a bicycle emerged out of nothingness and sat down
to enjoy the show. A little later, a family on a camel cart. Eventually a farmer on a tractor pulled up. I use the term 'tractor' loosely
here. Most of the outer structures by which one would recognize
it as such were missing, so that it looked like an insect some boys
had tortured. The farmer stood back and scratched under his
turban, assessing the damage to my vehicle. Then he took the
container of jettisoned diesel, lodged it under the bonnet, fixed it
down with bits of torn rag, pulled the connecting hoses out of the
damaged tank under the chassis and re-routed them up through
the body of the car, realigning the whole fuel system so that it fed
from the makeshift container, and started the engine. Not only did
it work, it got us safely through a couple of hundred kilometres of

sand and rock and was later, with some refinements of engineering, made a permanent improvement on the structure of the jeep. The farmer took a cigarette for his pains and refused food.

We drove on, met the important man, who introduced us to the important man, who took us to meet the most important Raika. In the meantime we had somehow collected another half-dozen helpers. The most difficult aspect of that journey for me was not the impossibility of understanding what was said or what was going on, or trying to breathe in a jeep full of men and burning grit, or even the sense of being an entirely useless human being. It was the fact of having bodily functions. Rajput ladies seemed not to have them. Narendra's sister Minu once told me that the princesses could hold their bladders all the way to Delhi if need be, rather than risk immodesty by going behind a bush, and she herself had only recently worked up the courage to demand to be let out of the car. To hell with that I thought. But euphemisms were necessary. 'Please, Khan ji, could you stop the car? I want to have a wash.' This, in the middle of desert with no water for miles. My companions would gaze out of the windows or at their hands and their faces would take on pained expressions as if I'd just said 'I want to strip naked and dance on the bonnet of the jeep'. And it's not easy relieving yourself when you know there is a carload of men dying of embarrassment not twenty yards away.

The important man of the village, a bearded and emaciated ancient, assured me that there would be no problem in my living with his community and yes I could travel with them. Why not? They used to take their camels into Pakistan, to Sindh, before Partition but now, usually, they went north-east to Uttar Pradesh. He popped a little greasy black stuff in his mouth and smiled beatifically.

'If you go with us you will live on nothing but camel milk. I myself once journeyed through the Thar for over a month without even water . . . but I had af-heem, of course.' He handed me some black stuff which tasted bitter but after a few minutes I, too, smiled and decided that for those who had to cross burning deserts with nothing but milk for sustenance, opium was a necessary part of the luggage.

'And how old are you, Haru Ram ji?' I was imagining he could tell me stories dating from the previous century. 'I am fifty-three,' he said, then added, when he noted the look on my face, 'The life of a nomad is very hard.' Mohan ji explained that opium improves the mind but destroys the body. Another noted that the women never took it unless they were ill, a point which initiated a general discussion about the intellectual superiority of Rabari women over their men. This mental dimorphism was remarked upon countless times throughout Rajasthan – Rabari women were clever, shrewd, outspoken and wise; Rabari men were quiet, simple and thick as planks. The explanation for this was that the men, from the age of seven, were out with the herds, hand-spinning wool and talking to themselves, while the women did all kinds of work, particularly bargaining and money management. Haru Ram ji tucked another piece of af-heem in his mouth and chuckled in a simple sort of way. Simple like a wolf.

'Do you smuggle it in from Pakistan?' I asked. I was assured that the Raika were much too innocent to do such a thing. No, the smugglers were mostly from organized crime cartels based in Bombay. Alcohol went north and heroin came south along the ancient silk-trading route, stashed in the chassis of fat-tyred jeeps with smoked windows which were now as commonplace as drome-daries in the desert citadel of Jaisalmer. Sometimes they sent rider-less camels home to villages in Pakistan, laden down with bootleg. If they were captured by the Border Security Forces, well, it was pretty hard to extract information from a camel. Later I was to find out that the Raika, who had begun migrating through the opium belt of Madhya Pradesh where poppies are grown legally, did indeed smuggle it across the state border tied to the bellies of their sheep.

We arrived at a 360-foot-deep well in the middle of low dunes where some young men dressed in rags were clustered around a pocket radio listening to the news. Apart from the turbulence in the country over the Ayodhya fiasco, the central government had recently accepted the findings of the Mandal Commission Report which recommended that the privileges of reservation (jobs or university placements) be given to 'other backward classes'. If the government acted upon this report the Raika stood to gain cer-tain privileges. But this seemed unlikely because so far more than

17

a hundred university students had burned themselves alive in protest and the carnage was continuing.

Haru Ram ji stared at the ground, followed some tracks and announced that the camels would return in half an hour. I was prepared to believe that pagis (trackers) could identify a camel's parentage by studying its footprint; I was not prepared to believe that Haru Ram ji could read the future on the ground. Half an hour later the herds came wandering in. Haru Ram ji picked an acra leaf, made it into a cup, milked a she camel and gave me the frothy drink. It had a nutty flavour and very little fat. I could think of a lot better things to live on but I could also think of worse.

Not for the last time I cursed my linguistic ignorance. At least one thing was evident as I sat under the trees and floundered in a swamp of sound. The Raika were in trouble and when it came to articulating their misfortunes these normally taciturn men became eloquent.

Previously, farmers and pastoralists had enjoyed a somewhat symbiotic relationship, the graziers providing the farmers with animal dung fertilizer. There was enough room for everyone and enough grazing to provide for visiting herds as well as local animals. The relationship between sedentary and peripatetic peoples had no doubt always required diplomacy but these days it could be explosive.

Today, there is fifty per cent less land available for grazing than there was just ten years ago. The enormous increase in government wells has meant that newly irrigated farms clog the migration routes, turning natural pastureland into salty wastes after only a few years. Small-scale peasants are usually close to destitution, so although they still want the animal's dung they do not want the herds eating the only crop standing between them and ruin, or decimating the grazing that sustains their own animals. During migration fights are prevalent, people are killed and when there is trouble the police almost always take the side of the sedentary folk from whom they skim off the bulk of their illicit income. And governments never like nomads.

Did the Raika have their own ancestral lands, I asked. Yes, these had been given to them by their Rajput rulers under the old jajmani system of feudal Rajasthan. But they were insignificant, certainly too small to sustain herds or to make farms out of. They grew a little bajri (millet) before monsoon and if the rains came they had grain to eat, if not . . . I had seen this stuff sticking out of the sides of sand-dunes, sparse as pubescent whiskers. In any case these men seemed to resent the idea of having to become farmers. They wanted to be allowed to do what they had always done so well and profitably – graze animals.

Many Raika were switching from camels to sheep which are less prestigious but more lucrative. Sheep feed on crop stubble or short pasture (thus doing more damage than the camel and enlarging the desert wastes), so migration patterns now tended to exploit river systems or farming country where the feed is best and also the safest. (In the jungle the animals are vulnerable to attack by jackals and thieves.) Droughts, military no-go areas, atomic testing sites, political boundaries, closure of government forests, the spread of subsidized agriculture – all these factors have forced the pastoral nomads to shift further and further south, out of the deserts and into the greener parts of the country.

My vision of whole communities setting off from the dunes of the Thar Desert with their thousand camels, their hearts set upon Pushkar as Jaisalmer melted into *fata Morganas* behind them, was badly moth-eaten. There were virtually no Raika left in the Jaisalmer area and those who remained, having diminished their herds during famine years, only migrated during exceptionally bad droughts. The old patterns of migration, which on a map might look like ancient river systems, were now more like feeble streams insinuating themselves around countless obstructions, whose beds changed continually and in which local eddies were formed by a backpressure of population. There was simply no room left in India, and the nomads, despite all their flexibility, pragmatism and skill, would be the first to be squeezed out of existence.

We all stared solemnly at the ground in front of us as conversation lapsed. Eventually I asked if I might meet the women. So far in Rajasthan, I had not so much as nodded to another female. They were either locked up in purdah or out in the fields working while their men sat in doorways smoking biri and yarning.

The Raika compound was beyond sight of the village and opened outwards to the 'jungle' – anywhere not cultivated or populated. A few small jhumpas were enclosed by a low wall. All the surfaces were pale ochre mud and dung which the women plastered over stone each year. Doors and lintels were decorated with whitewash. The roofs were made of sticks knotted to form a cone. Everything was neat, swept and aesthetically pleasing.

I was escorted into a jhumpa to sit with the men. The women poked in their heads from time to time to take a look at me. To do this they had to make a little peep-hole in the ornis (shawls) which hid their faces. They had never seen a European before and there was a lot of giggling and whispering outside the door. No one seemed to know quite what to do with me and the shyness was mutual. My companions talked among themselves while I imagined going to sit with Mornat who, being an untouchable, was not allowed inside the compound but waited alone at the perimeter, drinking from his own polluting cup. My reverie was penetrated by two devastating pieces of information which managed to scale the language barrier. Firstly, these women no longer travelled with the men on migration. It was too dangerous. Secondly, there would be no migration this year because the monsoon had been uncharacteristically generous here the previous season.

Dashed hopes lay all over the floor. I asked if they were taking any camels for sale to the Chaitri fair and if so could I go with them? Certainly but no women ever went to that particular fair. Well then, could I come to stay with the women here in the village, then take off with the men when Chaitri time came? Everyone agreed that this was a sensible idea. I could do that and still keep looking for people who *would* be migrating.

Eventually the women invited me into their jhumpa for more tea and as I left the men I sensed a tense expectancy, leading me to suspect that ornis or no, the females called the shots around here and that my plans depended upon their good opinion. The little round room was dark and cool. Handmade mats were stacked to one side and a tiny fireplace was set in the floor. There was no chimney but crooked windows set a cross-breeze, and recesses in the walls held personal possessions – some brass pots, wedding photos posed awkwardly in a studio, pictures of various gods, goddesses and deceased relatives in a shrine. I sat on the floor surrounded by at least twenty women.

Now, my kind of work is often made more difficult by the fact of my sex and I have found it prudent not to call attention to it when I'm on the job. For this project I had chosen neck-to-ankle-to-wrist cream cotton kurta pajamas. My hair was pulled back in a bun and I wore neither make-up nor jewellery. I looked as alluring as a cow pat. Crammed into that tiny room were the most glamorous creatures imaginable with kohl-rimmed eyes, perfect white teeth, bangles up to their armpits, earrings and nose rings and silver balls dangling here and there, a kilogram of silver around each ankle (women carry much of the family wealth in the form of jewellery, a habit which sometimes entices bandits to sever limbs from living bodies), calf-length skirts containing many yards of printed cotton, red-pink-yellow-blue muslin orni stitched over with silver – and from each of those Valkyries a reined-in energy which made me feel that if I lit a match the whole jhumpa would explode.

A senior woman (a widow and therefore dressed in demure maroon with only a few lashings of metal) shushed everyone and turned her attention to me. She did not believe that I couldn't understand what she said so she pushed her face very close to mine and repeated questions in a well-articulated scream. But gestural language is universal, so slowly we came to understand one another. No, I did not have children. (Consternation and muttering.) Why? I thought rapidly. Because my husband died young. (Sighs of commiseration and nodding heads.) Parents? Both dead. (General murmuring.) And how many brothers? I have one sister. What no brothers? No brothers. (A sense of tragedy in the air.) And does your sister have sons? Four daughters. There was respectful silence in the presence of one so persecuted by bad luck and my interlocutor pressed her hands together and indicated a celestial Bhagwan who, she seemed to suggest, moved in mysterious ways. I let out one of those noises which speak of suffering bravely endured, then leavened the mood by lighting a badly needed cigarette.

I already knew that a woman smoking was considered risqué but in this matter refused to make myself acceptable. When the riot had subsided I received affectionate hugs powerful enough to knacker horses and friendly shoves that toppled me over. Suddenly

21

we were talking or rather miming about sex. Two fingers hit the back of the opposite hand amidst ribald guffaws. Other, more explicit gestures were used. 'Could women in my country take new husbands?' Half an hour later I staggered out of that jhumpa drenched in sweat but holding the tree-bark hands of many new friends.

I returned to Jodhpur to prepare for my months in the village.

A week later Takat Singh informed me that the women had changed their minds about letting me live with them. They were flattered that I wanted to write about their lives and had talked of little else since my visit. But there was a problem: 'How will we open up to him?' they had said. 'We'll be too shy.' *Him?* Now I knew what all that chest-prodding had been about.

They had explained the problem to Takat. Three or four centuries ago a group of itinerant actors had asked for the protection of some travelling Raika. It was given and, as is proper, the female guests slept by the women and the male guests by the men. But there was something fishy about those actresses because nine months after they had left even unmarried girls found themselves with child. My friends had liked me but they did not want that to happen to them, thank you very much.

Narendra laughed and said that a few false starts were only to be expected; Minu sent a message suggesting I visit the Raika in Nadol, a village about thirty kilometres from her own village Ghanerao. She also suggested that I wear a skirt, a long skirt. I drove out to Nadol through typical Aravalli Ranges country: granite outcroppings, naked but for a few gullies of monsoon forest or a single, white-painted elephant stationed on a summit eternally surveying the farmlands below. Little temples burrowed into stone crevices; stairs were cut into rockfaces leading up to the sky. Not so long ago this had been jungle, where maharajahs hunted for the last of the tigers.

Originally the Nadol Raika had come from Jodhpur district but fifty years ago there had been some family disagreement so a brother and his family had moved south. Gradually others followed, marriages occurred and now their numbers were in the hundreds.

Nadol was much wealthier than Cherai. New brick houses

were being built to replace prettier but more fragile jhumpas. There was a little temple to Pabu ji, an important historical hero-cum-deity to all the Rabari. I was greeted by the men as usual and taken to sit in a separate compound. Tea was brought and yes I was most welcome to stay the night. But I could see they felt as awkward as I did. A long shadow fell across the ground in front of me. I looked up to see a most astonishing creature. I thought at first it was a eunuch or a man in drag. Could a woman be six foot two and have feet and hands like a Clydesdale? Could a woman have such a *face*? Woman she was, a boss widow, and her name was Teepu.

'Teepu ji, may I sleep at your house tonight?' Her monstrous mouth spread six inches to display two long, eighty-year-old teeth studded with gold. She lifted me off the charpoi (string cot), crushed my ribs in an embrace and marched me away from the men.

As evening fell I observed the village at work. No one hurried or strained yet each went about his or her tasks without pausing for rest. It was like watching the insides of a Swiss clock. Some women ground corn or wheat on huge round stones. Others carried head-bundles of leaves and grass for the sheep and goats now penned behind thorn fences beside the houses. Boys and girls shinned up trees to lop off branches. And where blue smoke curled up could be heard the rattling and patting of young married women cooking chapati, hampered by the weight of bracelets and the perpetual adjustment of orni over their faces.

At seven o'clock thirty camels came in. They were skeletal and covered in mange. A young man rode ringer around them; he had been out grazing them for ten days. He dismounted, picked up a front leg of each, twisted a rope under the hock, then hooked the foot to the shoulder. The camels were so passive they almost lifted their legs to have the ropes tied.

To the camel-herding Raika fate had been particularly unkind. With the demise of the Rajput rulers after Independence and the dissolution of the princely states, the rajahs could no longer afford to keep the herds of camels which had supplied their armies, or the Raika who bred and looked after them. Raika status was deteriorating too because the social and economic ties with the nobility (the Raika referred to themselves as 'younger brothers to the Rajputs') no longer existed in reality.

A pink moon rose, making the turbans glow and the silver shine. Teepu's family gathered around me: three or four younger women, a dozen children — tiny things with silver necklaces and no knickers, wrapped in red shawls. Groups of men came by. I slapped at some mosquitoes. The boy squatting in front of me, staring into my face as if it was the strangest thing he had ever seen, broke into an enormous grin. 'Anopheles. Malaria. Typhoid,' he said — the only English words he knew and he offered them like a gift. Another little boy began to cry. Everyone laughed at him and said, 'Oh, he's singing again. He's always singing.' The wails became louder, as did the laughter. His mother told him not to make such a big noise in front of the guest and put her hand gently on his mouth. Now his screeches could be heard in Ghanerao. His father came and cuddled him, his grannie kissed him, his uncles patted his cheeks, his feet, his hair, his mother wiped his tears with her orni. He was passed from embrace to loving embrace. I have a theory about Indian self-assurance. It does not originate in the comforts of religion. It originates in childhood when anyone under ten is adored beyond measure. Indians may tend to be anxious when away from their family or their group but they do not carry that bodily anxiety, the sense of never being quite at rest, that seems to bedevil so many westerners.

Six charpois were brought out from the two rooms inside the house and lined up on the porch. Now was the time for relaxation and conversation. The older people spoke in Gorwari to the boys who went to school, who then translated into Hindi while I searched in my dictionary or let loose with a repertoire of charades amid explosions of giggles.

'Are there sheep, goats and camels in Australia? What do they eat? What is the price of gold and silver in your country? Why are you interested in us Raika? We are poor people and you are very rich.'

I tried to explain to them what I wanted to do.

'But,' they said, 'we do not migrate any more. Only if there is a bad drought and even then the women rarely come.'

At least that's what I thought they said but later I thought they said they were taking camels to Pushkar, a journey which would surely last weeks.

'And will women go to Pushkar?'

'Absolutely,' said Teepu, 'and you can come with me.' So there it was, a new plan falling, fully formed, into my lap. There was tremendous excitement at the idea of my going with them and Teepu began to describe the fun we would have, ending her speech with 'And the bus fare is only twenty rupees.'

'Bus? You are going to Pushkar by *bus*?'

'Naturally. How else? Why would one walk when one can take a bus?'

'But the camels . . .'

'Two men will go with the camels and it will take them ten days to reach.'

Gradually the men began drifting away, children fell asleep. I hopped on to my charpoi and covered myself with a quilt. A child was tucked in beside me and Teepu lay in the cot alongside, a ten-foot pole in her hand. Everyone slept in what they wore: the women corseted top to bottom in bangles and plaits and rings and necklaces and pixie-hat contraptions and silver leg-irons.

Teepu slept four hours that night during which she would waken, alert, at the smallest sound, tend to a troubled child, pulverize the dogs with her stick or snore like the Delhi Express. As for me, sleep was a shore that could never be reached. I was kept awake by the dogs, the child in the crook of my arm, the coughing, spitting, muttering and the rat which tried to make a nest in my hair. Ten times I threw the wretch to the floor until, after a bitten finger, I did as the other women did – covered my head with a shawl and suffocated while the rat (and his friends) galloped along my quilt. At first fish-belly light Teepu was up and at work. Here a night's sleep was more like an afternoon nap, an insignificant pause in the eternal sameness.

By five the whole village was moving. The men doctored the sheep before letting them out to graze by throwing some powder in their pus-filled eyes, after which the women would spit in them and rub them. The camels were unhobbled; the young herder leapt on to the back of one, laughing and beckoning me up behind him. How dearly I would have loved to go thundering off into the hills on the back of that camel. But Minu had warned me about how a woman should behave. I had thought my clothes the last word in modesty but she suggested I cover myself more, that I do up the top button on my kurta, that I wear an orni, that I hide the string of my pajamas from view. She said, 'Everything has changed in India. People have no fear any more. And they are fed on these dreadful Hindi films. The Raika go to Pushkar and see western girls, drug addicts, going off with taxi wallahs for fifty rupees . . . You must be *careful*!' The camel herder disappeared into the dust, singing his head off and declaiming his manhood to the jungle. When it was time to go Teepu took me aside and whispered, 'Gold is cheap in your country. When you come back, you bring me some and we will bury it where no one knows.'

Six weeks sped by. I visited any number of villages gathering bits and pieces of information, all of it conflicting. Some groups had sold their herds and taken to farming, or gone to seek their fortunes in Bombay, or were selling milk — a taboo occupation until recently. And those who still migrated either went in a contrary direction, or had already been, or did not have to go because of good rains, or sent the men and left the women behind. The only thing certain about any plan I made was that a day, at most a week before execution, it disintegrated. That I was thereby participating in the reality of nomads whose movements depended on such vagaries as the weather and the corruptibility of politicians did not ease my anxiety. Whenever I thought I had found a group, some element essential to my own or the magazine's requirements would be found to be missing. Or the people themselves would think better of it because if something happened to me, wouldn't they be blamed? The graciousness of the rural poor which I everywhere encountered, their exaggerated courtesies which so charmed me and which at all costs they struggled to maintain, was a dignity of living which hid a reservoir of suspicion and fear.

I drove my jeep from village to village until the Gulf War started and India ran out of petrol.

2

If I had to be stranded anywhere Narendra's farm was as good a place as I could wish for. A little isolated perhaps as no one within cooee could speak English and my host was seldom at home. But I could put the empty days to good use by studying Hindi on the principle that once I had absorbed its syntax, it would be but a small step to picking up Marwari or Gorwari or Dingle – or any of the other related languages that the Rabari might speak.

I had a language cassette and accompanying book of grammar but what they hadn't told me in London was that this was 'shud' Hindi, that is, Hindi so high, flowery and convoluted that no one but newsreaders and professors could understand it. The explanations were so arcane I would have made more headway with a textbook on particle physics.

Eventually I abandoned it. No one on the farm spoke Hindi so it seemed more sensible to try to pick up Marwari from the servants. They were all illiterate so I had to invent my own written system for the tongue-torturing phonemes. They did their best for me, bringing tea to my room and staying for biri, jokes and reciprocal English lessons but the effort of communicating was exhausting. I found that when I tried to converse with them, French would come out or some mixture of Hindi and Japanese. Or worse, that all the languages would clog the speech channel so that nothing came out at all. Even Aboriginal words, unused for more than a dozen years, rose from the bottom of memory to muddy the language I so desperately needed to master.

As there was no one to talk to, and as the servants refused to believe that I actually enjoyed doing things for myself, the afternoons in paradise became a little boring. Servants cooked the meals, they sent the washing to the dhobi (launderer), they cleaned my room, they rushed to carry my bags, they were aghast at the idea that I should want to stack the log fire – and if I went to the kitchen to try to cook some food that wasn't flammable with chilli, they hovered and grinned in a pained sort of way. No doubt their Sahib had left instructions that I was to be well cared for and what might the Sahib think of them if he knew I was doing their job. I gave in to their ministrations of course, but the desire to run, to lift, to *do* – the habits of a lifetime – could not be quelled so quickly.

Sometimes I accompanied Mornat to a nearby forest. We would walk together for a couple of hours while he showed me the tracks of wild animals and tried to teach me their names. He had the habit of bringing his hands together in a namaste at the slightest acknowledgement of his presence. Any smile, any attempt to address him, and his body would shrink and the hands would come up – the tic of someone used to living on the bottom of the heap. But in the jungle, his true environment, his spirit expanded (though the hands continued to fly to his chest) and I was able to run, to lift, to do. Often his two sons would accompany us. They had their father's gypsy features – hooked nose and a gaze containing distances – but unlike him they had not yet been humbled. They stood proud as sea captains and looked directly into my eyes, laughing. Afterwards I would go to their camp to be met by fifty hunting dogs which Mornat beat into submission with a stick, then stroked with the tenderness of a St Francis when they came crawling on their bellies to his feet. I always took a bottle with me and the Jogis would dance, thumping drums and twirling handkerchiefs until thoroughly drunk, whether on music or rot-gut whisky it was difficult to tell.

If I heard Narendra's jeep arrive late at night I would peek through my curtains at dawn to see him performing his pujas (prayers) at a shrine by the well. The man seemed never to sleep. Once I had gone across to the kitchen at three in the morning to find him washed and pressed and sitting at his desk, working.

When I first met him a decade ago, I had imagined a kind of

rural establishment dandy dropping into the Legislature now and then for a chat with his fellow princes. But now, as I watched him perform, I regarded his political commitment with something approaching awe. He worked twenty hours a day and he wasn't even in office. (He had lost his seat in the Rajasthan Legislative Assembly, in the previous election, by eighty votes, and was now demanding a re-count.)

His kindness towards me was unflagging but the princely courtesy which, despite his anti-feudalist stance was as natural to him as breathing, made for a certain reserve. Besides that, on my rare forays into 'Jodhpur society' I had been unable to avoid the rumours circulating about him. No one seemed able to say exactly *what* he had done wrong, only that he *had* done wrong. I knew that he had broken social codes – he had divorced his wife, lived openly with his lover, had fallen out with certain members of his family – but none of these seemed heinous to me. All my instincts had led me to trust and like Narendra but the gossip made me just a tiny bit wary of him.

Whenever he was home one of the servants would come to invite me to an evening meal by the log fire with 'Sahib'. And as I prepared myself I would declare that tonight I would make up my mind about him. But inevitably, in the midst of the bounty of the meal, of the drink and firelight and stars, an awkwardness would descend. If I asked questions about his life he answered them openly but would offer nothing further. He never indulged in gossip or slander and if I hinted at the stories I had heard about him he did not defend himself but retreated into thoughtful silence. It was as if he had learnt to mistrust words early on, but had developed a compensatory gift: he could read others without, in turn, being read. On these occasions he seemed to be the loneliest man on earth and that in itself was extraordinary in a culture where everyone is fundamentally a member of a group. I was lonely too. Lonely enough to be delighted when his jeep arrived, yet equally pleased to retreat into my own little room after another inconclusive evening around the fire. As I lay awake at night pondering my strange circumstances, I felt as if I had strayed into an Emily Brontë novel.

So the days of trying to find something to do, of reading book

29

after book, of watching the progress of the war on Hindi television, wore into weeks. And into the spaces left by idleness, and by Narendra's silence, crept disquiet. The stories against him became more dramatic. There were hints of crimes — murder, gundahs, guns — but when I tried to elicit facts, it was like running after leaves in a storm. I understood, dimly, that I was being solicited in a kind of family war. But I did not know enough about the Rajputs, at the time, to understand the rivalries and intrigues that must have ignited in the feudal courts, and which continued to burn along extended family structures. The elaborate public displays of those royal families had always camouflaged the most ruthless power struggles.

One night after an evening meal I saw my host, through his lighted window, take a revolver from his bag and place it under his pillow. I felt a flutter of fear at the base of my throat.

It is salutary to find out that you are not as impervious to malignant gossip as you would like to think. Perhaps if I had not had access to people with a different perspective on Narendra I would have remained mistrustful of him forever. But you can tell a lot about a man from the quality of fidelity he inspires in the few friends he allows to get close. There were people who loved and admired him and from them I pieced together a rather different picture. It took a long time, but eventually I was to understand that the reason he was persecuted had less to do with his misdeeds than with his attitude. Within the community he came from behaviour is codified. One is not judged for individual good or evil deeds, but for whether one remains faithful to the status quo, to the old power structures and moralities of feudal Rajasthan. According to that older morality it is better for a man to be a hypocrite than to be truthful and risk making waves.

Narendra was some kind of new thing, a maverick, rooted in the traditional but open to new ways of being. In due time the flutter at the base of my throat would be reserved for the world in which he moved — political India, where people who made waves could be made to disappear beneath them. Pistols under pillows can be as much for defence as for aggression.

He belonged to the Congress I. But to think that explained anything was to betray an ignorance of Indian politics. It was as much the sclerotic old guard of his own party that Narendra battled as the opposition. The leaders of both sides were the real power running Rajasthan, the ones raking in the profits to be made out of politics. Some were members of old landed families or of newer nexuses of money and power. None of them wanted the corruption challenged.

To Narendra the most important issue confronting India was increasing Hindu fundamentalism. Even from the depths of my ignorance it had been impossible not to notice how the discourse had changed. Ten years ago another's religion had seldom been referred to. Now, from many Hindus, particularly in the middle class, I heard if not anti–Muslim sentiments at least a lack of outright condemnation of the fundamentalist wave. And from Muslims, who formed ten per cent of the population, the beginnings of a fear psychosis. It was like witnessing the spread of a disease, its effects too elusive at first to be frightening, then too powerful to halt. No doubt there had always been tension between the two communities inherent in their group identities. The British had exploited that tension for political ends and now the Hindu nationalist organizations were doing the same. Because of the decay of the state, disgust with the corruption of Congress (a corruption that has been cycled through a couple of generations since Independence, accumulating like DDT in the body politic), the insecurities brought about by the problems in Kashmir and the Punjab, and the pressures of modernization, people were more open to the idea of a party which promised a cleaner, more rigorous kind of rule, which appealed to Hindu pride by evoking a false past – and which, in its political use of the more fanatical revivalist movements, was similar in style to the National Socialists of pre-war Germany.

Only once did I manage to rouse Narendra out of his taciturnity. I said that I had always considered politicians to be the natural enemy and that Indian ones seemed to be a more vile species than most. He put his drink down firmly and said, 'For politics to be anything but filthy in this country, honest people who have the resources must get involved and not sit on the sidelines complaining. All your pressure groups and activists are fine and necessary, but it is in parliament that legislation is enacted and changed. Half a dozen good people in top positions can bring about enormous change. If they aren't on the take, the rot is stopped through the whole system.'

I didn't have a clue how to function inside that system. It was utterly bewildering to me. Whenever Narendra came home there I would be with a thousand queries, a thousand problems. 'Just leave everything to me,' he would say. But I did not want to leave everything to him. I wanted to learn the rules, to understand where I was and act accordingly. But trying to understand the intricacies of inter-family, inter-caste, inter-political, inter-communal, inter-personal relationships in a society that was going through profound upheaval was like being in a room of mirrors. Just when you think you have worked out what reality is, you bump your nose on glass.

All of them – Minu, the Colonel, Narendra – had often said I was very Indian in my ways. I did not quite know what they meant but I took it as a compliment. It was true that I had always felt at ease in this culture, had liked, for want of a better word, Indianness – the way people offered themselves to you, frankly, openly, warmly; the way in which one's being was as important as one's doing; the capacity to tolerate contradiction in human behaviour. But now that I had to live here, understand here, everything I saw only intensified my bewilderment. And this, coupled with my failure to make any progress with the Rabari, brought about something of a decline in morale.

Six months ago the way ahead had been clear. I would simply come to Rajasthan and everything would fall into place. I had written a very fine book in my head before arriving, without setting pen to paper. But had I come too precipitately? Shouldn't I have studied the language first? How could I take control of anything without the possibility of communication? There were three languages to learn and I was getting nowhere with all of them. Besides, how could I decide which language to concentrate on without first knowing which group of Rabari I would end up with? The editors were worried. My proposal had led them to believe that whole villages still left on migration. Somewhere in India this was true. The problem was finding out where, when and who without a telephone, common languages or fuel. The auguries had been irresistible. Now I wondered if fate had seduced me into this in a fit of spite.

I might have considered setting sail for England if there hadn't arrived, courtesy of Narendra, the handsomest twenty-five-year-old Rajput in India, with the largest whitest smile, the curliest, blackest moustache and the most amiable and serene disposition – Koju Singh, my driver.

Koju was an illiterate villager who had spent his life in the desert ploughing dust with oxen. How was it possible that this man who had never read a road sign could be so glamorous, so perspicacious, so wise and self-possessed? Privately I called him Dreamboat.

It was true that I could not see Dreamboat coming towards me, could not see that grin at a hundred yards' distance flashing through the trees, without feeling a warm glow. But I hasten to add for the benefit of the prurient that this flirtation never developed beyond one single, never-to-be-repeated handshake. Nor would it have occurred to Koju that anything other than a handshake were thinkable. He was my gallant, my protector. I was his job. And whatever attraction lay beneath our mutual regard, it never manifested itself beyond a proprietorial attitude in him and a barely concealed favouritism from me.

He owned only two ragged sets of clothes. When he washed at the well each day, a towel wrapped around his waist, he would also wash either a kurta top or a pajama bottom. I gave him an outfit of mine – nicely tailored cream cotton. The following morning he took an extra long time at the well. Brilliantine was applied. Moustaches were twirled. Preening behaviour occurred. Then he disappeared into the servants' quarters. I returned to my book, the hot feeling in my face returned to its rightful place. Ten minutes later I became aware of the smell of rose oil. I looked up and there was Koju standing beside me, his grin wrapped from one ruby-studded ear to the other, my clothes looking as if they'd been draped on an *Esquire* model.

'Koju ji,' I said in English, feeling the heat return, 'you look very handsome.' He grabbed a bunch of pink bougainvillaea and thrust it in a buttonhole of his new kurta. We had no common language but the bougainvillaea was eloquent. Then, perhaps feeling that his gesture was mawkish, he looked embarrassed, took the flowers out and backed away.

But there was no doubt that I had found the way to his vain Rajput heart.

3

Americans waved flags in their streets, Iraqis mopped up blood in theirs. The Kuwaiti ruling family came home to initiate the torture of anyone they didn't like. Arms dealers counted their winnings. In India those children who had decided not to immolate themselves as their chums had done in protest against the Mandal Commission went back to school. Religious fanatics cooled down temporarily, the better to incite hatred another day. Politicians threw chairs at each other in parliament. Petrol dribbled back into bowsers. All was right with the world again.

But was it really useful, I asked myself, to travel with a bunch of nomads no one has ever heard of? So what if the Rabari will be extinct within fifty years? Who in the world will give a damn? And what good would it do them even if a thousand people, even if a million people, *did* give a damn? And so what if nomadism was about to go out, phut, like a candle, the whole world over? The culture of the millennium had bigger things to worry about.

But I'd committed myself and there was no turning back. The Chaitri festival – an annual livestock fair – was to start in a few weeks. There, I could buy myself some camels and Dilip could fly in from Delhi or Canada or wherever he was to take his pictures. Along the way I would call in at Rabari dhanis (hamlets) until I found just that group . . .

Meanwhile I visited several villages with Koju but, as I had not been able to find an interpreter, the nets I pulled up were empty. Often I would drive for ten hellish hours for a prearranged meeting, only to find that my informant had disappeared to a wedding or a death or had just disappeared. And when I did find someone who purported to be 'the representative of the Rabari',

35

my obsession with the specific was usually met with vagueness or with promises of assistance which vanished when delivery time came. Others, lured by the smell of 'phoren' wealth, offered their doubtful services for fabulous sums.

Eventually I found one young man – Purnendu Kaavori – who worked at the Institute for Development Studies in Jaipur. He had travelled with a group of Rajput graziers into Haryana, later writing a thesis about them. He was pleased to offer advice and help but warned me that he, a local who spoke the language, had had great difficulty in persuading any group to take him on migration. They would be doubly uncertain about taking a woman.

Narendra as usual came to the rescue. In the middle of a schedule that would kill a person of lesser vitality, he had managed to find Bhairon Singh Raika – an ex-nomad, now constable in the Rajasthan police force – whom I could employ to liaise with the Rabari.

For our first interview Bhairon Singh wore Dacron stovepipes and a white nylon shirt which clung, sweatily, to his concave chest. When he boasted of the level of fitness required to enter the police force and how many other applicants less physically endowed than himself had fallen by the wayside, it was difficult not to smile. He was one of the half-dozen Raika in service, he could speak a little Hindi, knew all the Raika from Jodhpur to Jupiter and plenty of others as well, and would, he assured me, be able to explain the situation to less cosmopolitan members of his caste. He would accompany me to Chaitri livestock festival to assist in the purchase of the camels; he would most certainly find me a dang (migrating herd) to travel with. In the meantime would I like to attend a Raika wedding in his own village, Baabara?

The next day we all took our spoonful of the proffered jaggery and yogurt, Koju brought his hands together in prayer before starting the engine and, thus fortified against bad luck, Bhairon, Koju and I quit the farm gates. This time, I felt sure, the logjam was going to move.

A cool desert wind wrapped us in dust as we sped along the bitumen. There was no horizon. Trees emerged by the side of the road, to be swallowed up again by the dun pastel of our cocoon.

'Yesssss!' shouted Bhairon, ejecting me out of reverie with a bang on the shoulder. 'Raika!' The jeep flashed past a smudge of red and glitter, and camels concealed among the trees. The deeper we penetrated Bhairon's country the happier and more garrulous he became. Every Raika we spotted precipitated another bellowing 'yesss' and a lot of hysterical bouncing around in the back seat. Koju drove implacably on until we reached our destination – Baabara, a cluster of old stone bungalows.

Bhairon's people had previously been camel breeders from the northern deserts. They had arrived in this more fertile area a couple of generations ago, taken over an almost abandoned village, switched to sheep and were now better off and better organized than many others of their caste. Important resources were located nearby in Jaipur: merchants, wool depots, veterinary hospitals and various government agencies to control migration. Their flocks numbered in the thousands, earning them the nickname of 'migrating millionaires'. I had been told that some politicians and wealthy landowners were in the habit of giving their own sheep to these people to take on migration and that through these men the graziers could gain illegal access to protected (and rapidly disappearing) forests. When I asked Bhairon about this he pretended not to understand the question.

I was ushered into Bhairon's home. Up six front steps to a courtyard bordered by an L-shaped house consisting of a room for the buffalo, a kitchen and two bedrooms. Mrs Bhairon brought her only chair out into the courtyard. I was made to sit on it like a reigning monarch while Koju was given the charpoi. Crowds gathered, introductions were made. Bhairon bustled about and gave commands to his pregnant wife who, I imagined, wore a long-suffering look under her pink orni. All I had to do was smile a great deal and accept, graciously, his orgy of generosity. We were plied with the best food he could offer, drenched in expensive ghee. I wasn't hungry but not wishing to insult our host I watched Koju for clues. A rondo of etiquette ensued: Koju raising his hands politely to refuse the hovering ladle, Bhairon cajoling, Koju acquiescing to a tiny morsel, only to have a quarter pound of hot ghee dumped on his plate. Later he explained, 'For Marwari man, guest is most important.'

Our stomachs swollen, our belches politely thunderous, it was time to socialize. I was shown each of the rooms, all of the treasures. In the kitchen where Mrs Bhairon had been thumping dough over a tiny fire, smoke and chilli filled the air. Bhairon indicated his spouse and said, 'She is not a good cook. No, a very bad cook, I think.'

'She is a very good cook.'

'But she is very ugly.' He lifted the orni.

'Not at all. She is beautiful.'

'Then she is your servant.'

'No, she is my saheli (female friend).'

All this went down well and I had obviously passed the manners test. Even so, no one would let me help her with the work. I must sit and receive. Finally Bhairon brought out his *pièce de résistance* – a framed piece of paper on which it was stated that one Constable Bhairon Singh Raika had received twenty-five rupees and a commendation for bravery for helping to capture an infamous dacoit . . . One dollar did not seem a huge incentive for risking one's life in the badlands until I was told that the house next to his, a derelict but still beautiful building, had been bought for the price of a carton of my English cigarettes.

It was time to bathe and dress for the wedding. A partially closed-off corner of the courtyard was indicated and a bucket of well water brought to me. What to do? I was visible for a sweep of sixty degrees and anyone entering the courtyard would get a full view. I squatted down and hastily rinsed the bits I could get at, ending up with saturated clothes but mostly dry skin. Going behind the village wall for a shit was something of a test of ingenuity also. One had to step among the clustering turds, find a couple of square inches of spare dust and hope like hell no one came past. I now understood the logic of the village women's full skirts. As for using the jar of water to clean one's rear end, I never did learn the correct technique and it's not a subject about which one feels comfortable inquiring. I tried but never quite managed to conquer squeamishness. The world is divided between those cultures which touch their own faeces and those which don't. And it seems to me that those which do have a greater understanding of humankind's relationship to earth, our alpha and omega.

Ablutions completed, a quite spectacular gold necklace was placed around my neck. Next came Mrs Bhairon's second-best skirt. An orni was tucked into it and wrapped around my head. There followed bangles, anklets and bells and everyone agreed that no one would ever guess I was a European. We all took photos of each other: me with two brass pots stacked on my head, my legs cut off at the knee, standing at a thirty-degree angle to the horizontal plane of the photograph and looking every inch a European, albeit of the deranged kind. Koju never did learn to use that camera.

We squeezed our way up an alley to where the groom's party buzzed around a red tractor like Fabergé wasps, all ruby and marcasite. Every surface, saturated with the light absorbed during the day, was now giving it back to the night as a molten glow. Pigs ran about and squealed. Dogs fought each other. A man whose head and shoulders protruded a couple of feet above the crowd placed himself in front of me and grabbed the gold necklace. 'Giga,' he said, which might have been a threat to strangle me but which was, I found out later, his name. He roared with laughter and went about his business. Some women festooned in red and silver came out of a house singing. They were carrying a glittering bundle which, on closer inspection, proved to be a four-year-old child. Battery-powered lights danced around his gold brocade turban and his feet were pressed into gold-trimmed shoes with backward curling points. Every other part of him was covered in satins and tinsel. He was given to me to hold as if he were the most precious thing they possessed, as if all the pride of that vastly extended family were embodied in this exquisite, grave little boy – the bind rajah – the bridegroom.

Child marriages are illegal in India and one can see why this should be so. Among the Rajputs, for example, it is a matter of shame if a daughter reaches menarche in her parents' home. Consequently, girls begin producing children while they are still children themselves. But to the Rabari, who cling fiercely to the tradition, it is a sensible practice. First of all it is difficult for nomads to gather at one place so important events are made to coincide. Often deaths will be mourned a week before the marriages are celebrated ('mausar' feasts), to cut down costs but also, perhaps, to stress the cyclic nature of life. Tonight eight children would be married, thus forming important alliances and mutual support between families which would last lifetimes. After the marriage the girl would go to spend one night in her susural (in-laws' home), surrounded by affection, made to feel important and special, and then be brought home. There would be no consummation until well after maturity and, even then, she would go back and forth from susural to parents' home many times until she felt comfortable in her new role and until the communities decided the couple was ready to live together. Usually when the woman had her children she would take the newborn back to her parents' home, sometimes for months. Divorce in many communities was allowed, though frowned upon and usually had less to do with incompatibility than with infertility. Once again this would be a decision taken by the elders. If a husband died, then it was possible for a woman to marry again, though most often widows, particularly if they had children, preferred to remain single. All in all marriage was a pragmatic affair and individual desires came a poor second to the harmony of the group.

We were to take the bind rajah to his wedding in style. Fifteen people packed themselves into my jeep and we set off into the moonlight and dust, the women singing through their noses. When we passed a small shrine by the side of the track everyone let out an almighty whoop of greeting. The tiny boy smiled and blinked like a pampered cat.

The bindani's (bride's) village was a maze of small rooms and courtyards, a domestic logic that was difficult at first to understand. On a platform about thirty women were ablaze in primary colours and precious metals. I was taken to sit with them. When the woman next to me found out I had been married, she pulled the orni down over my face and pushed me to the ground. Shrieks of delight at this game which everyone joined in. I was instructed in the four or five methods a married woman must use to peep through her orni when there are in-laws or strange men present, using fingers deftly to form the little hole which allows just one eye to show, a most disconcerting gesture and, paradoxically, provocative. Once again there was much poking of my breasts, not as discreet this time, after which it was announced that I was indeed female. I was rescued by Bhairon and made to lie on a string bed covered with quilts in the courtyard. The groom was brought to me and although he occasionally nodded off in my lap, he never once whined or fidgeted. I'd shake him gently awake, as was my duty, and he'd stare at me for a second before breaking into a smile – dignified as a grandfather.

Into this courtyard forgotten in the depth of time came a skinny young man in Terylene flares and a message T-shirt. Pressed to his ear was a radio blaring out Hindi movie songs in competition with the women's voices. He knew a great deal about 'phoren' and announced to all present that western women had wicked morals and that they did not breastfeed their children. He was one of the educated élite and his only ambition was to land a government job so that he would never have to work again. He talked about money, disco music and was scornful of grazing as a profession. Was the future of the Rabari incarnate in this young man?

At the bride's compound (the bindanis were even tinier than the binds) some hired musicians were singing devotional songs to men stoned on opium. The Rabari, so sensible and shrewd with their money, do not practise the economically crippling – and spreading – system of dowry. Customs surrounding bride price (the opposite of dowry) vary from place to place but are usually more symbolic than financial. A family will try to marry all its daughters in one go, so although the celebrations may be lavish they only empty the coffers once. On this occasion the bride-groom's family displayed the gifts presented to the bride – a set of clothes, some silver anklets, foodstuffs and a little money. These were inspected carefully for any trace of meanness by various mothers, aunties and grannies, and pronounced satisfactory.

The night passed in a blur. People coming and going, bursts of singing, snoring from various charpois, hawking, coughing and spitting, the arrival of plates of food, rats nesting in hair or nib-bling feet. At some point I went to sleep under the spacious sky but was woken shortly afterwards by visitors coming by for a 'dekho' at the chief guest. At dawn there was corn gruel and yogurt, after which I was led to another section of the village where a thousand Rabari had gathered from far and wide for the party, dressed up in their very best. This was a death–wedding feast and it was a huge and expensive occasion. Along the flat rooftops, lined up like geranium pots, were rows of bejewelled heads. The joke about my married status had swept through the whole gathering. Banks of women pulled my orni over my face or tried to teach me the peep-hole trick. Dust rose into a sky as white as paper.

When I returned to the courtyard the groom greeted me by putting out his arms to be picked up, and with a heart-melting smile. No western child would have stood this stress for an hour. But this little creature, perhaps because he had never been separated from community life, did not once lose his composure during the whole four days. But then, grace under pressure is a valued trait among the pastoralists. In a few years this baby would be out with the herds, battling the world for his bread.

By mid-afternoon I found myself sitting in a small room at the front of a carpet of tightly packed men's faces. I had contracted some kind of stomach bug and was anxious about an undignified dash for the door using fifty turbans as stepping-stones. There were millions of flies, too many bodies, heat. I thought that a little food in my stomach might combat the waves of nausea, so in my exhaustion reached out to take a sticky sweet with my left hand. A common breath was held, an old man said 'aahhhh' and just in time I checked myself. I took it with my right hand, everyone laughed, the shyness eased and we began to talk.

There was trouble out on the dang. An old man had come back by bus with the news. The shepherds had had to bribe a forest officer with five thousand rupees to graze the flock – the equivalent of five months' income. Each owner would contribute a percentage of the money proportionate to the size of his flock but it was still a big financial loss to the village. That wasn't all. A few shepherds had been arrested for falsifying the number of sheep they had, so as to pay less tax to the state government. Now one of them had skipped gaol, and the police were looking for him. This, too, would require money for bribes. The top numberdar (leader of migration), who had returned for the wedding only two days before, would have to journey back to the dang immediately to sort out the mess.

I asked what they thought of politics and how they might vote. They replied that their only concern was survival and whatever politician might help them with that would receive their vote. On the other hand most of them didn't bother to vote, either because they had no belief in the efficacy of a democracy wormy with corruption or because they were out on the dang, hundreds of miles from home. So large a collection of shepherds was a rare occasion, most of them having little opportunity to leave the herds and come home. Their chief concern was with grazing rights, government control on the sale of wool, the loss of land to farmers and the dangers of migration. They made clear that these problems were common to all the pashupalak (animal herders) irrespective of caste.

But one man announced that he belonged to the BJP. He was fat and buttery, gold rings adorned his fingers and, although he was dressed in traditional Raika clothes, he looked like a badly cast actor next to his lean, sun-shrivelled relatives. He owned a shop in a nearby town. He could speak a little English and informed me that his fellow Raika were illiterate and ignorant, so there was no point in asking them about anything. He added that the reason the Muslims caused so much trouble was that they ate beef and therefore their 'brain temperature was very high'.

I wondered how much he influenced the others. He was, after all, wealthy and literate. He knew about the bureaucratic world. Did they rely on his judgement? From the way they listened to him respectfully but distantly, I suspected not. The nomads are the most tolerant of people and I saw virtually no communalist tendencies among them. They sell their meat to Muslims. It is Muslims who shear their sheep. There are Muslim graziers and so far the sense of comradeship with them, because of their common occupation, common problems, is strong. Besides, how can one find the time to stick to the finer points of Hinduism when one is out on the dang unable to wash or perform rituals? And how can one sneer at the cow-eaters when one sometimes indulges in a bit of mutton on the quiet? But when the nomads stopped wandering as one day they must . . .?

There were Muslim Rabari present at the wedding. Centuries ago when the Mughals invaded, they caused many problems for the Rabari, who often acted as spies for the Rajput rulers. One particular group was captured by the invaders and taken to Delhi. It was here that they were forced to eat beef thereby becoming instantly de-Hinduized. Their descendants were followers of Islam but they still performed ceremonies at various caste functions and their affinity with their original caste seemed as strong as their identity as Mohammedans.

I could discipline my raging stomach no longer. Blocking the door stood all seven feet of Giga. He grabbed me by the gold necklace like a New York mugger. (Rabari humour is sometimes opaque.) Hastily I took it off and made a dash for the nearest wall, to be followed and laughed at by children who were curious about a 'phoren's' body functions. Giga had lent the necklace and was no doubt worried that I was about to head for the hills with it. And yet it was he who, two days later, after I'd spent another sleepless, opium-filled night at his house, and was now saying goodbye to a hundred friends, took both my hands gently in his, pressed them together in front of his heart and said, 'We are your children.'

4

I had always had great affection and admiration for my body. While I realized that it lacked an inch or two in the ankle department and had other, less visible, aesthetic defects, it had, nevertheless, got me from many As to Bs without complaint and generally proceeded with its job of transporting the brain without needing to bother me. What had happened? Why this blinding exhaustion? Had I, somewhere in the last few months, become old? Or was India to blame?

I crawled into my room, closed the curtains, collapsed on to my back and decided India was to blame. Trying to accomplish anything here was like wading through glue. The simplest things – making a phone call, buying groceries, posting a letter – required superhuman patience. Why didn't people go mad; why didn't they stab and shoot each other, as they did in America; why didn't they pick petty bureaucrats up by the scruff of their necks and beat their brains out? How would I learn that Indian patience tempered through millennia? Above all, how would I learn to cope with the subcontinental stare? Wherever I showed my face, a thousand other faces immediately collected around it. If I stopped the jeep, even for a second, even if we were in the middle of nowhere, instantly faces crammed the windows, the windscreen; bodies shoved and jostled, cutting off air; fingers prodded, poked, tugged. Nothing I or Koju or anyone else could say or do made the least impression on that collective stare. Under it I might have been a performing bear or a monkey on a chain. It stripped me of my humanity, sucked out my vitality, and the only defence against it was to retreat inside myself, to psychically disappear. Or to lock myself in the kind, empty darkness of my room which is what I found myself doing after every foray into the world beyond the farm gates.

Being in India was like reading *Tristram Shandy*. Endless digressions from where you thought you were going. If I had given in to this form I would have been happier. But I had to impose an alien, linear form in which A progresses to B which progresses to C. India had its own way of telling a story but I was in no position to listen to it.

In a small village on the way to Baabara we had stopped to buy sweets for the children. To avoid the inevitable collection of stares, at least for a few minutes, I pulled an orni over my face, sank low into the seat and watched, as best I could, through the cotton. There were just a few little shops along the rutted street and, at the end of it, the village well. Rabari women were at the well, five or six of them, filling their pots. I imagined being with them, laughing as they were laughing, unselfconscious, unaware of being observed. I imagined going with them to the shop to haggle over the price of grain, felt the physicality of the heavy pot, the intimacy of a sister's arm around the shoulder, of gossip. I had imagined that I could become, over time, an element within the picture rather than an observer peering in. But it seemed more likely that I would never find myself there, inside the frame.

In the meantime my back felt as if it had been rearranged with a jack-hammer. Lumps of gristle bound muscle to bone and, when I walked, one hip ground in its socket like sandpaper. Not far from the farm was a dhani where, Koju informed me, a certain woman had a special technique for fixing backs. I hobbled to the jeep to find that Dreamboat had packed the passenger seat with cushions and was refusing to let me drive.

The old woman was frail as eggshell and blind. Her son led her out. I knelt in front of her and she took my hands, smiling. Then she turned me around so that my back was facing her. From the corner of my eye I saw her son hand her an enormous axe. Survival instinct told me to get up and run; manners proved stronger. I waited for the almighty thwack, which would kill or cure, only to feel gentle fingers run over my muscles.

'Where does it hurt?'

'Everywhere.'

46

'Achchha.'

Cold metal now followed the hand which seemed to intuit the most inflamed areas. Here the axe would pause, then begin softly tapping on flesh. The old woman began to chant. Once the axe was full to the brim of bad back spirits it would be banged on the earth to release them. The hand would find another spot; tap tap tap, bang bang bang and the mantras. This went on for fifteen minutes and I thought I did notice an easing of the pain. But perhaps that was the power of suggestion or perhaps the drone of the mantra relaxed me, giving the muscles a chance to unknit by themselves. Or perhaps her faith was powerful enough to over-come her patient's lack of it.

I thanked her and offered money but she would take nothing: 'This power is from God not from me, so how can I take payment from you? He took away my sight but in return he gave wisdom to my hands. In the morning you must give a gift of grain to the wild birds.'

Which I did.

To make the trip to Chaitri festival, the purchase of the camels and the meeting with the Rabari as smooth as possible, I em-ployed the services of various people. Narendra had found me an interpreter – a young woman Rajput teacher who spoke Hindi, English and Marwari. Her name was Raju ji. She would meet us at the mela (festival). Takat Singh ji, who had accompanied me on my first foray into the desert, would come for a day to help me choose the camels and gear. Koju would drive and cook. Dilip would bring his own driver-cum-cook. Bhairon would introduce us to the Rabari along the way until we found just that group . . . When he turned up on the day of departure the stovepipes had disappeared and he was Raika head to foot – tie-dye turban, long white shirt, white dhoti, pointed leather clogs, skinny legs.

It was night-time. Bhairon seemed to be lost. We were on one of those cart tracks through the sandhills north-west of Jodhpur. In the distance we could see fire glow coming from the door of a jhumpa and Bhairon went to ask the way. A group of men came out waving arms at him and saying the sorts of things that might be translated as 'Leave or we'll cut your throats'. Twenty minutes and many gesticulations and shared cups later, my policeman got back in the car smelling of deshi daru (homemade grog). 'They thought we were dacoits,' he said, 'and that we were going to steal their possessions and their women. (In this part of the world only government wallahs, police and bandits – none of whom were popular – could afford jeeps.)

We found the dhani and stayed three days. The people could not have been more charming but even so I sensed an undercurrent of suspicion. Alas, the more Bhairon boasted of my tremendous importance and fame, not just in India but in the universe (and therefore by association his own tremendous importance), the more the suspicion thickened. Without a language in which to explain myself, a smile at the wrong time, the lack of a smile at the required time, the offering of too much money or not giving enough money – these gestures could have as much impact as a hurled insult. Men would come and sit with me, polite as ever, and gradually get round to asking, 'You have lakhs and lakhs of rupees, and you have a jeep. Why do you want to live with poor people? Why do you want to *walk*?' I never found a suitable reply to this but it did indicate how far from enviable they saw their own lives and how incomprehensible they found mine. I began to notice that whenever I pulled out my notebook and maps, people closed like slamming doors and wandered away. Nevertheless it was finally agreed that I would set off with a couple of men and a small herd the following day and accompany them to the fair.

In the morning we waited as per instructions. And waited. The sun pressed down. Demoralization set in. Dilip was so angry I was afraid he might have a heart attack. By eleven it became obvious that the herds had cleared off without us, leaving us stranded near a waterhole, listening to Bhairon rant that these Raika were backward, uneducated hayseeds who didn't even deserve to have me write about them, but not to worry we would drive on until we found a more worthy group.

The community had decided we were government workers on some secret survey out of which they could only be the losers. Many of the families had been extending their dhanis and bajri plantations into government land. No doubt we were going to take the land from them, arrest them, beat them up, fine them, extract bribes from them – those everyday occurrences to which the poor become inured – so it was safer to be polite to us and divulge nothing. This was not the last indication I had of the level of dubiety necessary for survival in a world where there was no law on which you could depend for justice, where there was no security beyond family and caste affiliations, where disappearing resources, rapacious greed and endemic venality necessitated there be vastly more losers than winners and where one wrong move could mean the end of you and your family.

Drive on we did. Find a more worthy group we did not. I would have gone straight to the mela but a writer's needs and a photographer's are seldom the same. Besides, Bhairon's self-esteem was at stake. The thermometer showed a hundred degrees; tempers were a good deal hotter. I exercised non-violent non-cooperation with what I felt had descended into farce by staring at my feet in the front of the car. It was from this position that, looking up, I beheld Bhairon, transmogrified into a uniformed policeman complete with knife creases in his khaki trousers and cap set at a no-nonsense angle, directing, like a traffic cop, a group of resentful and protesting Rabari towards the jeep. I laughed till I cried.

I joined the three tired men and their two skinny cows (they had been walking flat out for three days to sell their animals at the mela) for the photo-opportunity, wanting to sink into the road under the weight of my shame. After a while they said, 'You take the cows and we'll go in the jeep.'

In the bluish light of dawn we entered the mela to be greeted by rear views of a thousand men squatting beside the road, water lotis (containers) beside them. On the other side of the dune was a soup of camels, turbans and dust. Everywhere groups of men sat under igloos of grass or awnings of coloured cloth, smoking biris, coughing and yarning, their camels tethered to pegs beside them. Takat Singh arrived and straightaway set off through the soup with me tripping along behind him. He waved his hands in front of the camels' eyes to check for short-sightedness, looked in their mouths to check their age (I wanted a two-toother, less than six years old), inspected their briskets and feet, and finally asked the price. It was always at this point that Takat seemed to suffer a stroke. Getting me a camel for the right price was what he said he would do for me and by hell he was going to do it. We trudged

49

around the sale areas for a full day until I would have bought a llama as long as I could sit down.

We both saw her at the same moment, the best camel in the fair – a black Jaisalmeri cow, with legs like a steel gazelle and eyes lit with a wicked intelligence. I lifted my eyebrows to Takat. He gave a nod and checked her over. Everything was in good order, a Rolls-Royce dromedary. We asked her owner to show her in action. He jumped on bareback, stuck to her like a leech and galloped her flat out through the crowd. Takat pronounced her 'notorious' and I said damn it I wanted her and I didn't care about the money.

It took another day to negotiate her price (my white skin automatically doubled her value) and to find a second beast. Finally the previous owners, myself and a hundred or so bystanders, crowded into a little office stacked to the windows with papers tied up in pink thread. We were told that we could not buy the camels because we had not thought to bring the right piece of paper. In the face of the great *no* of Indian bureaucracy I was undone. Not so Dilip. Surely he said, they knew of the most famous and prestigious magazine in the world? No? And they had not heard of Miss Robyn Davidson or Mr Dilip Mehta? Good heavens! So impressed were they by our fame and by Dilip's superior air that soon we were given tea and the whole business only took three hours. There were several forms upon which the previous owners – Ramu Ram of Jodhpur and Umaid Ali of Barmer – placed their thumbprints and upon which Miss Robyn of Australia placed her scrawl. Then I handed over the money, tucked the receipts in my kurta, drank a last cup of tea with Umaid, Ramu, the bureaucrats and the bystanders, and at last Momal and Sumal – named for two ancestral princesses of Jaisalmer, one of whom was gorgeous and one of whom was not – were mine.

Once out of the mela we walked into an Andrew Wyeth landscape. I looked forward to being on my own, even for a minute, but it was not to be. People coalesced out of emptiness, out of sky or dust or air and attached themselves to our little party like molecules building a crystal. Bhairon and I walked thirty kilometres the first day. (The others drove in the jeeps.) The only damage was a puffy knee, an aching back and a longing to be fifteen years younger. At every pothole Bhairon would snatch the camels' noselines from me in a fit of overprotective zeal. Resisting his chivalry took too much energy and I didn't have an erg to spare. It was on the second day that tempers, already frayed, finally ripped.

Once before when I had travelled with a photographer, I had been a bully. So I determined that during this project I would be the sort of person who looks to the light at the right time, who remains perfectly still for those difficult evening shots and who never complains that there is a lens up her nose. However, given that Dilip has a type triple-A personality, and given that I was worried about my animals, the potholes, the trucks, and that I hadn't slept the night before, and that the sun was burning holes in the top of my head, and given that I was sick of this whole venture, and wishing fervently that I had never begun it, and that Bhairon was shouting at me, so that I began shouting back in a language he could not understand, and that Dilip was now in front of me yelling, 'Turn your face to the left, to the left', while I was struggling to keep control of Momal – given all that, I think I said something like, 'Fuck *off.*'

When we pulled into a Rabari dhani that night my hosts said, 'Why do you want to walk your camels back to Jodhpur when all these people could do it for you? Why don't you go in your jeep? You have lakhs and lakhs of rupees. Why do you want to stay with poor people?' They left our queer party to itself. Dilip's bad humour showed itself in a surliness towards Koju whom he considered lazy. (Perfect Koju! Lazy!) Mine showed itself in a surliness towards Dilip. But this would not do. So I sat and more or less had it out with him, during which twenty minutes, Koju told me later, giggling, I had smoked two packs of cigarettes.

If the two-pack talk did not quite resolve the problems which were, after all, to do with differing work requirements which, being inherently in conflict, forbade any solution, it did make me realize that if future journeys were to be even vaguely tolerable for any of us – Dilip, myself and the people who worked for us – I would have to develop the emotional control of a sadhu. I must never again lose outward calm, no matter what. And although the effort cost me dear, from that day on, I never did.

Later I went for a drive, squashed between Koju and Raju, and burst into tears. Raju caressed my hands and Koju's face took on a manly expression. He said, 'Memsahib, you worry too much about all of us. Do not think of us. We are here to help you and we will do whatever work is required without complaint. And I would die for you if necessary.' I did not think that Dreamboat was silly enough to give up his life for one such as myself but I was deeply touched, and since we were speaking figuratively I, too, would have died for him.

Raju was not fluent enough in English to be a rapid translator but through her I at least got the gist of conversations. But, more importantly, I learnt from her how to behave in village culture, how to accept the generosity shown us with grace and how to return it without awkwardness. Previously I had not known who to give money to and those to whom I tried to give it more often than not refused it. And I had always felt clumsy because the giving of cash in my own culture is tainted. But in India money has no such faecal connotations. Now I knew to place it in the hands of newborn children, or if there were none then to give it to the youngest girl of the house. This money, too, would initially be refused but one joined in the dance of etiquette, insisting, refusing, refusing, insisting, until the money was accepted with a smile.

And when I came trudging into a village, exhausted beyond speech, Raju would be there to do the explaining for me, to gentle her way into everyone's trust. She would take me to the women, where we would cook together, rolling chapatis on little wooden boards, boiling spices in oil, or she would order me to lie down while she walked on my back. Dear Raju, how can I thank you enough for the sensitivity of your soul and of your tiny feet?

If I ever tried to venture even a little way outside the compound on my own, for just that second of peace to sort out my thoughts, Bhairon would be there. 'No need to accompany me Bhairon,' I would say, teeth clenched in a smile, 'I'm quite all right.' But Bhairon would not hear of it. 'You do not understand. There are gundahs here. You might be kidnapped or raped. When you go on migration, I will remain always by your side with a rifle.' The very thought made my spirits sink to my sandals. The only respite was pretending I needed a pee. Then I could have a ten-yard walk and two minutes behind a tree all to myself. Unless children had gathered to watch.

On the fourth day we were all in need of a rest. We camped early in a Raika dhani – a tiny nest of jhumpas lost amidst dunes. Our hosts bustled about, sweeping and tidying a little house for us to rest in, then bringing tea and buckets of water from the well so that we might wash. This was the kind of hospitality that only deserts distil from humans. Later, when we had refreshed ourselves and had lain our bones carefully on the cool floor, Mata ji, the oldest woman in the community, was led in to meet us by her great-grandchildren. There was not a hint of impatience marring their affection and pride as they helped her to sit and guided her hands to my face. 'She is old and lives in the shadow of God,' they explained. Mata ji smiled.

'God brought you to us. Guests, like rain, never come. But it is sad that I am blind because now I cannot see your face.' Soon the room was full of people, blocking the breeze from the windows so that sweat rushed out of bodies and collected into puddles on the floor. Mata ji kept my hands imprisoned in her own. Her nephew, the village story-teller, goaded on by an appreciative audience, a tape recorder and his first foreign guest, took the floor.

'All Rabari caste come from the first ancestor made by Ma-hadev (Shiva) on Mount Kailash in Tibet. When Mahadev made a bull to ride on, which had its fifth leg on its neck, Parvati (Shiva's consort) decided to make a plaything for herself out of sand. It was a strange misshapen animal she made and she put its fifth leg on its stomach. When she asked her husband to bring it to life with his special powers he said, "But Parvati this animal doesn't seem right. If he comes to life he will only cause trouble." But Parvati was adamant so Mahadev breathed life into it and said "uth" which means up, and that's why the camel is now called "unth". How-ever it couldn't walk because its fifth leg got in the way, so Parvati requested her husband to get rid of it. Mahadev cut it off with his chakra (blade) but a stump was left behind which you can still see. (Other versions hold that the leg was pushed up by Mahadev thus creating the hump.) Once that fifth leg was cut the unth would not sit still and Parvati could not catch it at all. She now asked Mahadev to make a man to look after the unth. Mahadev sighed and made a figure out of the skin dirt of his body, put nectar on it and brought it to life. Henceforth the man went around everywhere with the unth and Mahadev told him that he could drink the camel's milk whenever he felt hungry.

'One day the man and his camel got lost in the jungle. It was dark and cold. He saw a light far away, where a body was burning in the cremation ground. But being ignorant of burial rituals he took an earthen pot which was lying there, milked the she camel and heated the milk in the pot. He drank it then went to sleep.

'When it was very late Parvati ji woke up Mahadev ji and said, "That man hasn't come home and you must do something about it." Mahadev saw with his third eye that the man was sleeping in the cremation grounds. He and Parvati went and woke him up saying, "Get up Bhoot Rabari." ' (Bhoot means ghost and Rabari means, possibly, outside the road or way, thus signifying that the Rabari had done something wrong. There are other interpretations of the word's etymology – a Persian root meaning to graze, another meaning 'one who finds the pathways'.)

'Soon, the Rabari needed a wife. Mahadev told him to go to a particular river and steal the clothes of the fairies bathing there. This he did and the angry sisters chased him all the way back to Mahadev's temple. When they got there Mahadev explained the situation. Since it was he who was asking, two sisters, Avri and Bavri, volunteered to marry the Rabari. After a long time some Rajputs joined their descendants by marriage and that's why one finds many Rajput names in different Rabari clans.'

'Why are you called ghosts?' I asked.

Various people replied.

'Because our houses face away from the village and we do not follow the conventions of the village.'

'Because when we are with the dang we seldom wash so we look like ghosts.'

'Because we live in the jungle where ghosts live.'

'Because we practise different ceremonials and do not know all the Hindu rituals.'

The story-teller interrupted. 'There was one Rabari man from long ago who was told he must perform the seventh-day ritual after his father's death. He walked along not knowing what to do until he found a Brahmin and asked him to perform the sacred rituals for him, offering him two rupees to do so. The Brahmin smiled to himself and speaking in Sanskrit so the Rabari could not understand, said, "Here is a stupid Rabari who doesn't know anything. I will fool him and take his money." The Rabari returned home well pleased but when his neighbours asked him what the Brahmin had said, he repeated the sounds he had heard. Everyone laughed at him and called him an ignorant bhoot.'

Mata ji shushed us and said, 'Look, she is laughing to see us. She is laughing at our ignorance.' I assured her that I was laughing because I was happy to be with them and because the story-teller was very clever. She pressed my hands, stroked my face and said, 'It is our great good luck.'

Another woman announced to the gathering, 'We are called bhoot because we are afraid of nothing, not of snakes or wild beasts, and we travel where there are no people. We are the keepers of the way.' Sending a challenge to me from the corner of her eye, she added, 'It is hard to live with ghosts.'

Mata ji came to my defence. 'But this woman is courageous. She does work that men cannot do. She is strong enough to go with us.'

By now a horde of little boys in blue school uniforms had squeezed into the room. I asked why no girls went to school. 'A girl will go to live and work in her parents-in-law's house so an education for her is a waste of money. We are poor people and an income is more important than education. We usually only send one boy per family and then just until he can read and write. Even so he will still look after the animals proudly. After that we are not interested in school. We have not got the sifarish (influence) to get the jobs, nor the money for bribes, so what use would our education be? The animals are our living, they are our wealth.'

Next to me one of the boys was teasing his auntie. She turned to me and said, 'You see how he taunts me? He teases me because I am illiterate. We Raika are just like the animals, uneducated and backward. But one day I will educate my son and he will then be able to sit with educated people without shame.'

I asked if anyone here held other jobs. During famine years the Raika women (and any available men) were given work on drought-relief projects, building roads or sinking wells. And there was a boy who had gone to work with some relatives who owned a sweet shop in the slums of Bombay. 'Did he want to go?' I asked. People seemed bemused by the question. 'I mean, why *did* he go?' They looked at me as if I were retarded and said, 'For the money.' One forgets, in one's privilege, that poverty means the absence of choice. You do not go to cities because you are bored with country life but because you are a refugee of development or poverty or ecological destruction – and in the city you might be paid enough to send a little home.

'When God made the first Raika,' interrupted the story-teller, 'that man turned to God and said, "You're something else. You've given me two eyes, two ears, two feet, two hands but only one stomach. It isn't fair. Why did you do it?" God laughed at him and answered, "You foolish Raika, don't you realize how much trouble you're going to have filling *one*?"'

'And why do you sometimes call yourselves Raika and sometimes Rabari?' I was told that there was really no difference but that older people tended to use the older term Rabari, whereas Raika was perhaps more fashionable these days.

I asked if I might go with them this year on the dang.

'You are always welcome to live with us,' said Mata ji, 'but this will be a holiday year for us. Usually we migrate to Haryana. It is very hard work and we are pleased to come back. Haryana is full of badmaash (crooks). But this year the rain was so good we don't have to go that far.' In any case their herds were on permanent migration, a phenomenon which began in 1942 during a famine. The graziers had survived better than most by taking their herds great distances. It was impractical to bring them all the way home. Consequently, although people journeyed back and forth from the dang to the village, the animals never returned. During that famine, Mata ji told me, they had taken some children from other castes with them so that they could drink the animals' milk and survive.

When it was time to go I asked Mata ji if I might buy some camel feed from her. 'Areeeee, if I took money from you I would not go to heaven. You are my guest.' Pointing to the three tiny gold suns in each front tooth she said, 'When I die, this is the only gold that will go with me. What does one take after death? Just one's good deeds and the love of others.' In the end I gave the payment to her grandson who belonged to a generation which had learned to temper generosity with pragmatism.

Walking the next morning, the phrase 'keepers of the way' kept returning to me. As it implied something fixed and rigid I had thought it a mistranslation. But if it was, it was a felicitous one revealing, now, a deeper truth. Rabaris were the keepers of the original way – nomadism.

On the second last day Dilip drove to Jodhpur to stay in a hotel. He would meet us in the morning to do the 'camels coming past Jodhpur castle' shot. I decided like a good captain to remain with my men. Raju had already gone home, so Koju, Bhairon and I camped by a small white temple. Poor Bhairon had been trying his best to satisfy the requirements of the lunatic white woman and the demands of a photographer. And what had he got in return but mouthfuls of dust and sore feet? He had that look that cats sometimes get when they are disgusted with you – flat around the ears. He said nothing but I was pretty sure he was close to tears. Or to murder.

Koju tactfully went to heat him some water and I began to prepare the dal. 'Bhairon Singh ji is angry,' I said, but there was no reply. He sat cross-legged on the steps of the temple and began to shave. Afterwards he disappeared behind the temple for a bath. I busied myself with the cooking until I was interrupted by an exquisite baritone. I looked inside the temple and there was Bhairon, standing before the goddess in his fresh white clothes, cleansing his being with song.

When, the following day, we limped into Narendra's farm, he lifted his arms to heaven and proclaimed, 'Bhairon Singh Raika – History ka hero.' And I put out my right hand to Koju who took it shyly in both his, bowed, grinned and delivered me to Narendra.

5

History's Hero went back to being a policeman. Dilip returned to Delhi. Momal and Sumal were tethered in front of the house. And I, at last, had someone to talk to. The moment I saw Narendra all the repressed speech of the previous weeks came out like sulphurous gas from a geyser. There he sat in his rattan chair, nodding gravely, smiling occasionally as I babbled on without breath, dropping my mania into the well of his being without ever hearing a splash. I talked to him the way Bhairon had sung to his goddess. And with the same depth of gratitude. After the first bout of verbiage I disappeared inside my room and slept for a day. On the following morning Narendra sent a message that someone had arrived whom he would like me to meet.

From my small contact with India's godmen I was not predisposed to holding them in high regard. If I thought of them at all, I thought of them as greedy charlatans who drove around in Cadillacs exploiting spiritual vacuums. Then there was the other kind which mixed politics with religious fanaticism and preached tolerance to all Indians except Muslims, Christians, Jains, Jews and Sikhs. Nor had I, like many other westerners, come to India to find Bhagwan. But when I sat in front of Bhawani Shankar ji and looked into his face, there was no mistaking that I was in the presence of a highly evolved human being. Everything about him was sweetness, selflessness, clarity, vigour and humour. Metaphorically speaking, you could see straight through him to the other side of the room. He was dressed in a scrupulously clean but threadbare dhoti and he wore a pale blue turban which exactly matched his eyes. He was very old.

We talked for a while, Narendra interpreting. Then they

1. *Koju and me with the new jeep*

2. *Walking my new camels back to Jodhpur*

3. *Mornat, king of the Rajasthan Jogis*

4. *Takat Singh and Chutra training Momal*

5. *Bhopavand, a Rabari village*

6. *Phagu*

7. *Nakki, 48 years old*

8. *Latchi gathering the lambs*

9. *Parma wears my hat and glasses*

10. *Jaivi, Parma and me*

11. *Parma, Jaivi, Latchi and me sewing*

12. Collecting firewood

muttered something to each other. Bhawani turned back to me and said, 'You must not be anxious about your work. Everything will turn out well because you are not doing it for selfish reasons. You must learn to be calm and to help you with this, I will give you a mantra.' It was an ancient Sanskrit verse, an appeal to Devi. I was to learn it off by heart and say it every day.

'But Bhawani ji, it is not much good my saying this prayer when I don't believe that Devi, or anything else, is there to listen.'

He burst out laughing and replied, 'But you are quite right! There is no one listening; there is nothing. Only the creation itself which is ineffable. Imagine it as an engine, pushing the universe along. Think of it in terms of science if you like, but say the mantra anyway. You will see that it will do you good.'

He refused to take anything from me and, by way of explanation, told the following story. The Maharani of Jodhpur wished to thank him for some help he had given her by having a velvet coat made for him. He refused the gift, saying that he would become dependent on the warmth and luxury of the coat but that when the coat wore out what would he do? It was better never to own a coat than to miss having a coat.

'When my child died I might have given way to grief as I loved him very much. But that would not bring back my son nor do anyone else any good. It is better to proceed with one's duty in the service of others than wallow in the pain attachments bring.'

It is disconcerting to meet someone to whom it is impossible to give anything because he has no desire for anything. He cannot be charmed or won over because the love emanating from him is already unconditional. I rarely said my mantra but when I did, I said it for Bhawani ji whose heart was as pure as a temple bell.

'You brought him here for me, didn't you?'

'He comes to visit me anyway. But as you were here . . .'

'That's so kind of you, Narendra. But, tell me, all this puja business you do. What goes on inside your head when you do it? I can't imagine what it is like to have a faith.'

'When the old man dies I shall probably stop doing them.'

'But what do you *believe*? Do you believe in the soul surviving after death?'

59

'No.'

'Do you believe in karma?'

'No. There's just one life.'

'Then do you believe in a God who is conscious of you, who listens to you?'

'No.'

'*Then who the hell are you praying to?*'

'Not *to* anyone exactly. I remember Jesus, Buddha, Mohammed, Parvati. The earth has been kind to me. So it's a way of just . . . being by myself, returning to myself and . . . giving thanks.'

There was no point in asking thanks to whom as the Who or What of the matter was obviously irrelevant. The point was that Narendra's prayers gave him a kind of ballast as he sailed through the storms of life.

'You will need someone to look after the camels.'

'No, I won't. I've owned camels before . . .'

'Hmm. But that was in Australia and now you are in India, and in India you will need someone to look after the camels. You won't have time to take them out to feed so I've taken the liberty of employing a Raika . . .'

'If someone has to be employed, then I'm doing the employing . . .'

As always Narendra got his way and a few days later Chutra Ram Raika arrived, a man whose diminutive size was in reverse proportion to his ego. His people no longer wandered but worked, when they could, for local landowners. He wore his turban at a jaunty angle, strutted on dainty legs, had been educated to tenth class, could speak Hindi and a dozen words of English, pronounced himself honoured to be my unth wallah (camel handler) and demanded double his wages.

For the first time I found ignorance of the language useful. 'Kya?' I said. I had enough Hindi now to be able to imagine Chutra's speech in English. It went something like this.

'I am the luckiest and most honoured of men to be able to work for such an important and rich a person as yourself. I will work as hard as a thousand men and I will protect you and look after Momal and Sumal because I know everything about camels.

And you will give me twice the wage that Sahib has offered. I am an only son and I must look after my mother, who is very poor and very old and very sick. I must build her a new house to live in.'

Chutra sighed deeply, then began to pick prickles off my kurta – an intimacy which made me distinctly uncomfortable. Besides that, he used the intimate form of address, tum. In Hindi tum is used to address those younger than oneself or close friends or those in an inferior social position. Servants, for example, are always referred to as tum by their employers. This linguistic hierarchy went against my grain. Consequently I used tum only with children and always addressed the servants as aap, the more polite and respectful use. 'Kya *aap* ne bole?' I said pointedly but Chutra was impervious to innuendo. I backed into the house to discuss the matter with Narendra.

We had had similar discussions before. I wanted to pay my employees more; he forbade it.

'But why?'

'Because if you pay Koju more, or Chutra more, everyone will have to receive an equivalent raise and hundreds of people work for me. Besides, they are already well paid. The ones at the top receive more than a government salary and all of them get three months', holiday a year plus many perks. Please don't wreck my system.'

'A feudal system,' I muttered.

'Don't you worry about it. I'll deal with Chutra. He's already getting twice the wage of his previous job and the rogue only has two camels to look after.' He laughed. 'But you have to admire his pluck.'

Later Koju came in bearing tea. He had a brooding look. Piecing together the bits of his mumbled Marwari, I supposed him to say, 'If certain people are being difficult, then there are thousands of others in need of a certain person's job. Certain people should be thankful for what they are offered which is more than other people get to do more work.'

The notion of solidarity among workers had not penetrated rural Rajasthan. The Marwaris working here were entirely lacking in that prerequisite for class-consciousness – envy. Koju was identified with Narendra and, by default, me. What was good for us was good for him. Our enemies were his enemies. He would boast to everyone we came across that *his* Memsahib spent the equivalent of a day's wages on cigarettes. And did the recipients of this information regard me with loathing and contempt? Not at all. My profligacy was an indication of my high status and the proper response to a status higher than one's own is humility and respect.

Chutra did not give up despite the tacit censoriousness from those around him. I took to sneaking across to my room like a burglar, hoping not to encounter him. But he was able to divine my presence and there he would be, cajoling, flattering, harassing.

'Chutra, you must take up the matter with Sahib. He says what each wage will be.'

'Not at all! You are my benefactor. You are rich and I am a poor man. You can say how much.'

No one was more conscious than he of the multitudes pressing against the gates of this farm. I could have had ten thousand camel men for the price of a carton of cigarettes a *month*. But Chutra Ram Raika was educated to tenth class and though he might own just one dhoti, one fraying shirt and a ratty turban, he was Somebody. To show how indispensable he was he got up at five, fed the camels, clipped their coats into pretty patterns then took them out to the fields to feed on the ketcheri trees. Wherever I looked Chutra would be there, loudly finding something to do. As for the camels, never have I seen animals so pampered. Their bellies became huge, their humps obscene, their tempers horrid. My camels in Australia had been spoilt, no doubt, but they had manners. Any insurrection was met by a hefty blow. Not so, Momal and Sumal. If I tried to go anywhere near them, Chutra would be there fussing, telling me what to do and how to do it, grabbing lines and leather out of my hands. Now, camels are not stupid. Very quickly these two understood that they could persecute anyone they cared to as long as they sucked up to Chutra. I would dearly have loved to take them out bush and teach them proper attitude with a hobble chain, but the unth wallah was omnipresent.

Chutra had already told me the story of the princesses for whom the camels were named. Momal was the princess of Lodvara, the old capital of Jaisalmer. She was famous for her beauty.

Sumal, her sister, who was not at all beautiful, dressed like a man and loved to go hunting. Mahendra was a prince of Amarkot, the old capital of Pakistan. He was extremely ugly, had only one eye and was very dark. But he loved Momal and wanted to marry her. The love was returned in full measure. Mahendra owned a very wonderful camel called Chikal who could travel the six thousand miles in a night and cross the Kaak River without any problem. At midnight Mahendra would ride to his mistress, stay with her until four and then return home.

One night Momal and Sumal had been gossiping together and became so tired that they fell asleep in the same cot. When Mahendra arrived, they were curled in each other's arms. Mahendra saw that his beloved was sleeping with, as he thought, another man. He became very angry and galloped home.

At four o'clock Momal awoke and said, 'Where is my Mahendra?' The servants told her that he had come but had left in a very angry mood. She thought to herself that it must be because he had seen her with Sumal and sent a message to him to come so that she could clear up the misunderstanding. But he would not.

The next night Momal determined to go to him. But the rains had come and the river was swollen. Every minute the flood became higher and higher. But so desperate was she to see her prince that she plunged into the water and drowned. Mahendra never married anyone else.

Chutra had to struggle against tears when telling this story. Later he boasted that in the good old days Raika had been messengers to kings and were allowed further into the royal houses than other castes. Raika had accompanied their rajahs on the battlefields of yore; indeed, the nobility had depended upon Raika intelligence, Raika bravery, Raika skill.

I could follow his line of reasoning. By a stroke of good fortune the old days had returned and he, Chutra Ram Raika, was now employed by a member of the Jodhpur durbar (court) and by his guest, a fabulously rich European. Ergo the camels had to have the best and most expensive food, the best saddles, had to be decorated with bells and silver and tat, had to be seen to be superior in every way to hoi polloi camels. But this was not what I had planned. I wanted hard-working, safe, affectionate camels. Camels you could share a joke with when the going got rough. I did not want these autocratic, fat, foul-tempered, gaudily attired, malicious and, above all, dangerous princesses.

But my ideas were based on ignorance of the natural order of things. I was not to handle my own camels. That would be beneath my standing and would imply that he, Chutra, was incompetent at his job. I was to behave like a kind of white-skinned rani to whom such things as tightening girths and punishing dromedaries were unthinkable. But the root of our difficulty was this: I, his boss, the person from whom he was supposed to accept orders, was a woman.

Our horns were locked from the beginning but I could only lose ground. Chutra had behind him the weight of tradition, fluency in Hindi and Marwari (it is very difficult to be commanding when you cannot say the commands) and the skin of a crocodile. Thus Momal and Sumal became his camels and I gave up my last hope of controlling any aspect of my life in Rajasthan. Was it character-building to be made impotent? Was I learning how to let go the old habit of total self-reliance? No. I was learning how to resent bastards like Chutra in the privacy of my little room at night.

Of all the servants, the only one who really understood my need to do things for myself was Koju. Indeed, so well did he understand it that he could now lie back quite happily, smoking my cigarettes or playing Marwari songs on my cassette recorder while I did all my work myself, and his as well. Somehow I just hadn't got the hang of this servant business.

I could not get used to the idea of there being classes of people inherently inferior to oneself, to whom one could be as odiously condescending or downright brutal as one liked, yet with whom one lived as intimately as family. I had seen otherwise perfectly decent people in Delhi abusing their servants as if they were pets. Deep within I held the Protestant notion that one should do one's own chores and that, if you divided the world into masters and servants, the masters became incompetent at looking after themselves, and the servants incapable of independent thought. Perhaps, in my own culture, the ideology of egalitarianism was compensation for the chasm separating one individual from another. The structure of Indian society provided a kind of psychic security as well as imposing order. Every person knew where and who he was in relation to every other person.

It was a different morality to which I must adjust. But how was I to find a place within the structure that was tolerable for me and would not cause problems for the people around me? Without the ability (or desire) to recognize high from low, close from far, I gave equal attention to all, thus exhausting myself, confusing the recipients and upsetting the balance of a system that had worked perfectly harmoniously before I came.

Yet it was the servants who were my closest companions, the servants who laughed at my jokes, tried to teach me their language, told me their stories, who were there when I needed company, who tactfully withdrew when they sensed my inwardness – the servants who were my friends. But those friend-ships contained so many cultural subtleties of which I was unaware that it was only by their acceptance of the boundaries imposed by difference of birth, their understanding of the correct relationships among each layer of the social pyramid, and their tolerance of my ignorance, that trouble within the ranks was avoided.

Narendra had asked Takat Singh to train my camels. Tractor loads of sand had been deposited in front of the jhumpa in prepara-tion for the event. On the morning it was to begin Sumal almost took my hand off at the elbow, a piece of evil at which Chutra had smiled benevolently. Takat arrived at six in his blue safari suit, dynamited the hills with his laugh and said, 'Just see if she wants to bite anyone after today.' I took a seat ring-side to watch the perform-ance. First the camel's front legs were tied with rope, so that she was forced to crawl. This she did, roaring and fighting, until her back legs quivered and she sank to the ground, at which point Takat, displaying neither anger nor sentimentality, belted her with a rope until she crawled again. Chutra's heart was breaking but I felt the tiniest sliver of satisfaction at the sight. By the end of that first day's training my princesses would crawl on command with-out so much as a rumble of protest. These morning circuses were to continue for four weeks until Momal and Sumal would lower their heads to the ground on command, roll over on command (a useful tactic in the desert when you are under fire though I rather hoped I would never have to use it), pace, stop and walk on command – and any thought of chasing, biting or kicking anyone seemed to have vanished from their pretty heads.

When Takat was around, Chutra was the essence of humility not to say obsequiousness. But as soon as Takat was gone he would grumble that only Raika knew how to handle camels and that all this training was a waste of time. Takat had given him strict instructions to exercise the beasts every day and to follow through with the routine. Predictably Chutra did not comply. But at least I had my way about riding them every morning at five.

I always rode Momal, the Rolls-Royce. Off we would fly at a brisk pace, Chutra, naturally, taking the lead, his turban set at an even more rakish angle, his back straight, his little legs gripping like fingers, singing Marwari songs in a frightful falsetto, waving his whip in the air like a battle flag. Mists rose off the chilli fields, water birds paddled in the irrigation ditches, the castles in the distance were tinged pink by the rising sun.

Whatever faults I could find with the beasts on the ground, once on their backs I adored them. It was like riding clouds, or silk, and they responded to the merest touch, the softest word. The difference between Jaisalmer riding camels and Australian plodders was the difference between gold and lead. Chutra became a tall man in the saddle. To be seen on the back of such elegant camels as these compensated for his littleness, his poverty, for all the humiliations of being an intelligent man employed far beneath his abilities. I almost came to like him during those rides until one day he said, 'Madam Sahib can ride very well.' Amazing how a compliment can sound like an insult when delivered with the correct amount of sarcasm. I said nothing.

'Of course,' he went on, 'Raika women can ride without a saddle and jump on to the animal while it is standing.'

You little arsehole, I thought, and longed to boast that I had galloped my own camels bareback down creek-beds in my youth. But I didn't know the words.

Whenever I came back from my forays into the desert I would find that the camels had reverted to their old habits and that I might as well eat air as hope to have any influence over my camel man. Let's look on the bright side, I said to myself since there was no one else to talk to. You have the two best camels in India, you have the assistance of an ex-minister and countless helpers and hangers on, and it is against the laws of mathematical probability that with this much effort you will not find, somewhere, across six states, just that group . . .

A couple of weeks later History's Hero visited. He had, after much thinking and worrying on my behalf, discovered exactly the right place for me to centre my story and it just happened to be his very own village, Baabara. Knowing that self-interest lay at the bottom of his proposal did not prevent my being grateful.

Thanks to an overdeveloped sense of responsibility towards the magazine's photographic needs I had been very choosy till now. In locating a group of Raika I always took into account such things as desert vistas, pretty jhumpas, dramatic photos of arrivals in Pushkar — that sort of thing. Bhairon's people, I knew, lived in boring, eaten-out farmland, and would take their animals along the Chambal River beside factories, sewerage outlets and leaky nuclear power stations, and on into the dacoit-infested badlands. Not exactly the sunset sand-dune descriptions with which I had secured the magazine's interest and cash.

Then there was Bhairon to consider. Although I felt sympathy, even fondness, for the third policeman, on our previous adventure I had sometimes found myself wanting to strangle him quietly and bury him in a dune. Naturally this feeling was mutual though, from his point of view, shepherding me was infinitely preferable to being bullied by his superiors in Jodhpur, especially if he could convince me to focus my research at his village thereby providing himself with a paid holiday and his family and friends with who knew what perquisites. While I understood how much this erstwhile nomad loathed being a cop, how he longed for retirement as a marooned man longs for a ship, the thought of spending a year with him hovering over me and answering my queries with wildly incorrect information was not compelling. On the other hand time was running out.

Bhairon was going to introduce me to one of the most powerful numberdars in the whole of Rajasthan — a man so clever that even local politicians courted him. The numberdar would,

Bhairon assured me, be delighted to take me with his dang but there was a hitch. The badlands along the Chambal River were crawling with bandits and therefore a pistol, a rifle and himself, Bhairon, would be essential baggage.

'Surely you're exaggerating the danger,' I said. 'If your people don't take rifles on the dang, why on earth should I?' He got that flat look around the ears again. 'They do take rifles if they can get them. In any case everyone, men, women and children, is armed with lathi and stone slings. Last year the dacoits kidnapped a man and broke both his legs because his family could not afford the ransom. We Raika are trying to convince government to set up armed posts along the migration route to protect us. Apart from stealing our animals, the dacoits often capture women for their pleasure and you would bring in a big price.' Somewhere in the small residue of my romanticism I had been harbouring the delusion that the dacoits were Robin Hood types with attractive moustaches and incipient socialist tendencies, who might, if encountered, be interesting to chat to and who would at the very least provide good book fodder. Bhairon was setting me straight. If their chivalry had ever been real (a perception which depended upon whether they cut your feet off or shared their booty with your village), it was no longer. These days they were more likely to be arm-breakers from the Bombay mafia. About as pleasant to come across as a nest of vipers. That the Raika were willing to risk their lives pushing their flocks along this new route indicated their level of desperation and the daring that has allowed them to survive since time immemorial.

I had already met, clandestinely, a retired leader of the dacoits but even he, being of the old school (moustache, incipient socialist tendencies), could not guarantee our safe passage. Besides not fancying the idea of having bits of me broken, I worried that my presence on the dang would place my hosts in greater jeopardy. Which in turn made me curious as to why the numberdar was so anxious to have me along.

Never mind the hitches. A new plan was taking shape. I would hurry to Baabara to catch an interview with the numberdar before he returned to the dang. From there I would meet up with

Dilip in Jaipur and head on out to the dang, a hundred or so miles away, to photograph the shearing. I thanked History's Hero, rang Dilip, hired Raju as interpreter and arranged to go to Baabara the following week.

6

On the way to Baabara, Bhairon took us to a village where some of the Raika's genealogists, the Raos, lived. The formalities of introduction completed, the Rao was ready to talk.

'So, Madam, what is your business here?'

'I would like to know about the Rabari.'

'I know nothing about the Rabari. The Rabari of Gorwar and Gujarat have their own genealogists. I am Rao for the Raika.'

'I see. Well, then, I would like to know about the Raika.'

'We, the Raos, know many things about the Raika which are secret and we will not tell you. But there are other things I can explain to you if you will come with me. But first you must take tea.'

We drank the inevitable tea, surrounded by a sea of smiles so freely given, so sweetened with charm and refinement, so charged with expression as to make speech almost redundant. It is difficult, when you first encounter these smiles, not to believe that their owners are not a higher form of humanity. Of all the smiles in the room that of the Rao was the most numinous.

We were taken to a room in another building which soon enough was packed to the rafters with people. The Rao opened an untidy book filled with beautifully crafted Hindi.

'When the first Raikas were created in this world, so was my family to record their history. They are called Raika because the name of the first Raika's wife was Rai. She was a fairy. This man and woman had one son and twelve daughters. The daughters were married to Rajputs and from them emerged the thirty-six official sub-castes of the Raikas. [In fact there were hundreds. No one knew how many because a new sub-caste might be formed each time a son moved away with his family to settle somewhere new.] Each day I fill my book with new information. It is my job, as it was my father's and grandfather's.'

Every five or six years Rao ji and his father travelled all over India to record the births, deaths and marriages of their Raika clients. (Each sub-caste had a separate book weighing approximately thirty kilos.) As payment the Raika gave gifts of animals, clothes and money. Rao ji said that the Raika called themselves Rabari out of bad habit. They were Raika or Devassi. The caste was split into three main branches: the Rabari of Gorwar, the Devassi or Raika and, later in history (or further up the trunk), the Rabari of Kutch.

I knew that many older Raikas still referred to themselves as Rabari and the Rabari of other states might use either name, though Rabari was more common the further from Rajasthan the caste had spread (and the longer its separation from its origin in Jaisalmer). But I had only recently been able to determine why. There was an attempt by the more politically astute numberdars in Rajasthan to federate the whole caste under the name Raika, in the hope of establishing enough power to lobby governments. The term Rabari, they felt, was less glamorous than Raika, even derisive. According to folklore the word Rabari carried connotations of an innocent blockhead, whereas Raika, as Chutra had so often pointed out, was an honorific to be proud of – heroic. It was true that Rabaris had never attempted to climb within the Hindu hierarchy but there was no doubt that they were proud of their connection with the high-caste Rajputs. Though I was never able to find out exactly how many Raika/Rabari there were, the general consensus was that there were about half a million spread throughout India. Not a bad power base if it could be unified.

'Do you know how camels first came to India?'

'No, Rao ji. Please tell me.'

'Pabu ji protected the honour of cattle and women. He had a niece who was to be married. She wanted some camels as a wedding present but there were none in India. So he journeyed to Sri Lanka, the home of camels at that time, disguised as a hermit. He stole some animals from Ravana and was chased into the sea. But he strew the water with peacock feathers and the camels crossed

71

over them like a bridge. Meanwhile the niece's new relatives were teasing her, saying, "Oh, ah. Better put away our spindles or they'll be knocked over by all those camels who are coming."' I asked the Rao whether, as Sindh was in Pakistan, and as the word means sea or over the sea, the story indicated that the camels really came from the north. Not at all, he assured me, the story he told was literally true.

We had been in the room for an hour. Raju had been valiantly trying to translate what was said with limited success. It was time to go. I leant across to her and asked whether I should pay the Rao directly and if so how much. She said payment was not necessary but perhaps a gift of twenty-one rupees would be a nice gesture. I decided on fifty-one. (The extra one rupee is for luck and probably derives from the ancient craft of numerology.) The Rao's smile took on a peculiar twist which I could not read.

So far, if I stayed with a community, my policy had been that any payment or gifts should go to the whole community or to the head of a family who had looked after me or to the children. I gave the money openly for all to see. If I received specialist informa-tion then I endeavoured to pay for that within a framework of acceptability, always veering towards the top of the range because I knew this was expected of a European. It was extremely difficult for me to judge this because without language I often could not work out who were the principal leaders within a kin group or indeed which of the informants was the important one. When Raju was with me I relied on her diplomacy which was impeccable.

We went to the car and waited for Bhairon who was involved in an intense conversation with the Rao. Eventually Bhairon came to my window and whispered with embarrassment, 'He wants two hundred rupees.' No one said a word. I handed over the money. Quibbling about it would mean a loss of face for Bhairon and added irritation for me. Rao ji's evolved and generous smile returned and he bowed to us deeply as we left.

Koju's moral outrage expressed itself in a clenching jaw and a white-knuckle grip on the wheel but there was one salutary effect of the exchange: Bhairon kept quiet for at least fifteen minutes.

We arrived in Baabara and went straight to seven-foot Giga's house. It is a curious thing that when one cannot communicate through language one relies upon less dominant, perhaps pre-lingual capacities for judging people. It may be some chemical exchange which scientists have yet to discover that encourages instant rapport, or perhaps in this case it had to do with gold necklaces. Whatever the reasons, Giga and I met each other like long-parted family. I liked him for his size, his laugh, his gentleness, his self-confidence. But most of all I liked the way he was with his wife. When I first met her she had been hurling abuse at her daughters-in-law who took no notice whatsoever. Then, on seeing me, she transformed from Witch of the West to Wendy. She grabbed me with her rough hands, led me through her house to admire her beautiful things – shelves of brass pots, jewellery locked in boxes, a camel decoration made of goat hair and cowrie shells – and all the while Giga grinned at her, admired her, *liked* her. Our stocktaking over, she lit up a biri which she inhaled through one nostril. I asked why she should be the only woman to smoke.

'Because she's a badmaash,' Giga said, laughing. Later Koju told me it was because she had lost both her sons during migrations. 'So who will criticize her for enjoying her cigarette?' From then on I decided that whenever I smoked, I would say that I had lost two sons.

Giga could not understand my desire to migrate with them. 'Why do you want to do this thing and risk yourself? You will end up looking like us.' He ripped off his turban and tugged at prematurely grey hair. He then informed me that he would not be going on migration this year but, if I waited until next year, he would come with me as bodyguard and so would his wife. Bhairon sent daggered looks and hustled us along to the numberdar's house.

Bhopal ji was as thin and white-haired as a grannie but his intelligence radiated like body heat. We all sat in the courtyard at the front of his white stone house. I asked him how the migrations were organized.

Two numberdars only would meet in Kota, a town about a hundred miles away, to decide where all the thousands of flocks

73

from this section of Rajasthan would go. Scouts would be sent out to reconnoitre grazing land and to set up deals with various village panchaits (councils) for grazing rights. Once one group had approached a panchait another could not do so. In a very short time this information would spread by word of mouth until every pastoralist would know his own route and the whereabouts of every other dang. It is almost impossible to comprehend how this feat can be carried out so efficiently, without mistakes or quarrels, without telephones, jeeps or letters. Only later did I come to understand the efficacy of the lakri o tar, the walking-stick telegraph.

The numberdars would buy a kind of entry visa from the Madhya Pradesh government and by this method the flock was regulated and controlled, the numbers known. At least theoretically. But, as the numberdar said, everyone considered this payment an unjust bleeding of precarious income and lied about the size of their herd. I was beginning to understand that from his point of view it could be quite useful to have someone like me along. I had connections and might be able to grease their way through tight places.

One of their major concerns was the slump in wool prices. With the troubles in Russia and China much of the wool trade had closed down. Synthetics were taking the place of wool. Meat was sold to Arabia but there were problems. 'These days,' said a gnarled ancient, whose white beard was rolled into two sausages and tucked behind his ears, and whose feet attested to many years plodding through the wilderness, 'everything depends upon marketing.'

Some time in November all the people who had decided to migrate from this village – women and children included – and all the sheep held close by, would set out for Kota where they would join up with the larger flocks. It was agreed that I would go with them under the aegis of Bhopal ji who immediately understood photographic requirements. Yes, we would pass through deserty areas. Yes, the photographer and myself would be welcome to come to Pushkar with his people just before they left on migration.

'One more thing, Bhopal ji. When I am writing up my notes

perhaps I could rent a jhumpa?' I had fantasized about setting up my typewriter in one of these little round houses, so simple and pleasing, like a cubby-house from childhood, but the numberdar snuffed out my sentimentality immediately.

'You want to live in a jhumpa? Why? They wash away in the floods and have to be rebuilt each year. These stone houses,' he said, pointing to his own, 'are more expensive to build but less costly in the long run. Even the Raika must change with the times.' He suggested that it would be better if I were to live at his house. He would teach me all I needed to know and would look after me when it was time to migrate. In the meantime the shearing was about to start and he had to return to the dang immediately, but I was to meet him there to finalize arrangements.

I had been through the alphabet of failed plans. Now everything was being handed to me gift-wrapped. My responsibilities to the magazine would be fulfilled, an end to anxiety.

But I had met some other people involved with these particular Raika and I could tell that there were power struggles going on in which I could be a pawn. I admired the numberdar immensely. But while I respected him for being able to manipulate the system to his people's advantage and wished him luck, I did not want that manipulation to include me.

I said to Raju after the meeting, 'The numberdar is a very shrewd man.'

To which she replied, 'Who would respect a fool?'

I parted from Bhairon and Raju, proceeded with Koju through gathering rain and picked up Dilip. The following day we reached the Chambal River whose banks were occupied by miles of factories and refineries spilling their muck into the ominously rising waters. 'Development' in Rajasthan favours industry and large-scale agriculture and therefore is of benefit mainly to people in the top section of society – industrialists, the new middle class, rich landowners. Rural villagers are usually pushed aside or down into deeper poverty. Through the interstices between the new world and the old move the nomads, finding chinks and niches, adapting, surviving, until such time as the last pathways close.

When we reached Kota we found out that our road had been cut off at Baran and the bridge leading to the dang was covered by ten feet of water. Had Dilip not been with me I would be sitting on the banks of the Parbati still, gazing at the flood. He knew exactly whom to go to for help, exactly what to say to him and how to say it. The Superintendent of Police, Dr Bhopinder Singh, organized a jeep and driver for us on the other side.

Our transport was a heavy, wood plank U-boat, perilously leaking and ferried by four small grunting men pushing two oars on each hind flank of the boat. A tanker had been swept over the bridge just before we arrived. Men waved from the top. A cow hurtled past, horns showing above the torrent. It managed to reach the bank. A little later a dog, with less luck. On the other side the oarsmen leapt out into the mud and hauled us up to the jetty.

We drove to the higher ground on which the flocks were being held. It was typical overstocked sheep country – eaten to the bone, trees bonsaied by constant nibbling. New shoots covered the rocks with a fuzz of chemical green. Rain clouds tumbled around the sky, heavy and bad-tempered. Lifting a finger made the body erupt in sweat. There were small dangs everywhere here. A couple of months after the shearing they would move to another holding ground near Guna, then off they would go again into the migration.

The first line of defence on a dang is the dogs. Given that death by rabies was more likely than death by dacoits, I stood petrified as twenty mongrels stared at my ankles or throat with teeth bared, slaver flying. As for the Raika, they all looked as if they'd walked to hell and back. Skinny, tired, dirty, harassed. And yet, when they found out that we were friends of Giga and the others, the friendliness and generosity came out like sun behind clouds. Most of the women were camped next to their charpois, sitting in the sun, huddled over fires, cooking for the men. I was almost at fainting point with the heat. Yes, they agreed, smoke and flames licking at their faces as they punched their dough, it was hot. Don't worry about the dogs, they only bite at night. Here, come sit with us. Have tea? Chapati? No, you must not help us, you are our guest. I did what I could to help, which amused them. And perhaps a good laugh was the best contribution after all.

There was rather less attention paid to the refinements of

76

purdah out here, perhaps because there wasn't much to be gained by having physically hampered women around in a situation where everyone has to pitch in, everyone may have to fight, everyone is performing at the very limit of their physical and mental capacity.

The children were hardly children, so capable and sure of themselves were they. The girls were miniature women with babies almost as big as themselves tucked on a hip. I had a magazine with me, full of boring pictures of boring politicians. They clustered around and demanded to know who each one was. I made up some very strange names which sent them into hysterics. These tough little creatures had just walked a thousand kilometres or so on nothing but milk, chilli and flour. Why did they behave like live electrical cables? Why weren't they listless?

The sheep were all suffering foot-rot after the rains. A few shepherds were injecting antibiotic straight into the sheep's hooves but it looked to me like these skeletal woolbags did not stand a chance. Many had been lost through disease or in the floods or to thieves.

Despite the fact that it was impossible to sleep that night – coughing, bleating, gurgling, barking, snoring, sweating, slapping anophelese mosquitoes – I was, for the first time, excited by what I was doing. Whatever the discomforts of dang life, here one could breathe. Here would be continuity, friendships. The women were up before first light and called me over for tea.

I was assured that Bhopal ji would be arriving that day. In the meanwhile there was shearing to watch. Each dang had hired shearers belonging to a Muslim community, bussing them from northern Rajasthan down here to the south-east. There were about twenty shearers per dang, each man shearing fifty to sixty sheep per day at a rupee per sheep.

The shearers sat behind a thorn-bush windbreak and clipped with hand shears, very quickly, never leaving so much as a scratch and constantly sharpening their tools with a large file. The wool was weighed on a huge balance hanging from a branch, put into a pile, then transferred to the one-hundred-kilogram bale inside which a turban was bobbing up and down – the wool-presser. Young girls were stacking the wool or going about like hens, picking up any little bits left hanging on shrubs. A number of sheep were held by one shepherd next to the shearers. When they were sheared, they were let out to feed and another lot brought in. After all the wool was sheared from all the dangs, merchants would send trucks to take it to factories in Bikaner for dyeing.

I asked why the Raika didn't shear the animals themselves. A shepherd replied that they couldn't afford the numbers of men to do the work; they were all too busy herding the sheep. Another told me that the work was gunda (ritually unclean).

'And don't you wash the sheep before shearing them, as I've seen it done in other places?' The shepherd laughed, pointed at the lowering sky and said in English, 'Automatic.'

After lunch a young man arrived to say that Bhopal ji was fifty kilometres away on another dang.

'We'll drive there then.'

'You can't drive there. The roads are cut.'

'Then how did Bhopal ji manage it?'

The boy smiled at me as he might at a child and said, 'He walked.'

It was the end of August. I had about a month before the Baabara dang was to leave. The fact that I had not been able to make contact with Bhopal ji, and probably would not be able to do so, made me a little anxious. I knew how readily plans could slip through your fingers if you didn't have a stranglehold on them. I would have to rely on Bhairon.

Narendra said, 'In the meanwhile why don't you go to Kutch? I've heard the Rabari there swim their camels in the sea.'

'But Kutch is on the other side of the world.'

'Only a three-day drive from here.' (I had been on enough of these only-three-day drives to know that you reached the end of them more dead than alive.)

'What language do they speak?'

'Gujarati, I should think. Or a version of it.'

'Then I'm not going. Unless I can find a translator and that's impossible with so little time.'

'Not entirely. I speak a little Gujarati.'

Once, just after I had met him all those years ago, when I was still overawed by him, he had been showing me through his house and had picked up, casually, a solid silver box as old as his name and handed it to me. 'Please accept this small gift. For your bravery.' Then he had turned and glided away, leaving me with my jaw hanging open. Now, with exactly the same insouciance, and with exactly the same effect on me, he disappeared inside the jhumpa.

PART TWO

Migration

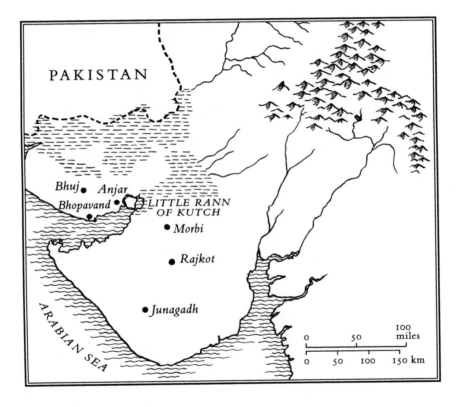

7

A squiggle of smoke, a figure in billowing robes, a camel and a bed silhouetted themselves against the horizon. To the east a moon squeezed into the sky; behind me the sun dissolved in the Arabian Sea. This was where I wanted to be. These were the people I wanted to live with. The previous year of doubt and confusion lifted off my back like an outgrown skin.

It had taken us three days to reach Bhuj, the ancient capital of Kutch, in northern Gujarat. Dreamboat and Narendra had done most of the driving which left me free to appreciate the landscape, a labyrinth of desert and sea as barren and beautiful as Mars. The instant we crossed the state border the roads became strips of aerodrome perfection. Gone were the death-trap potholes, gone the ridges, bumps, two-foot-high shoulders, gravel patches suddenly appearing on hairpin bends. Gone the overloaded trucks littering the sides of the road like dead cockroaches, their guts spilled, their wheels pointing skyward. Why? Because in Gujarat, unlike Rajasthan, the money for roads did not go directly into someone's pocket. Some of it was actually spent on building roads. In Gujarat one could see women. Unveiled women. Women riding scooters! And you could see forestry plots by the side of the road that contained real trees, rather than phantom trees which, in Rajasthan, only exist on paper. But best of all was having Narendra with me. Not only could he translate languages, he translated what was buried beneath them – the gestures, cultural forms, shared social signals. Besides that, he was the least flappable companion I had ever travelled with, the most patient, the most generous.

I had had in my possession one hastily scribbled name: Dr Rama Krishna, Assistant-Director Gujarat Sheep and Wool

Development Programme, Bhuj. Experience had taught me to place little hope in such names. But on meeting this South Indian and the saints-among-bureaucrats who worked for him, I knew I had struck gold.

Dr Rama Krishna had immediately brought us to a shepherd whom he particularly liked, Rangka bhai Rabari. It had taken us a day to find him, camped on this windswept little plain just a mile outside his village. His mother spread her best quilt on the ground for us and brought tea.

'I have no home but these camps,' she said. 'I live under the sky, no matter whether there is rain or sun. The village is not our home, the dang is our home. That is where our property is.'

Rangka assured me that there would be several dangs leaving from his village and setting out for Saurashtra. He would not be going this year but he would talk to his community on my behalf. His mother suggested that I would do better to remain here in Kutch, wandering the local area with her.

Rangka's wife Jasu laughed, dazzling the company with her beauty, which was not merely physical but an emanation of her whole potent self. 'Yes, stay with us here. You carry the water and I shall carry the flour. But be warned, if you travel with us your skin will become as black as ours. Even your hair will go black.' She tugged at my blonde straw then took me to see her 'equipment' stacked neatly on the cot. Thickly embroidered blankets, appliquéd flour sacks, a marriage smock for a little brother which would take years to complete, a blouse studded with fragments of mica into which she tried, unsuccessfully, to squeeze my bulk. This was the finest embroidery I had seen anywhere and aeons of wandering were coded in its patterns.

Rangka would not be migrating this year because he was on his honeymoon. He had waited for his wife for over twenty years, travelling back and forth to his in-laws' house, begging them to send her to him. He and Jasu had been together for just four months, so I can be forgiven for seeing him as a man undone by love. She had cost him forty-five thousand rupees, most of it in jewellery, but by the way he looked at her from under his brows, checking whether his words received her approval, it was clear that he thought she was worth that and more. They were a handsome couple and you wished, when you saw them together, that the feudal tales of desert romance were true: that Jasu and her husband found deep pleasure in each other out there on their bed under the stars. But it's unlikely. For one thing, there was always someone else around – his sisters, mother, visiting children, other shepherds. For another, there weren't the necessary hours to spare. And it was the women and children who shared Jasu's bed, not Rangka.

Two ancient shepherds came hobbling in. They worked for a local landowner for a yearly set of clothes, their tobacco and flour, and a hundred and seventy rupees per month. We teased them by asking if they were married, to which they laughed good-naturedly and confessed that they weren't wealthy enough even to get engaged. I did find myself wondering if they enjoyed carnal knowledge of their ewes but I found out later that though the practice was not unheard of, it was considered immoral and punished accordingly. Sex was not a right but one of life's bonuses. Like wealth, you were lucky if you had it but if you didn't, you got on with the task in hand – surviving.

It was not uncommon, I was told, for a woman to be in her mid thirties before her parents finally relinquished her to her husband, usually at the behest of the elders. The reason may well be economic as a daughter is a valuable worker. But from what I was to see later on, the detaining of daughters had as much to do with affection as it did with finance. Or, perhaps in a community like this, one's ability to work and contribute is inextricably bound up with the love and respect one receives.

Dr Rama Krishna thought that the Rabari women had a hard time being kept in their parents' homes until they were 'old'. But I interpreted the phenomenon differently. Here were women whose value as human beings was reflected in the heavy bride price. They owned property in their own right (receiving sheep from the husband's family at marriage and inheriting the mother's jewellery) and although they did not sit in panchaits or attend the men-only smoking/yarning sessions, no one doubted the ferocity of debate back home. They were not burdened with child-bearing during their teens. Their work was as valued as the men's. They could shop and do business in villages and towns without being chaperoned and without covering their faces. I do not mean to say that individual women were in any sense capricious regarding community law. Only that the power between the sexes was balanced, so producing a confident sauciness in the women and a humorous appreciation in the men that were delightful to behold.

The Rajasthani Raika women I had met were freer than females of many other castes but, even so, I had been somewhat taken aback by those little peep-holes they made in their ornis and the way they covered their heads and went silent when their men were present – so unlike their Kutchi cousins. Perhaps this was due to their links to the higher caste Rajputs, who are such sticklers for purdah that women may be locked up for their entire lives. It seemed to me that the Rajput influence had other negative effects on the Raika. While the Rabari of Kutch were patrician in their demeanour – the servants of no one – the Rajasthani Raika boasted of being servants to kings and were quick to dissociate themselves from Rabari who were not.

These were the first people who had wholeheartedly supported the idea of my travelling with them. When we rose to bid farewell, the mood was one of excitement, pleasure, satisfaction. Narendra took out two hundred and one rupees and gave them, with a certain flourish, to the youngest child who accepted the money with equal graciousness.

'How do you do it?' I said as we got into the car. 'Please, tell me the rules.'

'There are no rules. It was a happy meeting. The money was a way of acknowledging that. It is only done once and then only if the feeling is good. I gave it because they impressed me, because we liked each other. You don't have to feel nervous of doing the right thing. Just do as you feel. Be spontaneous. What they respect is genuineness.'

We drove to Anjar or, as it is otherwise known, the Paris of Kutch. (There was a Copenhagen of Kutch, a Jaisalmer of Kutch, even a Venice of Kutch.) It did not look at all like Paris but like a dusty little medieval town with a Portuguese influence in the architecture. Kutch is more or less cut off from the rest of the country during the monsoon and Kutchis tend to be faced, psychologically, to the sea. The thriving ports, the huge ships with foreign names, give the people an outward-looking character, a cosmopolitanism that is not shared by their land-locked neighbours. There was room to breathe here. I did not get stared at quite so much. The population was thinner too because Kutch lacked water and without it people cannot live.

Narendra provided everyone around us with a glass of tea (cobblers, cloth merchants, beggars, shepherds et cetera) and we sat on wooden planks outside a tiny shop made of beaten tin and cardboard – Anjar's version of café society – to watch street life. It was the wedding season and the streets were packed or rather, I should say, garlanded with Rabari grooms, ranging in age from two to twenty. The old man slurping next to me grumbled that he was fed up with the wedding season because the young shepherds were showing off their finery instead of helping him with the sheep. He grumbled but he watched me watching the young men and smiled with satisfaction.

Beauty is a poor standard by which to judge human beings but how could people who looked like that not be beautiful inside as well? What flair! What sense of colour and design! What magnanimous display of self for the delight of others! First, the turbans. Purple red gold black silk, tied so that they had a slightly triangular shape lending the faces beneath a Pharaonic cast. Next, a long-sleeved smock made of thick white cotton drill, embroidered in minute stitches of every colour – purples and reds dominating – edged in gold or silver, tight fitting until gathered beneath the breast to flare at narrow hips; the sleeves pushed up into wrinkles at the wrist. Beneath the smocks, white lawn dhotis, one of the oldest forms of dress in the world, were tucked into pink-, red- and black-striped nylon socks which disappeared into high-heeled leather clogs decorated with brass studs, the toes curling backwards into Sindbad points. They hung around together in groups like adolescent boys anywhere, shy and giggling one minute, swaggering the next. And, in among the riot of masculine colour, groups of women in black wool and silver, black ornis swelling out like jib-sails, strode past whitewashed walls.

Here, Rabari marriages all occurred on the same day, the second of September. Usually, auspicious times for Hindu weddings are ascertained by Brahmin priests who are paid to consult the stars. But the second of September is Krishna's birthday, so how could it not be auspicious? This bending of the rules was typical of Rabari thrift and good sense.

Dr Rama Krishna and the others held no illusions about the innocence of the nomads but they felt deep admiration for them and worked unceasingly on their behalf. Building up trust with their clients and at the same time challenging certain traditions which were no longer useful to them (for example, convincing them that the goddess would not punish them if they gave their sheep medicine for pox infections) were no easy tasks. That they had successes in both was a tribute to their commitment and vision.

'If they can rook you of fifty rupees they'll feel happier with that than if you paid them a hundred. But you can't blame them. They behave to others as others behave to them. Everyone tries to exploit them.'

A fieldworker, Mamu bhai, a Rabari himself, laughed and added, 'There is a Gujarati saying about us. We will ask you politely to lift your foot so we can pick up a stone. Then we'll hit you with it.'

The Doctor had tried to protect his clients from exploitation by the merchants by adding some competition to the market and thereby stabilizing the prices. But the Rabari still preferred the more traditional relationship with the banias (merchants), even though they were forever being ripped off by them.

A merchant would fix a price with a mukki (the Kutchi word for numberdar) for the wool of all the sheep under his jurisdiction and the bania would pay for the shearers. But because the wool was bought per sheep not per kilo, the merchant would wait an extra month before shearing so he would get seven months' growth for the price of six. In that extra month the poor mukki would be forever visiting the merchant to plead, thus adding to his expenses. On top of that the bania would not pay straight away but would wait, sometimes months, until the market price had fallen. Thus were the Rabari being 'fleeced'. However the banias often acted as financial backers for migrating shepherds. If anything went wrong in a distant state – fights or arrests – the mukki would send a message to the bania who would come to sort it out. The money from the wool was not enough to keep the community going if there was an emergency (income from wool has fallen one hundred per cent in the last four years. It is coarse wool for carpets because the sheep which produce the finer garment wool can't survive the rigours of migration), but they could borrow from the merchant whose surety was the sheep.

Perhaps the most important reason for continuing to deal with merchants rather than government agencies is that the former do not require banks or documents – a big incentive to people who resist any kind of regulation and who, if ever they have surplus cash, quickly buy gold and bury it.

The next day we were taken to visit a Rabari camel herd out in those wild and lovely but denuded hills. Mamu bhai said, in response to my query, 'There are two animals for every person in Kutch and the land just can't support the numbers. We tried to contract out a livestock-culling programme which the Rabari were in favour of, but the Jains are very rich and powerful here. Killing animals is against their religion so, under political pressure, we had to cancel the programme. During the bad seasons the numbers do fall off but as soon as a good rain comes, the count shoots way up again so the country is never rested.'

The owner of this particular herd of camels was relatively wealthy. This meant that he would not take them on migration himself but, having reconnoitred an area ahead by bus, had handed the animals over to members of a Muslim caste, the Juts, to whom he paid six rupees per camel per month. The camels would leave Kutch thin and come back fat. In the meantime he would take the stronger, healthier camels on small local migrations.

The two communities, despite their different religions, had helped each other out and travelled together as long as anyone could remember. The Juts were considered a little lower on the social pyramid but a wealthy Jut could just as easily employ a poor Rabari as the other way around. The Rabari preferred to hire the Juts rather than members of their own caste because if something went wrong on migration then the trouble remained outside the 'family' and would not sow discord within the community.

Out of these herds one or two female camels would be dedicated to the goddess – Mata ji ki Meri. The milk of those cows would never be sold, only given to children, and the animals themselves never sold even when they were old and useless. The camels belonging to the goddess would always be kept with the Rabari, never sent away with the Juts.

Back in Bhuj I collapsed in a heap in the Prince Hotel whose air-conditioning, fine service and chicken tikka masala I would come to depend upon in the months ahead. But today the very thought of chicken tikka made me want to die. Narendra sat on the side of the bed and forced me to drink nimbu soda with sugar. I hated him.

My policy in India had been to eat anything and to drink whatever water was available on the assumption that sooner or later my body would learn to accommodate the bugs. And it worked. I had had only two bouts of illness, both of them mild, and this was one of them. Besides, from what I could discern of what lay behind various village walls, it wasn't only visitors who suffered intestinal troubles. And if Indians could cope without dubiously bottled water, so could I. I had had my shots of gamma globulin, rabies vaccine and tetanus, and sometimes remembered to take my quinine. More precaution than that seemed obsessive.

Dr Rama Krishna had been hunting the whole of Kutch for a certain mukki, Pala bhai, whom, he felt sure, would be the best person to take me on migration. He 'lived' in Rangka's village but, as the Doctor put it 'The Rabari are never at home.' I knew my friends in the department were working very hard on my behalf and I also knew that once Pala bhai was located and brought to the office I would have to be there, as I might never get another chance to meet him.

The phone call came through. I leapt off the bed in excitement and found myself flat on the floor. I made it to the jeep but the earth was spinning off its axis. Narendra said I was the colour of a banana. We arrived at the office but I decided I would lose more face by fainting in front of them than by staying away. I asked Narendra to cover for me and I drove back to the hotel. I made it to the bathroom and struggled with my trousers. My body erupted – Mount St Helens at one end and Vesuvius at the other. It was so violent and so surprising that I didn't even have time to feel disgusted. I spent the next half hour cleaning myself and the bathroom, then I headed back to the office. Oh the European stomach, that organ of sabotage, proof of racial inferiority. At all costs I must conceal the inadequacy of my stomach from Pala. It would confirm his doubts about me.

I entered the Doctor's office. Everyone was waiting. Narendra said, 'Did your international call come through?' 'No,' I said, improvising equally quickly, 'but I cancelled it because I could not miss meeting Pala bhai.' Even if I had not recognized him from his bearing, the huge silver bracelet made up of the English letters of his name would have given me a clue.

He wore the traditional white turban and white embroidered smock, and carried his wool shawl draped over his arm with the air of a man who has his clothes tailored in Savile Row. His eyes shifted from face to face, reading them. I beamed, brought my hands together in a namaste and said, 'So what have you all been talking about?' The Doctor replied that they had not reached a decision because it was very difficult. I said in Hindi, 'What is the problem?' Without missing a beat Pala answered, 'What problems aren't there for us travelling people? Shepherds and sheep killed on the roads. Bhils (tribals) stealing our animals; bandits stealing our money. Fights with locals and police. Thirst and hardship and the closing of grazing lands. Too many deaths each year on migration.' There was not a trace of whining in this speech. He spoke as if ticking off a shopping list.

Naturally money was an incentive to having me along, but what if something happened to me. Would he and his people be held responsible? How could he trust us when we said that they would not? What guarantees were there? What might the repercussions be of this unprecedented state of affairs? Not just a stranger with them but a European stranger. A *female* European stranger. He said, 'If I make the wrong decision my face will be black with my people.'

And so the bargaining and convincing went on. Each man present put forward his point of view and there was much bantering and laughter. When anyone made a good joke or said something 'true', Pala would rise to shake hands with that person – so gently, so gracefully. But I could sense his confusion. He must base his decision on instinct, monetary consideration and trust in this roomful of people, none of whom was a shepherd. Every now and then he would whisk the Doctor's colleague, Praveen Singh ji, into another room for a private conference. When they returned the discussion would continue, back and forth, and during it I would feel Pala regarding me, trying to size me up.

'It's all very well what you people say,' said Pala, 'but I am already more worried about her than I am about my own sister.' But after two hours, it was clear that he was coming round to the idea. He insisted that I have a man with me. I had not particularly wanted this but it would give them more confidence and the man would be able to teach me how to do things without my having to pester the group.

I prayed for my body to behave but exhaustion was getting the better of it. It grabbed hold of bones and bent them. It compressed the brain. Not only must it be endured, it must be hidden. At last the price was fixed − two thousand rupees a month. I must provide my own food and buy my goat milk from them. They would provide camel, saddle and gear. Narendra proclaimed, 'From now on Pala bhai's family is your family,' and everyone stood up and shook hands and ordered tea in celebration. Pala asked for my name. When I told him he frowned as if to say, That is not any kind of a name, and announced that from now on I would be called Ratti ben − sister of blood, or passion. I handed over a thousand and one rupees, a down-payment, and offered to pay his fare home as we had delayed him.

Mamu bhai Rabari insisted on showing Pala my hotel room which, although I loved it, could only be described as luxurious when compared with the competition. A bed, a hot water tap, a window, an air-conditioning unit, a couple of bare light bulbs, a Laminex coffee table and a Vinyl sofa. But the point needed to be made that if I were willing to forego such opulence for the Rabari, I was obviously a serious sort of person. We all sat around, stiff, nervous and giggling, waiting for the food which Pala, having never tasted such things before, then could not finish. Mamu bhai teased him saying, 'You'd better finish your icecream or you'll make a bad impression.' Afterwards, in the bathroom, Pala burnt his hands in the hot water. We all laughed at him, the laughter of the sophisticated towards the simple. He said, 'Well, how was I to know? It started out cold.' As they all filed out Mamu bhai surreptitiously reminded him to bid me farewell. Pala went to shake my hand while I brought my hands together in a namaste. Then I went to shake his hand while he namasted. I did not kid myself that the first two weeks alone with them was going to be anything other than a nightmare of mutual awkwardness.

The next day Narendra had to return to Jodhpur. After saying my goodbyes and thank yous, I closed the door of my room and confronted empty space. I would be forty-one in five days' time and no one in the world knew where I would be. Not even me. Many of my birthdays and Christmases had been spent in happy solitude, so I wasn't sure why I should now feel . . . well . . . sad. And wouldn't it have been nice if I could have celebrated my birthday with someone like . . . say . . . Narendra.

The marriage ceremonies would occur the following day. I had forewarned Dilip, who was anxious to photograph a child wedding. He was on his way from Delhi. The Doctor had gone to a good deal of trouble to locate a village where such ceremonies were taking place and to negotiate with a certain man regarding the delicate matter of taking photos.

It is not easy getting from Delhi to Bhuj – a long plane journey via Bombay – then from Bhuj to a village, carrying all your camera gear and squeezing it, along with half a dozen people, into a single jeep, especially when back in Delhi you have a wife and a newborn baby with whom you would prefer to be.

At village Varshameda we were greeted politely but not warmly. Word had spread that child marriages were to be photographed and this had caused some ructions within the community. Might we not show these photographs to the government and land the people in trouble? The women regarded me sourly. Our contact, Naka bhai, was doing his best to help us but even he was having a difficult time with his relatives. He said, 'Most of the Rabari are innocent but I've lived around the ports and I am more knowledgeable. It is hard to change them.' Naka was aware of the difficult future facing his caste. He had sold all his sheep and bought a truck, and was trying to convince others that they should follow suit. Slowly a knot of men formed around us, anxious that we should hear their problems.

An old retired mukki began, 'Our children will always herd sheep. What else can they do? They are not educated. And how can we abandon our way of life, it is all that we know?'

A young man took up the theme. 'There is no future for us Rabari. The government tells us we destroy the forests but they said they'd replant those forestry areas twenty years ago and they've done nothing, so why can't we graze our sheep there? And why do they plant a tree that is useless for everything except cooking fires? The thorns get stuck in the sheep's mouths during the drought when they eat them in desperation.' Hoping, perhaps, that his words would travel further than Varshameda, perhaps even as far as the Raj Sabha itself, he declaimed, 'If the government doesn't help us, we'll go to Pakistan.' The discussion became more heated, the old men, confused by the politics, giving way to the young hotbloods. Finally, the anger exhausted itself.

To lighten the atmosphere I addressed the old men. 'So when are you going to make this young man a leader?'

To which someone replied, 'How can we make him a mukki, yaar? He might land us all in Pakistan.' And everyone fell about laughing.

We waited several hours for the ceremonies to begin. At last Naka came to us full of apology and said, 'They have decided that you cannot photograph.' Dilip went off like a cracker but it was no good. The decision had been made. It was final.

I worried for Dilip. As he said 'you are only as good as your last photograph' and he felt he wasn't getting the material he needed. The Rabari were not making it easy for him. But what more could I do? During the long periods of waiting, events would happen without warning, leaving no time to call him from Delhi. Or, as on this occasion, I would summon him and nothing would happen. My responsibility button was being hit with the force of a jackhammer. Very well then, one thing I could promise him – pictures of camels swimming in the sea and of the last traditionally built Rabari village in Kutch. But not just yet. I had been told the people of that village were suspicious of outsiders. Therefore I would go to live there myself for a couple of weeks under the auspices of Dr Rama

Krishna, so that the inhabitants would get to know me and to understand what was being asked of them. I would prepare them for the rather more dramatic arrival of a photographer.

8

Bhopavand (the place of priests or mediums) consisted of five hundred or so round, beige houses decorated with whitewash. The roofs were pointed cones of grey straw, so that from a distance the village looked like a tight cluster of narrow toadstools. It had a defensive appearance but once you entered it, it opened to reveal its life. One hut blended into another, linked by terraces and platforms. Emerging from and disappearing into the houses were men in white and women in black. The little oval doors and windows showed that slight lopsidedness which is so pleasing to the eye: everything here had been made by hand from earth, wood, straw, dung, stone.

But behind each stark exterior lay fantasy and fairy tale – round white palaces containing Moresque cupboards moulded of mud plaster, inlaid with mirrors, glass paintings and baubles, old light bulbs set in rows. White quilts bordered in red or blue lay stacked against walls, brass pots shone in a gloom fractured by patterns of light from one or two windows. Here and there pale blue or pink wash framed recesses where the deities lived.

The village sat on a shoreline as if it had reached the end of something and could go no further. An enigmatic landscape stretched beyond – sandy islands and tidal flats across which the sea came creeping so fast and so thinly that watching it sent tingles up the back of the neck. The water was light brown and opaque. A mile or two away a line of froth delineated the beach and along it Impressionistic strokes suggested stick and hessian shelters. A camel cart creaked its way across the flats, delivering drums of water to the Muslim fishermen camped there. The land seascape had an abandoned quality and a largeness that made the heart swell out to fill it.

Bhopavand had perched on the edge of this sea for several centuries and very soon it will have dissolved into the past for ever, which may go some way to explaining the prickliness of its inhabitants. They are camel breeders and were once quite well off. Their deity, Goddess Vankul Mata ji, rides on a camel and specifically bequeathed the animal to them. Although there is little profit now to be made from their herds, they cannot abandon a way of life which has sustained them since their beginnings, which is intrinsic to their identity. They cannot betray Mata ji.

I never did get to the bottom of Rabari religious beliefs but I did know that for all the folkloric jokes concerning their ceremonial ignorance, despite the variations in local beliefs and practices, and even though the etymology of Rabari can be interpreted as 'one outside the conventions', it was, nevertheless, a caste famous for producing ascetics. Why this should be so, I do not know but I suspect that if you have lived your life alone with the herds you develop a propensity for speculating upon, and talking to, God. Out on the dang there may be little access to ritual apparatus – temples, specialists and intermediaries – but this does not mean that the faith of travelling people is less potent. The gods are always present and Rabari attachment to them is strong, even though, during migration, the dialogue with those deities is necessarily internal.

This community was unusual in the sense that the principal deity was worshipped externally, and collectively, and surrounding that worship was a complex ritual apparatus. Besides the camel, Mata ji had bestowed a singular spiritual superiority on her people so that all the men of the village inherited the title of bhopa. She demanded strict ritual performances from them, a proper place to live, sacrificial objects and so on.

One could say perhaps that the Rabari of Bhopavand were uncharacteristically orthodox. Their Mata ji seemed a rather unforgiving version of the goddess, forbidding her worshippers to build in anything but traditional materials, forbidding even the use of kerosene let alone electricity. But lately she had been loosening up a little, feeling, possibly, that it was better to bend to the modern world than be entirely shattered by it.

I arrived on the day Bhopavand was celebrating the opening of its first cement temple, which sat amidst the dun houses like an Italian wedding cake. The way Mata ji had given permission for this rupture of tradition was as follows. Her bhopas tied a goat by the front of the old temple, a toadstool house like the others. Then they stroked the goat up and down, themselves going in to trance and asking Mata ji if they could build in mortar and brick. If the goat shivered (and it would be an insensitive goat who did not), the answer was yes. In any case if the goat refused to comply another would be substituted.

Around the temple banners and bunting were flying, and visitors from miles around were milling about the stalls or being fed under an enormous open-sided tent. Beautifully dressed Rabari men dished out the food on thalis: dal, hard noodles, some sticky sweet stuff – all topped with a liberal helping of salty dust. Afterwards, near the water truck which had been donated by the government for this day – the village well being such a long way off – men were doing the washing up. Behind them was the open-air kitchen: giants' cauldrons made of rivetted iron, bubbling over fire pits. I wondered how they managed to afford such a huge party. The Doctor told me the first man to open the door of the inner sanctum of the temple had paid nine thousand six hundred rupees for the privilege. Another paid five thousand rupees for tying the flag on top.

Now that Mata ji had given the OK, progress in the form of electricity, pumped water, breeze-block housing and, eventually, television will reinvent Bhopavand. Whether this is ultimately a good or a bad thing, who can say? But one can certainly say that it is the unique being devoured by the homogeneous, a process characteristic of our age and, to me, a cause for grief.

Dr Rama Krishna waited with me all morning and introduced me to the person who would be my 'contact', a new field officer whose job it would be to explain to the people of Bhopavand why I was there. After they left Koju and I set up a tent a quarter of a mile from the village. Only later did we discover that we had camped near the animal graveyard, where the dogs came at night to scavenge and to howl until dawn.

In the afternoon we went to the burial ground to watch a

ceremony. (The Rabari here bury their dead just as Muslims do.) On one side were the women like a noisy congregation of rooks. On the other were the men. Coloured flags flapped in a heavy sea wind. Drums beat out a pulse. Towards the front, some of the men had gone into trance, waiting for the goddess to possess them. They would shake, then suddenly leap up and dance, flagellating themselves with thick leather ropes but only for a few seconds, after which another man would gently embrace the dancer from behind and take away the rope so that no real damage was done. One could not help but be a little envious of such intimacy with God. I had asked the older men and women if I might take some photographs to which they readily agreed. (I loathe taking photos in such situations but as Dilip was not there I felt it was my duty.) But when the time came a man screamed at me to go away. I slunk backwards into the crowd, ashamed and upset. Another Rabari from a distant village could speak a little English. He said, 'These are jungly, jungly people. A wild tribe. They always make mischiefs.'

On my first tentative foray into Bhopavand alone I was met by the children – a gang of over-excitable little fiends who spoke at screaming pitch. I submitted to their teasing. Seru was leader of the pack. In another culture he would be branded hyperactive. Or perhaps a prodigy. When the shrieks of his gang became too much, he lifted his hand and his face took on a furious look. The laughter died instantly and everyone waited in expectation. He pulled me close to him and began playing a rhythm on his face. Fingers drummed on his puffed-out cheeks, his tongue clicked in syncopation, eyes bulged. I was made to copy. It took great dexterity but those years at the piano came in for some use after all. Hysterics from the monsters. Young women came and joined in, everyone popping fingers on cheeks and clicking tongues. I noticed that the women and children were never still. It was as if they were electrified. Yet they were covered in carbuncles and boils. No doubt they had been working since they could walk and high energy output was a habit. They asked me where my husband was by twirling an imaginary moustache, looking questioningly at me and slicing the hand sideways, as if to say where? Or what? Then they indicated my camp. I realized that they thought I was married to Koju, or if not married to him, then doing things with the handsome young Rajput of a morally questionable nature. Older women came by but they stared at me sourly. Or was I just imagining that? When I went back to camp, I passed an old lady rebuilding the platform of her house – mud, dung and water, smoothed and plastered by hand. She came to show me those hands. They were raw and suppurating. She asked for medicine, so I took her to my tent for antibiotic dusting powder and from then on doctored her every day. Officially Mata ji could cure anything but perhaps western medicine hurried her along?

I waited a few days, not knowing what to make of the conflicting signals. Some people wanted me to visit them and were very friendly. Others cast flick-knife looks. There were, as always, the perfect manners but underneath them lay a queer kind of tension. The whole village was turned inward. I invited some of the ladies to my camp for tea but no one came.

Life can get pretty dismal sitting beside a tent on a flat surface that stretches brownly from horizon to horizon, in 110-degree heat, thinking about what normal people do on their forty-first birthdays. So Koju and I decided to walk across the mud to visit the Muslim fishermen on the beach. From them we would try to hire a boat by which to cross the channel, and on the other side hunt for the camel herds which, we were told, would soon be swimming that channel on their way home.

The fisherfolk lived for six months of the year in their home village fifty kilometres away. The rest of the time they lived here, under these flimsy shelters, by the shade of a stunted and half-naked tree. The men stayed out all day on their heavy wooden boats, netting fish or catching small lobsters which they sold to America for big money. Half a dozen women and about a dozen children remained behind on the beach, salting and drying the fish on stinking racks, then packing it in crates to be sent to Bombay. There was no fresh water for bathing (each delivered drum cost ten rupees), no vegetables – only what the sea provided and the milk from a couple of goats. As for the boats, God knows how they weren't all lost at sea. The channel was a calm stretch of maybe five hundred yards' width but when we came to land on the other side, there was a slight sea chop. The boat heaved wildly; Koju clung to the mast looking most unnautical. Getting out, we sank up to our crotches in mud. From there we walked across several kilometres of squelch, searching the surrounding mirage for any dromedarian shapes. Koju walked a few hundred yards ahead, his shape becoming thinner and thinner until it melted into light.

When we returned, the fisherwomen had gathered enough courage to ask us to tea. How different they were from their Rabari neighbours. There was a gaiety in them, an outwardness, that belied the adversity of their lives. The boys dug up some crabs for me. I gave a young girl seventy-one rupees. After that I visited them almost every day, not for the crabs so much as for their company.

On the fifth day Koju drove off to replenish our water supply at a well several kilometres away. It was early morning. The salt pan stretched away to clouds on 150 degrees of the compass; the remaining angle contained a line of palm trees and the clustered cones of the village. A figure in fluttering black emerged, then vanished. Tiny birds ran through the marsh grasses; the earth was holding its breath between the exhalation of a land breeze and the inhalation of a sea breeze. Gradually the day's mirages were forming, making it seem as if the ovenlike tent was surrounded by cool water. A herd of goats appeared and crossed the flats, heading for little islands of salty grass, creating an optical illusion in the heat shimmer. The thousands of legs looked like the legs of one creature – a monstrous millipede – followed by a lone goatherd.

There was a noise from the village. I turned around to see two hundred women heading towards me. I rose to greet them, wondering how I would provide tea for such a multitude. All went well at first. But soon the excitement grew into something unpleasant. The children whipped up a kind of hysteria and it grew and spread through the women. They began going through my things, grabbing at them, and when I tried to stop them I realized that any action on my part would only increase the frenzy. I stood in front of the tent, arms folded and stared resolutely at the horizon. I wasn't frightened, not exactly, but it was deeply unsettling to be confronted with crowd hysteria in the face of which I was entirely powerless. The old lady whose infected hand I had been doctoring tried to calm things down but without effect. At last the jeep appeared in a whorl of dust and the women and children fled, screaming, inside the mute walls of the village.

Dear Koju. He took one look at me and knew just what to do. He fixed the radio and turned on the English news, made tea, said he'd throw red chilli powder into their faces if they came again, said, 'By night dogs, by day children.' He said that he had never liked these people but, shrugging philosophically, added, 'Dusare desh, dusare loog' (different countries, different people). I accepted the tea with shaking hands and soon we were laughing.

The next morning I decided to go back into the village on the falling-off-a-horse/getting-back-on principle. Besides, I had promised to take medicine to the old lady. The children were waiting for me, a hundred or more, and this time they grabbed at my clothes and bag, pinched me and chanted, 'Boopin! Boopin!' (which was how they understood my name). Chills up and down my back – this was the pack hunting and my terror of it was atavistic and profound. I pretended unconcern and slowly made my way towards some huts where previously I had been welcomed. As the pebbles started flying, a woman pulled me inside. I waited there with children and women pushing and shoving at the entrance, blocking the air so that those of us inside could barely breathe. But the lovely person who saved me did not lose her equanimity. Quietly she talked to them, explaining who I was, why I had come and that I was not an enemy. Then some old women placed themselves at the front of the mob, alternately calming the children and half-heartedly chastising them. My protectors apologized abjectly but it was clear that staying any longer at Bhopavand was neither profitable nor wise. Only later did I find out conjecture was rife that I was a government spy.

To those who have a romantic view of travel or who, longing for the liberty they imagine it brings, wish that they, too, could throw off old jobs, old husbands, old responsibilities and head for wilder climes where, they feel sure, both life and themselves will be entirely different – that is to say, better; who do not understand that one carries the self like a heavy old suitcase wherever one goes; who think of travel not as a line of inquiry, a satisfaction of curiosity or as a method by which to better understand the world but as an escape from banality, I have this to say.

When you are so tired, frustrated and filthy that you would like to cry but cannot because people are watching you; when your period has come and you are in pain but you must not display it; when you do not know what is going on because you cannot understand the language but you sense the atmosphere is not right; when you are operating on twenty levels at once and not sure if you are correct in any of them; when you have entered a place where the people are suspicious of you, or frightened of you, or hate you because you represent something evil to them; when you cannot make your intentions understood; when there are children, hundreds of them, pressing up against you, shouting, pulling at your hair and clothes, or pelting you with rocks; when you are so fed up with humanness that you would like to shoot everyone you see, including your self; when the village dogs race towards you howling and slavering; and when, finally, you make it back to the tent to have a cup of tea, the only luxury you have, you find that the milk has turned to yogurt; when there is no one with whom to have a sensible conversation, nor is there likely to be anyone for months; when you realize how very far away from you are the places and people you understand and who under-stand you; when your Celtic skin, which blushes even under a weak northern sun, has been baked into pottery by sun and salt so that you have to stop yourself thinking of the cancers which surely must be forming, let alone the years you are adding to your face; when the little beasts that have taken up residence in your stomach double you up in a cramp so that you have to run behind a dune even though there are people everywhere watching; and when you have so lost touch with why you are doing what you are doing that it seems you are trapped in a machine of meaning-lessness in which moral values are mashed to a pulp and yet, because of an overdeveloped sense of responsibility (or perhaps a lack of courage), you cannot liberate yourself by cancelling an article for a magazine; when you have plumbed the very depths of banality, then, you begin to wonder if it is worth it.

If *what* is worth it, exactly?

Moments. You might be walking along a beach where there are

no footprints. There is a little girl, a fisherman's daughter, holding your hand. You see some shapes in the distance along the rim of the sea and you think you recognize those shapes from pictures you have seen. You take in a breath, just loud enough for the girl to look at you questioningly, and you point to them and she nods and you walk together into the brightness. And there, for the first time in your life, you see them. But they are not pink, you say, and hurry towards them. Their stride, too, quickens – long hinged legs elongated in the mirage. You reach to within ten yards of them before they float off the sand, insect legs slowly pacing, slowly lifting them up in a blaze of flamingo red.

It's not the same as seeing them in a zoo.

Or, you might be walking through mud to the hips and you are laughing at your friend Koju who has never seen the sea and who poses for a photograph with a shell on his head. And then you sit on the sand floor of a tent with the fishermen who stuff you with as many hot fresh crabs as you can eat, plus tiny curried fish, tea and fellowship, and you eat five crabs before sheer embarrassment at your gluttony forces you to stop. And the lady of the house hugs you and laughs, and takes you to the sea to wash your face.

It's not the same as eating at the local restaurant.

Or, you have been walking through a wilderness of sand. The silence and the rhythm of the walking have sent you into a reverie in which you seem behind yourself, watching yourself watching reality. The wrinkling action of water on sand brings a thought to the surface which echoes the pattern itself. What is the force driving matter into ever more complicated, ever more improbable forms? Why does it do this, and why are you here to observe it? What you see is so astonishing that you are grateful simply to have life, to have senses with which to witness the event, even though the seeing hearing smelling touching wondering must end in nothing-at-all. Then another thought washes up through that thought and you recognize the rightness of it, of yourself being one of an infinite series of forms coalescing out of matter, returning to it, so that before and after lose their meaning and their terror, and the soul is allowed, for the time it takes for a sparkle to flash on the sea, to feel connected to everything that ever was or ever will be. Something solid forms in you again and holds you strongly to life.

I retired to Bhuj's Prince Hotel to lick my wounds. I had two days to do so and what better way to pass them than to stay in bed watching videos, reading, sleeping and eating chicken tikka masala? Through the gullies of Bhuj I went searching for the video shop. I found it and took out six videos. But back in the hotel room I found that every one of them was so damaged that only a scratchy grey surface came up on the screen, across which human-shaped ghosts sometimes strayed. The sound was something like a pond full of croaking toads. Back I went to request a refund or videos that contained videos.

'But you have already taken them out, Madam.'

'Yes, I *know* I have taken them out but I am returning them because they are unwatchable, and I would like you to give me back my money please, because I paid the money to watch videos that had something on them, not videos that had nothing on them.'

The man behind the counter looked as if he might break down under the weight of sorrow I had just placed upon him. He pulled out the piece of paper upon which earlier I had signed my name. Would Madam care to regard the piece of paper and realize that there was nothing he could do? It is mysterious to me now, when such incidents formed the fabric of everyday life, why one incident rather than another should light the fuse of that startling anger.

'It is true that the videos are empty but you see, Madam, that is not my job. I am not the owner.'

'Then please may I speak to the owner.'

'Yes, but he is not here.'

'Where is he?'

'He lives in Bombay, Madam.'

I did not care about the money; I cared about logic. I felt my chin tremble stupidly. I raised my voice. His features acquired that impassiveness which is impervious to plea or rage. He had gone away inside. I left, defeated, and through the window watched him replace the videos on the shelf ready for the next customer.

Fortified with some friends from Dr Rama Krishna's department I returned to the village, apologized for any misunderstanding and once again explained my position. Now, it seemed, I was the most popular person in Bhopavand. I was glutted with tea, apologies came from right and left – all of which, I suspected, had more to do with fear of reprisals for the stoning than any heartfelt affection for me. Nevertheless it was agreed that a photographer could take pictures of the camels swimming the channel. Instead of remaining near the village I set up my tent on the nearby farm of another Rabari who maintained a house in Bhopavand but preferred to live outside the ambit of its restrictions. He worked from before dawn until after dusk on his farm, as did the rest of his family, but any profits immediately went to paying off his loan for the purchase of the land. Please, he asked, would I find him a job in Kuwait or Saudi Arabia? I promised I would try.

Dilip's approach to the cantankerous citizens of Bhopavand was that they could be bought off and he was, of course, right. Money flowed out of his pocket and in return the world was offered. We were led on camel-back to the shoot. After it was over, and everyone else had returned to the village, I gestured to the little boy leading my camel. He grinned, got up behind me and we galloped back across the flats. The whole village was waiting, wearing the kinds of expression that said 'If she can ride a camel like that, she can't be all bad.' And Seru, the leader of the pack, the one who had been the first to play with me and the first to stone me, made a bow so full of sarcasm that I could only laugh and bow in return.

After Dilip left I went hunting for Pala bhai. At the village where I heard he might be, I was greeted by retreating backs. The men did not know where Pala bhai was. Had not, it seemed, ever heard of Pala bhai. The women began to cluster around me. A fat, surly one sized me up and pronounced, 'She'll never make it.' With a contemptuous air she rose and flounced away, her minions falling in behind her. The old ladies, sympathetic in the face of my humiliation, had not travelled to the edge of the world and back as she had done and therefore deferred to her. Usually migrations were local, though some dangs journeyed outside the Gujarat border, depending on seasonal rains. But in one particularly bad year many people had abandoned Gujarat altogether and travelled deep into Madhya Pradesh, returning, like this woman, only for ceremonial, ritual and cultural ties. Eventually these links too will sever, as they have in the past. The fat lady had been 'out' for three years. During her time away, she had learnt some Hindi and she had become worldly, which in these times meant defensive and rude.

A couple of her lieutenants came back, instructed in what to say by their leader.

'We'll take her if she'll wear black wool like us.'

'We'll take her if she'll agree to be tattooed – neck, face, hands and legs.'

'If she'll have large holes made in her ears for the silver.'

'If she can drink ditch water that's green or black.'

'If she can go for days with no water at all, nothing but sheep or camel milk.'

'If she can walk on even with her blisters bleeding.'

A crone with pebble glasses set askew on her face stopped the taunting, touched my hand and said, 'You see, we cannot take you because it is too hard and too dangerous for you. Besides, others will think we have kidnapped you.'

Pala's dang had left with my money but without me. I had missed the Baabara exodus in Rajasthan. I called Narendra and wailed into the phone. Yet when I put down the receiver, I found myself leaping around the hotel room, yelling things like yippee and hooray. The door to the dungeon in which I had been living for a year was open. I would write a long letter to the editors apologizing for my signal failure to come up with the goods, return what money was left, and that would leave me free to do this thing in my own way, at my own pace, on a shoestring, without the pressure of photographs or story line. I would stay here for a year, study the language, live with people, write my book.

But I couldn't, because underneath the joy, like mud, lay Protestant guilt.

Two days later Narendra, prince among men, arrived. He had driven straight from Jodhpur – five hundred miles.

We went back to Rangka bhai, the first Kutchi Rabari Dr Rama Krishna had introduced me to, and whom I had liked so well. His uncle Phagu had left with his dang three days before. He, Rangka, would go there immediately with the Doctor and Narendra, to talk to them. Meanwhile I should stay with Rangka's wife, Jasu – a proposal which, I realized, was a kind of test. It was she who would have the final say as to whether I was migration material or not.

We huddled together under the shade of a spindly tree – Jasu, her sister-in-law and several baby goats which curled in my arms. My head was on the girl's stomach; Jasu snored. When she woke she took a mirror from her blouse and added kohl to her eyes, then to mine. We managed to communicate about the important things – clothes and make-up. Did I happen to have any nail polish with me? I had been told that the Rabari were 'very innocent of relationships', which was why they had few children. When I asked these two why they had smaller families than other village people, they replied that it must be God's punishment because they broke the law by eating mutton. How Rabarilike that answer was. They are consummate dissemblers to the outside world, truthful to the death with each other. Rabari women use whatever birth control technology they can lay their hands on; I knew this from the doctors and nurses at the local hospital.

I had brought fizzy drinks but both women spat the stuff out, having never tasted it before. Tea only, please. They took their sewing out of coloured bags, stitched away and asked questions. The younger woman broke tiny mirrors on the side of a tin for her embroidery. The mirrors, she said, were to scare away tigers. But there are no tigers in Kutch I pointed out. Yes, she agreed, but before (eight hundred years or so) her people had come from Rajasthan, and in Rajasthan there were tigers.

When the men returned Jasu suggested that I buy a goat from them for five hundred rupees (fifty rupees above the market price), then she would get her Muslim friends to kill it. She would cook it and everyone would eat it in celebration of my becoming part of the family. I offered to take them into the nearest town for tea. They mimed sashaying through the streets of Anjar, swinging my hand and showing off to the lesser mortals who did not possess a pet 'Angrez'. I had passed the test.

108

Rangka brought good news and bad news. Yes, Phagu would consider having me with them. However, I would have to provide my own camel and gear as they had none spare. Koju and my friends from the department went off in search of a camel to purchase, Narendra and I went back to the hotel to pack. Everything I needed, including two camels, was back in Jodhpur. I would have to wing it.

By afternoon a camel had been found – a young bull owned by some Juts. We went to check him out. Just as with people, one can take an instant liking or disliking to particular animals. Ram Rahim was willing, sweet-tempered, obedient, and he didn't chase or bite people – a hoi polloi camel. I hopped on his back, went for a fast pace in the evening light and decided that I liked him very much.

He would have to be trucked to the dang. And I would have to hurry to catch up with it. There was no time to sort through my luggage of which there was far too much, and no time to think. Phagu bhai had trucked his lambs across the Little Rann of Kutch, a vast stretch of salt and mud flats inundated, once a year, by seawater and floods. The flocks, shepherds and some of the women with their camels had pushed along at thirty miles a day, there being no feed to stop for. We caught up with them as they were pulling into camp in a river-bed. Immediately they asked me if I would drive back a few miles to pick up three men and some sheep who were too exhausted to move any further. The men had no food.

When I went to collect them, the sheep seemed barely conscious and the men looked like corpses. Back at camp, night was falling and the women were bringing in huge bundles of African thorn on their heads for the cooking fires, or thrashing the piles with ten-foot sticks to blunt the prickles. Others had walked a mile to a well and were carting back three large brass pots stacked on their heads. The men were bringing in the sheep, five thousand of them. Everyone had been working non-stop since five o'clock that morning. Yet the sounds of laughter and greetings rose above the clamour of the sheep.

Each family clustered around one or two charpois on which the gear, food and saddles were placed, and on top of which were various handmade quilts. The women and children slept on these, between two and five to a bed. Each camp was maybe twenty yards away from the neighbour's, far enough for a little privacy but not so far that a shouted joke could not be appreciated. Each family's camels were tethered twenty feet away from the camp. Three rocks in a triangle formed the stove, behind which was the bundle of hellish sticks and in front of which sat one or two women in their black wool, facing inwards, heavy silver balls dangling from the rims of their ears, swinging to the rhythm of rolling, slapping, patting, pounding dough. Around this *tableau vivant* stood sheep and goats, so tired and so stupid they singed their noses on the fire.

The negotiations were done in their own language so I had no idea what was going on. Pala, the mukki who had disappeared with my money, had been a bhopa and had carried himself with the self-consciousness fitting to his station. Phagu, on the other hand, did not project godliness. He projected naughtiness — if it's possible for a tall, thin, stooped, elegant man to look naughty. He glanced at me from time to time, his eyes narrowed with speculation, then crinkling in amusement. Eventually it was confirmed that I could travel with them and the fiscal arrangements would be as follows: Phagu's daughter and niece, Jaivi and Parma, would cook and fetch water for me, and Nakki, his wife, would load the camel. I would provide my own millet and I would pay two thousand five hundred rupees a month. This was a large amount of money for them, though as Rangka said later, 'If they didn't like you, you could offer them ten times as much and they'd turn you down.'

We drove back to where the lambs were being held and where my friends and I would spend a night. Nakki greeted me taking both my hands and leading me to the fire for tea. Somehow it was easy to tell that she was head of the women's world, just as Phagu was head of the men's. There were just a few older women and children here, camped by the side of a thunderous highway, close to a pit full of faeces and festering water, and two hundred yards from a stone-crushing mill which churned out decibels and dust. This would be our 'resting place' for a day or two while everyone recovered from their race across the Rann.

In the morning Narendra was uncharacteristically glum. 'I'd do anything for you but, please, don't ask me to camp out again. God, was I uncomfortable.'

So, I thought to myself, there's a trace of the palace left in my anti-feudal friend after all.

He kept pulling things out of his luggage saying, 'You might need this. Better take a few of these.'

'But Narendra I've got too much . . .'

'For once in your life, yaar, don't argue.'

Ram Rahim arrived by truck. I tethered him next to my own camp − a fold-up metal cot sagging under the weight of suitcases, bedroll, tent, saddle and supplies. At last the goodbyes could be postponed no longer. I waved to my vanishing jeep and turned to face my 'family' with whom I had approximately twenty words in common.

9

There is nothing so frustrating as being with people upon whom you depend for survival, from whom there is much to discover, whom you like a great deal and who seem to like you, who want to know everything about you – and having to behave as if someone had cut your tongue out and a bit of brain as well. 'Kya?' I would say, right ear craned forward, mouth hanging open. The ladies were patient, as no doubt they always are with village idiots. Questions would be repeated louder and slower until eventually they would sigh and shake their heads, or peal with laughter and give me a clap on the shoulder before going about their business. 'Samji natti,' they would say (doesn't understand) whenever someone new tried to address me. Previously I had tended to learn languages very quickly, although I forgot them at the same speed when I had no use for them. But India's one thousand, seven hundred mother tongues had defeated better linguists than me.

And yet how quickly one learns that other language of gesture and inference, in this case augmented by a few precious words and some phrases from *Teach Yourself Gujarati*, a fascinating little book which contained such sentences as: 'the lock of your musket is rusty', 'you will be hanged tomorrow' and 'a sepoy shot himself' – but nowhere mentioned grammar. I had also thought to bring slates and crayons for the children and books of the Gujarati alphabet for me.

Thus equipped I was now made to understand that I should teach the children how to read and write. As you do not need to speak a language to make a sound and draw the symbol for it, I thought I would try. We sat for a couple of hours under an acacia, the women occasionally mock-threatening their offspring if they didn't work hard, until an older boy came in from the herds, asking his brother, a twelve-year-old, to return to work. The boy ignored him, earning himself a tug on the earring. He howled and literally threw himself into his grannie's lap, sobbing and clutching at her black skirts while his brother, caught between compassion and not wanting to cave in to the boy's histrionics, laid a couple of reluctant clouts to his back thus making the sobbing louder and the burrowing deeper. This was the first and last time I ever saw a child chastised. Grannie, unable to resist so direct and physical a plea, gently told the brother to leave the boy alone. The shepherd went off to the animals muttering; the boy jumped up, tears forgotten, and once more applied his attention to the slate with a kind of frenzy. But he wrote the letters sideways or upside down, and how do you explain that the alignment of a letter is as important as its shape? We moved on to numbers. I drew one dot, two dots, three dots, with the number beside. They repeated the drill until I thought that I wasn't such a bad teacher. Then when I asked them to write down the number of pebbles I held in my hand, they drew three dots. Phagu's and Nakki's youngest daughter, Hatti, a ten-year-old with such healthy self-esteem she risked being a pain in the arse, had been showing off abominably by writing every letter perfectly. She was being tutored by Parma, her auntie, who in turn had been taught to read and write by another member of her family when she was a child.

The children were, every one of them, delightful company but it was Nagji with whom I had fallen in love. He was the sweetest little boy imaginable. He had only to look at you and his whole face opened in a smile. He was dressed in bright floppy trousers, tightened at the ankle with embroidery, and an embroidered vest laced with silver. He stood gazing off into vistas, legs apart, arms folded across his chest and thought deep thoughts. Even the weeping sores around his mouth could not detract from his lovableness. He was almost seven years old and smoked a chillum like a professor.

It was to take Nagji to a doctor that we women walked into Morbi that afternoon. They were exhausting, these larger towns, not just because of the noise and pollution and chaos but because they elicited, at the same time, contrary emotions – excitation and boredom. Confronted with the main street, I took a breath and hesitated. Someone gave me a little shove between the shoulder blades, as you might to a child standing on the edge of a swimming-pool.

'Where is the hospital?' Nakki asked a passer-by.

'Which hospital?'

'Private,' came the reply in impeccable mid-counties English.

There were about twenty people waiting in the surgery, sitting on the cement floor. We found places for ourselves and then the doctor, seeing a European among his patients, summoned me into his office. For ever after, the Rabari, shameless about queue-jumping, would want me to accompany them to clinics. Nagji submitted to the probing but when the nurse put him on a bed and brought out a tray of instruments of torture, he permitted himself a silent cry.

'You must feed him fresh fruit and vegetables,' said the doctor tersely, first in English, then in Gujarati.

Oh sure, I thought. Grown on a camel's hump, I suppose.

After that it was down the steps like released birds and across the street to the chemist to pick up the medicines. The owner of the shop, fat as befitted his social position, sat at the front by the till, in a state of somnambulance. His second in command, thinner than he, took the order and shouted it to a third person, an emaciated little man, who ferreted among the shelves, cabinets and boxes of the miniaturized shop. There were forms to fill out. Everything seemed to proceed in slow motion. The time is money mode has not yet invaded rural India. When the purchases were complete I had gathered the usual crowd. 'From which country?' could be heard from various mouths, along with giggling and the inevitable demands for money and pens. If you answer this question as I had, innocently, in the past, the question is then repeated by everybody within earshot and the laughter crescendos. More people gather, more people shout 'From which country?' and begin to jostle each other to get a better glimpse of the freak, until you find yourself the focus of a mildly hysterical mob. Dignity demands that you pretend it is not there. It is, I suppose, divine retribution for the treatment your whiteness receives in certain doctors' surgeries.

The phalanx of ladies drew me away from there and up a gully. A man sitting at the front of his jewellery shop cried out, 'From which country?' We hurried past but he called after us. 'Please come. I speak English. No need buy. Take chai with me.' The word 'tea' stopped Nakki in her tracks. She led me back to the man who, on learning I was Australian, listed every cricket hero my country had produced. He ordered tea for us all (Nakki demanded coffee), which came in glasses in a wire crate delivered by a little boy. I was given one chair, Nakki another, and the remaining women sat on the steps. Had Nakki lifted the glass to her lips with little finger crook'd, I would not have been surprised. I could read her mind. Having me around contained hidden benefits. A little later when she was choosing plastic sandals for Hatti, the shoe wallah threatened her with raised arm for fingering the merchandise. But the moment he saw me Nakki could touch as many sandals as she liked.

If I had to name the quality which I most admire and envy in the majority of Indians, it would be the capacity for patience, which is another way of describing an ability simply to be, without anxiety. I admire and envy it because I am devoid of it. Those hours spent sitting on the ground waiting for my friends to purchase their stores, with nothing to read, unable to converse, shooing off flies and beside myself with tedium and restlessness, were, in the end, salutary. I learnt to forget how mentally and physically uncomfortable I was by forcing my attention outwards. I might focus on life's diversity sifting past or strike up a halting conversation with a beggar who had come to pick at my sleeve. Or I might pull an orni over my head and half drowse for sixty seconds propped against a doorpost. Or, fearing that madness might arrive any minute, and take me screaming down the gullies ripping my hair out, I might repeat Bhawani ji's mantra which got me no closer to God but at least took me away from my self.

But I did not develop those techniques for some time and on that first shopping expedition the hours had cannon balls attached to their heels. At last came the final purchase, my millet seed. The women took tiny pinches of it to chew, then threw the remainder back in the sacks in disgust – the preamble to bargaining. As I was to learn, the banias were no match for them. They gave up in exasperation, yet by the time the last grain was measured out everyone was smiling and chatting, just as I imagined the Allies and Italians did on that Christmas Day my father told me about, when guns were put away and men remembered they were all made in God's image. Jaivi tied my millet in a piece of cloth, placed it on her head along with the other purchases — sugar, sweets and oranges for the children, onions, potatoes and coriander — and we proceeded to the miller.

'Paisa. Ek pen.'

'From which country?'

'Greg Chapell, Ian Botham . . .'

'Memsahib paisa, bhuk lagi, das rupee . . .'

We took refuge in a ten–by–six–foot room containing a dozen or so women, the mill wallah and his electric mill, which you could barely see through the flour mist. The grain was turned out on the floor and we sat around it on gunny sacks, then sieved it through large colanders several times. Weevils, bits of stick, chaff and dirt were picked out by hand while sweat ran down the body in runnels, chaff itched the skin and eyes, and a kind of glue made of flour dust and sweat clogged every orifice. But none of that mattered because here women could make contact with each other outside family or community boundaries — the wise old witches and the young wives — and exchange information. The preliminaries were always the same in these situations: how many children each woman had, how many brothers and sisters, and where everyone was from. My worth as curiosity piece soon waned, the town women proceeded to pump the Rabari women for news of other places and everyone got down to serious female politicking or, as it is fallaciously known, gossip.

An hour later the clean seed was given to the miller to grind, the flour was caught and tied up in cloth. We dusted each other down and then it was time to walk home. It was hot, even at five o'clock and our bundles were heavy. I bought everyone a drink from a roadside vendor who, behind his tiny cart, squeezed lemons the size of golf balls, mixed the juice with carbonated water, then chipped pieces off a block of greenish ice — a luxury more deeply enjoyed than a bottle of Krug could ever be. After which Nakki, to my delight, hailed an auto–rickshaw. Seven of us squeezed into this contraption, which wheezed along at about ten miles an hour, coughing blue fumes. There was a good deal of price haggling before we got in and a little more at journey's end. Then it was time to gather firewood, fetch water and cook. Our day of rest.

The first major communication problem occurred on the morning of departure. I had far too much luggage for one camel and had understood that Phagu would distribute some of it among the other animals. But when it was time to break camp, it was loaded on Ram Rahim. I mimed concern. Phagu mimed back that we had no choice. He and I would take a short route, through the centre of town, leaving the dang to go the long way, thereby avoiding the bribes they would have had to pay to the officers 'guarding' the roadside forests. Phagu had already wasted five hundred rupees on the police.

The road was a maelstrom of trucks, buses, jeeps, Ambassadors, scooters, scooter-rickshaws, bicycles, carts, people, cows, buffaloes, camels, goats and dogs. The second time the saddle swung under Ram Rahim's belly, scattering pots, pans and bedding over the road, I decided to take the excess luggage back to a café near where we had camped. Phagu would wait and guard the remainder. I went through the gear very quickly, throwing what I thought was extraneous into a large suitcase. I tied the camel up outside the 'restaurant' – a breeze-block shack open on one side and full of flies and tin tables – and carried the suitcase in on my head. The proprietor tucked it under his own bed in the corner. Ram Rahim was still overloaded and by now so terrified that he shied at passing trucks. The luggage came off again. Phagu and I reloaded hundreds of pounds in minutes. The camel's nosepeg bled. I lost a chunk of my shin but remained oblivious of it until later. A noisy audience had gathered by the time we reached the dang camped on the other side of Morbi beneath a skyline of chimney stacks, on a patch of earth littered with broken bricks, glass, garbage and human excrement.

Magically everyone knew just what had happened. Phagu indicated, 'Ratti ben, *you* unload the luggage, *I'll* tie up the camel.' When I obediently turned to do this, they burst out laughing and Phagu said, 'No, you rest. Nakki will unload.' He patted me on the shoulder, then walked away cackling to himself, organizing the shepherds, wading through a sea of several thousand hungry, screaming sheep and picking out armfuls of lambs to be tethered for the night. He had not rested since dawn.

There was a sense of urgency getting all the work done by nightfall. The women ran barefoot over stones and thorns, chasing the lambs. I tried to help them but the dogs attacked me as soon as I touched the animals, especially one psychotic brute with yellow eyes. Nagji pulled me around by the hand, threatening the dogs, trying to explain which lambs belonged to which camp and how to tether them by the neck to the long goat-hair ropes radiating from each bed. I went to a well with the women but townspeople followed me like a pack of howler monkeys. I wanted to crawl into a hole and die. Jaivi put her arm through mine, smiled her father's wry smile and said something like, 'Are you sure you want to live with us?'

That evening around the fires there was a lot of talk about the day's problems. Nakki in particular seemed very concerned and kept repeating the word 'chor', which means thief. She also repeated 'biscoot', one of the commodities I had abandoned at the truck stop café. She seemed to be saying that my luggage would be stolen and that I should return for it. I did not have the energy or the capability to explain that stolen luggage was low on my list of priorities just now and if the restaurateur wanted to eat my biscuits he was most welcome to them. Nor did I realize that conversations were usually far less complicated than I supposed. It was agreed that I ride Ram Rahim back in the morning to retrieve the luggage before the dang set off. Again, it seemed that the excess would be distributed. I went along with everything, nodding, smiling, agreeing, without really understanding what was being said, until at last I climbed on to the mountain range on my bed, rested my head against my saddle and yearned for unconsciousness which finally arrived at three o'clock. Two hours later I was woken by men whistling, clicking, trilling and hooting their music to the flocks. All night they had been on patrol, hitting sticks on the ground and rattling things, taking turns sleeping on the stones or giggling at me punching and cursing the sheep which rubbed themselves against my cot without cease. The goats liked to use the corners of the bed to scratch between their horns, the bony part used for butting which is not only impervious to the human fist but can crack knuckles as if they were eggs. They accepted my punches as a sensual bonus – proof of my affection – and leapt on the bed for more.

Each shepherd had slightly different calls, variations on a theme, and the overall effect was something like Amazonian woodwinds with percussion. There are morning calls to move out, a call to bring the sheep to water, and so on. The basic signals are the same but each area has, as it were, its own dialect of calls. Muslim graziers will have a different dialect again. Each man knows his own sheep, which might number in the hundreds, and vice versa, and his particular flock will disentangle itself from the larger flock and move out behind him in the morning.

As the sky lightened people could be seen disappearing with their lotis (water containers), then we gathered at the fires for tea. Nakki asked if I'd cleaned my teeth, handing me a stick of acacia for the job. Chew spit, chew spit, for half an hour to the rhythm of dough being slapped into shape. Every morning the same: hot millet roti (flat bread) with a soup of masala, ghee, salt and butter-milk. At night the same. Fresh goat milk, of course, if you could stomach it and the inevitable tea, drunk as an aperitif before meals, so strong and sweet it was like an injection of amphetamine.

Phagu clipped the goats and wound the hair into skeins which he would sell for ready cash in town. After breakfast he sent the shepherds off with their flocks – and instructions. The camels were let go for feeding under the charge of one unth wallah. Then he directed me to take off with my oh so hungry little camel. I was rather pleased at the idea of going back on my own. But no, Phagu had only been kidding. He would come with me and nothing I could mime could dissuade him.

At the café I had a bucket-bath in a corner of the kitchen, offered Phagu a meal which he refused, retrieved my suitcase and back we went to the dang. I would have given anything to really communicate with this man, tell him how much I appreciated what he was doing and how apologetic I was at being such a nuisance. But the words were not available. We took tea together in Morbi, standing outside a dusty little dabar (roadside eatery). I bought some lucerne for my camel and as soon as we reached the dang, Phagu explained to everyone that although the restaurateur had offered to heat me some water to bathe in, I had made do with cold. This won me brownie points, as did the sharing out of biscoot.

At around three o'clock we loaded up to leave. But this was too absurd. All the luggage was again placed on Ram Rahim. Confusion and helplessness. Out on the road, after spilling luggage for a radius of ten yards, after almost losing a finger in a snarling of ropes, after shouting at local children to stay away from the camel's legs in a language they could not understand, or at stupid young men who yanked Ram Rahim's noseline so that he roared in pain, I handed the line to Parma, indicated that I would catch up with them at the next stopping place a mile or so further on, tried to ignore the cacophony around me and my luggage, waited for a passing rickshaw, heaved everything into it, squeezed myself in on top of it and pointed in the direction of the dang.

I reached camp to find Phagu waiting for me. He looked at my finger, inspected my shin and said, 'This is bau taklif (big trouble) for you and taklif for us.' 'Bau taklif,' I agreed. Was he thinking better of his decision and sending me home? I had to admit, the idea had a certain appeal. My body ached, I was ready to drop, I wanted to cry. I wanted to kill the morons who gathered around me gawping, pointing, shrieking, even now, within the precincts of the camp. There was no respite from them, nowhere to hide from them. They pressed ever closer, pointed me out to their children, scratched their balls and stared. But most of all I could not bear the feeling of being such a liability to my hosts or of attracting these locals inside their world.

'I tell you what I will do,' I spoke/mimed. 'I'll take the luggage back to Morbi and wait there until a jeep comes to pick it up. Can I leave the camel with you?'

'Yes, you can, but how will you stay on your own and where?' Even the simplest conversations took time and effort, so how could I explain that being alone in cities was my natural state. I tried to say that he must not worry about me. I would throw myself on the mercy of the circuit-house, usually reserved for travelling politicians and sundry bigwigs. Phagu did not like the idea of abandoning a woman under his protection to the evils of a town but he had no choice. Nevertheless, he insisted on coming in the rickshaw with me and the luggage, making sure I got through to Dr Rama Krishna and that I found a safe place to stay.

We rang from one of the tiny STD booths that can be found in the remotest corners of India. That they exist is something of a miracle, so one should not grumble that the lines are often inaudible. I have rung the world from these boxes and feel a great affection and gratitude towards them. I screamed into the receiver until my face was redder than the heat had already made it. Send . . . jeep . . . Morbi . . . circuit-house. At last the message got through. Then I handed the phone to Phagu, thinking he might want to add something. He took it dubiously, held it a few inches from his gold earring, whispered a few words at it, shrugged and handed it back to me.

At the circuit-house a most extraordinary thing happened. Phagu began to shrink. On the dang I thought of him as an imposing man in whose face a heightened intelligence and authority was manifest. Someone you felt a little in awe of and wanted to hug at the same time. Someone so special that his qualities would leap across any division of class, caste, culture. While Phagu shrank in this environment, with its gardens, bitumen driveways and offices, I began to fill out at the edges. I was in my territory, explaining in English how grateful I would be if the rules could be bent a little as I found myself in a strange predicament. The man agreed, then glanced over to Phagu, indicating that he should pick up the luggage and follow us. I went to pick up luggage too, but a porter came and took it from me. In the fluorescent light of the room I was ushered into I could see what the manager saw when he looked, or rather didn't look, at Phagu – grubby turban, huge earrings, humbled shoulders. One of those colourful little dots that make up the great backdrop of Indian life. He was not rude to Phagu, not at all. But under his gaze Phagu ceased to exist.

I had told myself that I would get used to this ordering of the world. Told myself that the curtness, or rudeness, or bullying, from one higher to one lower down, was not necessarily hurtful to the one beneath, who, in his turn, would behave in the same manner to those beneath him. It was simply a signal stating one's level in the pyramid, recognized by both sides in the interchange as correct form. But I did not get used to it, then or later. And it gave me another reason for liking the people I travelled with. Although they were proud of themselves as a caste, they seemed to exist somewhere outside the more rigid hierarchies of settled people. In the months ahead I never once saw them show discourtesy to another human being, no matter how lowly, nor gratuitous cruelty to another form of life.

Phagu returned to the dang in the rickshaw. I bolted the door, closed the shutters, turned off the lights and hid.

10

'Narendra, I'm at Morbi circuit-house.'

'I know. I've been trying to ring you. Don't worry. Everything will get sorted out. Now, what I suggest is . . .'

Rangka bhai, the first Rabari I met, Mamu bhai, the Rabari field officer and two other men employed by Dr Rama Krishna arrived the following day in the department jeep. I was so grateful just for their presence that soon I had them in stitches, charading the loading of luggage, the running after lambs, the punching of sheep at night. Mamu explained in Hindi that everyone, people and animals, had been very tired after their fast days across the Rann, so problems were particularly unmanageable for them at that time. As to the confusion over the retrieval of my suitcase, he explained that 'chor' does mean thief but '*chhor*' means to abandon. In the linguistic muddle they thought that *I* wanted to go back to get the 'biscoot', and I thought that they wanted me to. This indicated how far the Rabari had extended themselves on my behalf, without complaint, without question, and at a time when it was most difficult for them to do so. I also understood a difference between myself and them. They had known life was difficult, accepted it, since they were children. And this being the case, they didn't waste effort fretting about it.

When the others went to buy food Rangka and I were left alone and fell into that mutual shyness brought about by an intensity of liking. What is it, this force of attraction, that leaps across every barrier humans have ever been able to construct? In situations like this, when you are receptive to the point of rawness, you become acutely aware of it. We respond to each other as individuals for reasons no one yet knows. Finally he said in his halting

Hindi that perhaps, if it were too difficult for me, I would like to come and live with him and his mother and Jasu? They would be pleased to have me and I wouldn't have to pay anything either. I explained to him as best I could that I did not mind roughing it and that the only real hardship was not being able to speak or understand.

But this was not true. Everything infuriated me. The stimulation and uproar, the skinny bodies and staring faces, the plucking, whining beggars, my own stifled outrage at so much *unnecessary* suffering, so much callousness, so much indifference masquerading as spiritual refinement.

If I had any kind of creed in regard to living among strangers, it was this: one could criticize one's own place, indeed one had a duty to do so, but when crossing a cultural border one left behind judgements as to how life should be organized. Especially when you belonged to the culture that has the power to describe, and misdescribe, Other. In my own wanderings I was happy to surrender parts of what had originally formed me in exchange for the new perspectives offered by difference. But lately, battalions of judgements had been arriving unbidden from some less evolved self and nothing I could do would fend them off. So strongly had I adhered to the previous point of view – that you cannot judge until you understand – that this new species of thought frightened me. What would I become if I allowed them their space? Would I become the kind of person I despised? Were they truly new or had they been lurking around before?

Always I'd been driven by a compulsion to make contact with the world, to be as aware of my life as I could be, to wrestle meaning out of event – and that compulsion lay at the heart of everything I did. Yet here I was in a town layered with the sediment of centuries, a town full of marvel and novelty, and the thought of exposing myself to its pressing, hounding crowds was more than I could bear. I stayed instead in a dark, sealed room, conserving energy for the next onslaught.

Yet the following day, after I had said goodbye to Mamu and Rangka, and turned to take my place in the line of women, children and camels setting off into nowhere, some ancient part of the spirit stirred in recognition, said this was what our species was built for; this makes everything else worthwhile.

The procession moved along like a train on its tracks, halting only at its destination – a withered valley beside a dam in which buffalo wallowed and people washed themselves or their clothes or their bicycles. Around the rim of the dam, twists and curls of excrement slowly leeched disease into the water. Our drinking supply.

Shit is rarely mentioned in tourist guides to India. Nor are those public loos in which faeces fill the corners and line the walls as far as the ceiling in such positions as to beggar imagination. Shit in the gutters, on the pavements, around ruins and tombs, in public gardens, sticking to your shoes, littering the banks of dams and rivers, encircling villages, piled in gullies and beside the door stops of the wealthy, recycling its way from body to body – omnipresent, human shit.

I carried medicine for dysentery and a few of the other things I hoped I would not get. But of all the things I did not want to get, I did not want to get Guinea worm the most. Guinea worm is endemic, I was told, among travelling people who had to drink from open water. The parasite enters the system, finds its way through the body to the skin, usually on an arm or leg, transforms into a lavum and builds a little house for itself in the form of a boil, where it proceeds to replicate. The boil eventually bursts, releasing packets of eggs which get washed into the water, ready for the next pick-up. Sometimes, however, the parasite loses its way within the body and pops out, instead, on an eyeball or inside an ear. I had brought a water filter with me but within a few days I gave up on it. We might have to move quickly, so that a walk to the well and the half hour spent filtering was out of the question. Or we might reach water after hours of walking without a drink. To wait so long for a clean cup of water was beyond me. Eventually I de-livered my health to chance and drank whatever my companions drank.

On that first evening everyone was especially welcoming. Women from other camps came by to share prashad – sticky sweets made of flour, milk and jaggery. How the hell had they found time to take the food to a temple for blessing? How had they found time to cook it?

'This is your dang now,' they said. 'You will see. You will enjoy living with us.'

Nakki explained, 'I am Rangka bhai's piu and therefore I am your ben, because Rangka is your bhai and that means Jasu is your babi, so you must not call her Jasu ben, you call her Jasu babi,' which initiated a general discussion as to who my other fifty or so relatives were. They wanted to know my age and looked amazed when I said forty-one. I asked Nakki how old she was. She looked at the ground for just a moment too long and everyone went silent. I had thought she was in her mid seventies. She was just seven years older than me.

My own camp was wedged between the two branches of my immediate family. On one side, ten feet away, were Nakki, Phagu, Jaivi, Latchi, Hatti and Arjun; on the other side, Lakhma, Parma (her niece) and Lakhma's husband whom, it was quite apparent, she found an unspeakable bore. She would let out exasperated little grunts whenever he came to sit by her, fan her hand in front of her face and cough as soon as he lit up his chillum. Thankfully he was too dim to perceive the effect he had on his beloved and puffed smoke lovingly at every sourness.

Although I was closer to Nakki in age, it was really the two young women, Jaivi and Parma, who were my peers and with whom I was to spend most of my time. Jaivi was Phagu's oldest daughter and secretly my favourite. She was in her twenties, had the same dry humour as her father, and a face round and open as a sunflower. Parma, my 'cousin', was tough and uncompromising, her beauty more masculine and ambiguous than Jaivi's. Latchi, Phagu's fifteen-year-old, regarded the world with that superior, bored air that is so tiresome in adolescents and spent most of her time looking into her mirror or being chivvied for laziness. All were gruff in manner, so that to get my attention they would dig a finger into my arm or ribs, leaving a bruise. A friendly pat was a thump. A playful touch, a whack. But then, at other moments, they would display the utmost delicacy in kissing a palm or touching a face. What made these women so beautiful was that they were incapable of making a movement that jarred.

By the light of the flames I watched them intently and was struck by the singularity of each character, here where there were no books, no films, no travel outside of Gujarat, no notion about the rest of the world – none of the things one might associate with the expansion and enrichment of personality.

As the faces came more into focus they became queerly recognizable. I could see Phagu standing at a blackboard teaching particle physics. Or Parma, where had I seen her before? On the stage somewhere? Jaivi, I now saw, was my friend Jenny but ten years younger and wearing a black wig. That broad face, which I had thought of as belonging to Jenny alone, was here repeated in Jaivi as a variation on a theme. Over there was my niece as an old, old woman. Then I saw that Phagu was not a physics professor at all but a painting I had seen somewhere. A Vermeer perhaps – that sideways glance, so familiar. There are only so many families of face in the world.

In the light of the fire similarity shifted to difference and back again. Which was paramount: our similarities or our differences?

On the second day I tried to take a bucket-bath but the children followed to watch. Sacrificing cleanliness to modesty, I left my trousers on. Later I learnt how to bathe by watching Nakki. She sat outside the tarpaulin, rubbed her hair with ghee, then filled a basin with water and a little buttermilk. She took off orni and blouse, revealing her breasts, but kept her skirt on throughout. Then Jaivi poured the mixture through her hair and over her back. She washed the upper part of her body and her legs and feet, then squatted over the basin to clean beneath her skirts. Afterwards she combed out long grey curls which turned into ringlets in the sun. When her brother-in-law walked past, Parma cautioned her and Nakki lifted her black wool to cover herself but in a lackadaisical way – a mere gesture to form. Here on the dang strict purdah is impractical and everyone understands this, brothers-in-law included. He tactfully looked the other way and did not pause in his stride.

Nakki's ablutionary methods were not much good to me, however, as I wore pajama rather than skirt. So, whenever I could manage it, I would carry my bucket far into the scrub, hide myself as best I could, crouched in a ditch perhaps or behind a ruined wall or spindly tree and furtively wash, patch by patch. A cavalier attitude to purdah was one thing; for a woman to be seen exposing her nether regions quite another.

The daily routine went something like this. Before first light I would wake vulnerable and disorientated and look across to Jaivi, expecting her ironic grin – my landing light – only to see a Gorgon. Lots of Gorgons. I have been told that my early morning face can fill a grown man with dread, yet I know that far from glowering I am almost unaware of any other human presence and am still surfacing from the depths. But somehow one does not expect nomads to suffer from early morning liverishness. However, after scouring pots with mud and grit, churning fresh goat milk by hand into buttermilk and ghee and clarifying the ghee over a fire, the gears of social intercourse were oiled enough to proceed with the more genial activity of cooking. Then tooth-cleaning, followed by breakfast around the fires. Later the shepherds would pack some roti in a cloth, take a pannikin for water and begin to separate their flocks. Lambs would be put to mothers for a drink; the newborn and the sick kept behind with the women to be transported by camel. The men would go off to sounds of bleating, baaing and woodwinds. If there was any work to be done with the flocks – injections, drenching, shearing – this would be done before they left or in the evening when they came in. Phagu and another man would go off scouting, leaving the camels to feed, guarded by the unth wallah, and the women to sew or walk into nearby towns or villages for supplies. Sometimes the women would wait almost all day under tarpaulins; sometimes we would leave in the late morning, the timings and distances designated by Phagu the night before. Half an hour before leaving time the unth wallah would bring the camels in, they would be fed a few pieces of roti, then loaded up.

At first Nakki insisted she load my camel but gradually I convinced her I could do it myself. Even so, someone would usually give me a hand or watch, with amusement, from the corners of their eyes. During the first week or so, they would check what I had done – whether I had tied the ropes tight enough and with the correct knots – less out of concern for me than the thought of time wasted on the road, reloading. First, those enviable hand-stitched quilts (gudios) would be placed on the camel's back, the saddle on top. A huge goat-hair sack would then be thrown over the saddle, forming two deep pockets either side. Into these went the cooking gear (shiny brass dishes and round clay pots, earthen hotplates for cooking the roti, and little stainless steel tea cups) and across the top, embroidered sacks of flour and food, and the few little personal possessions each person carried. Once this was strapped down, up would go the charpoi, its four legs poking at the sky. On top of it, the tarpaulin, tied in such a way as to form pockets into which the lambs would be thrown. Upside-down brass water pots decorated the four posts of the bed, ready to be filled quickly if we passed a well. Anyone too ill to walk (and you had to be almost dead for that) lay tossing about amidst the lambs, groaning like a seasick sailor.

For some reason I was never able to work out, fifteen-year-old Latchi always rode. She would climb up on the huge old bull, one foot on his knee, the next on his neck, then whoosh, on to the charpoi perched ten feet in the air. Her black orni would float off, revealing backless blouse and creamy skin. Once aloft she would brush out her plait and preen into her mirror. Sometimes little Hatti would be lifted up behind her sister; sometimes she walked with the rest of us.

At first I found it hard to do without water. It was impossible to lift my canteen down from the saddle while we were moving and it was unthinkable to stop the camelcade for such a triviality as thirst. I thought to conquer this problem by stocking up on oranges whenever we went shopping. During loading up I would secrete one or two in my pockets to suck, surreptitiously, as I walked along. But someone would always see, so that I would be obliged to share. (I noticed that they, too, experienced this problem and if they had bought anything very special in town would try to hide it because if it was seen, it must be offered. I once saw Nakki curse under her breath when she saw some local Rabari approaching just as she was about to tuck into her biscoot. But when the women sat with her, polishing off the biscuits, you would have thought Nakki had brought the packet out for them alone.)

We would proceed without stopping unless we passed a well, to which several women would run to fill pots while others kept the camels moving. If we stopped to water the camels at a trough, Latchi would swing down from her perch as if she were climbing down vines to fill the four pots. We might pick feed from wayside trees to feed the baby goats at night or, if there was a patch of particularly nutritious fodder, allow our ravenous camels to browse for a while. Sometimes we would walk two miles, sometimes twenty, in a straight line or in a circle, depending upon where we were to meet the flocks or where the walls of cactus and stone – the squares and rectangles of sedentary folk – directed us.

Once at the designated camp we would seat the camels and unload. The charpoi would be upended on the ground, the lambs tied to it by the neck along long leads, then the gear stacked on top, culminating with the beautiful quilts. My own gear was a downmarket version of theirs – a fold-up aluminium bed, an odd assortment of bags, a couple of old eiderdowns, cushions and sheepskins, and a tent which remained in its wrapping. I soon discovered the reason for stacking everything on the beds. If you leave anything on the ground, which I did in exasperation one night because I could no longer stand lying on a luggage rack, it will have been eaten to dust by white ants in the morning.

As soon as the unloading was done, some women would go to gather thorn bush using a long wooden pole to pick up the sticks and add them to the pile on their heads, which spread six feet wide and four feet high in a tangled mass. Other women would walk to a water supply, anything from two hundred yards to a couple of miles away. Then to the cooking: dough worked to a large slab in a metal dish, pieces of it taken and rolled between the palms then right over left, left over right, throw it about, pat it, turn it, throw it again until a perfectly round, nine-inch-wide roti without any rents was ready for the hot plate.

At night when the animals and men came in, when the lambs had been separated from their mothers and tied to the ropes, when the newborns had been brought to the relevant camps, the camels caught and tethered, when each camp had lit its incense and waved it around the outskirts of the dang to ward off evil, when little jobs like hafting new sticks from eucalyptus boughs, or plaiting new ropes, or giving medicine to the animals, or mending equipment was complete – then, at last, the shepherds could rest with their families, the happiest time of day. They would sit down with the same expression with which they got up – a deep sigh and 'Eeeh, Bhagwan', usually followed by an exhausted silence, then laughter and a recounting of the day's events. This was the only time they got to lie on the beds, though most often, they, too, sat on quilts on the ground. After food, there would be a general discussion of the next day's plans. Our camels were tethered to pegs in the ground at night, Ram Rahim so close to my cot that we could whisper to each other in the darkness.

Usually I would sit by the fire with my family and try to participate in the cooking and the talk. But often this effort of concentration was too much for me. I was sleeping an average of two to three hours a night. When the day's work was done, I would sometimes go to my cot and pretend to doze but my mind ground along, filled with a grit of anxiety, which must be akin to the frustrations of the newly blind, or invalided. I could not speak. I could not understand. I must speak. I must understand. Then I would hear, 'Ratti ben, food is ready!' and my stomach would knot up as if I were about to enter an examination for which I was unprepared.

One evening I showed them an article I had written in a magazine. It contained pictures of me and my camels in Australia. Phagu held the book upside down or inquired again and again if the person in the pictures was me, if the pictures were in my country or another. I saw the immensity of the gap of comprehension between us, the gap of meaning, where before I had seen only our affinity. The faintest look of wistfulness came into his face. When I thought of his education of his daughters, of his striving for and pride in them, I suddenly wanted to put my book away, as if my joy in reading emphasized his exclusion from the world of the literate. But this protective response of mine was mirrored by him whenever I betrayed ignorance of the modes of existence in his world, whenever it became obvious to him that I was treading water a long way from shore.

One night I was huddled on my cot feigning sleep when suddenly the dogs went berserk. The moon was so bright I could see a figure running flat out up into the rocky hills. Two shepherds took off after him, waving their sticks. All I could think was how brave the thief was, or how desperate. As it was only the loss of one lamb, and as there was obviously no chance of getting it back, the incident was an occasion for fun and excitement more than anger. Parma crept up behind Hatti, lifted her arms in an archetypal gesture and, leaping in front of her, said the Kutchi equivalent of *boo*! Hatti squealed and dived under the quilts of the bed.

She was the most loved (and the most spoilt) of children. She ordered everyone about, hand raised in a fist, chin out, flouncing her skirts imperiously. Her older sisters plaited and decorated her hair, encouraging an already overdeveloped vanity. And at night, when her big brothers came in, the first thing they asked for was Hatti, who climbed all over them, gave them cheek. A hand raised to slap would send her into hysterical giggles; she knew it would never be delivered. Her rudeness was seen as a charming independence of mind by her family – a necessary training in stubbornness. I liked Hatti but from a safe distance. And it was clear that to her I was the stupidest person on earth. Not only could I not talk, I could not cook a decent roti.

'How come yours are perfect and mine are like this?' I said to Jaivi one evening. Phagu answered, 'Because she has been doing it since she was a child.' But they appreciated the effort – another occasion for hilarity. They laughed a lot these people.

The children accepted my dumbness more easily than the adults, chatted on as if I could understand them and seemed not to require too many replies. Everyone was aware of my particular fondness for Nagji. He was teased about it but nevertheless would fetch up most evenings on my cot, smoking his chillum in companionable silence.

I watched Hatti playing with a green plastic doll which she had dressed in bits of rag and old dog chain. She dragged it around in a leather clog with upturned toe – a chariot travelling across continents, worlds perhaps. Dry camel droppings tied in bits of plastic bag were gold and precious gems. On another day I had observed her in deep contemplation of a dead lamb. She dropped a rock on its head experimentally. There was an inscrutable look on her face which was chilling nevertheless.

The dang was a training ground for the children. The little girls had their own pieces of play embroidery and carried small brass pots on their heads. At night they made pretend roti. The smallest boys smoked biris and chillums. Soon these angels would begin leaving camp in the mornings with the men, wrapped in their white turbans, carrying their sticks, calling to the sheep – married and responsible men, earning their own living at the age of eight or nine.

One night after the lighting of the incense we visited Phagu's brother Pala's camp for bhajjans (devotional songs). One man would start the first line of a song, his companions joining in. Then the women would begin, huddling together under their black wool, competing with the men, keening their lungs out, laughing when someone got the words wrong, or felt a little shy. They sang a song about Ratti ben, my ancient namesake, who had lain between the bodies of two slain men – one a Rabari, the other an enemy – to prevent their blood from mixing. They drank tea and sang until the stars swung past midnight. They sang themselves into intoxication.

It was as if they took a spiritual bath in the music, their troubles washed away with songs as old as the subcontinent. And I was struck once again at their intimacy with each other – the bonds among them continually strengthened, like calcium laid down in a bone, by singing, or sharing prashad, or sewing each other's mats, or smoking each other's chillums. How comforting it must be to pass through life's storms always with the support of the group infusing every action and every thought with one voice extending from the time of one's ancestors down through the generations, saying, 'It is all right. We are all here. There is no such thing as alone.'

11

But the ancestors were too far back in time for their voices to reach me and with each day my isolation from my companions grew. They had welcomed me into the warmth of their communion; now I was out in the cold watching them through a window. They would see me peeping at them and turn away as if to say, Why are you looking at us? Go away! What had begun with good will was atrophying for the want of language to nourish it. I had imagined I could understand, through a kind of pre-lingual sign language, quite complex interactions, as if I could just manage to stay afloat on an ocean of incomprehension. The truth was I was going under.

There were more than forty people on the dang. Jaivi said disparagingly, 'We can remember all our sheep. How come you can't remember our names?' She made me draw a map of the camps, then write the names and the degrees of relationship. They tested me. Who is that boy over there and who is his mother's sister's daughter?

'Samji natti!'

During the day we sheltered from that poisonous sun under a tarpaulin. The wind rushed under it, gusting hot grit into our faces. Hour upon hour of unparalleled boredom as we waited to shift camp. Time stretched out as it does in dreams. I buried myself in Proust, his cool, privileged world. Marcel was waking up, enchanted by the songs of peasants selling their wares beneath his window. He lay in white sheets; soon he would pull the bell for Françoise to bring him his morning coffee. I tiptoed out of the bedroom in Paris and looked up. Pressed against me, the women stitched, blew snot out of their noses, spat and belched.

There were a couple of men under the tarp with us, shivering with fever. One crawled out to vomit. Nakki rubbed his legs and arms with raw onion. Baby goats covered in sores drank from our water pots and urinated on our mats. The air was mostly dust. The horizon promised nothing but dust. Where was I? Why was I here?

I tried to write notes but the words ran out, evaporated into the blue above. I heard them talking about me. In that forest between sleep and wakefulness I understood, with immeasurable relief, their words. I tried to fix them in my brain for later, knowing the futility of the exercise. My everyday mind would close over that fertile place like parking lot cement. I was suspended in a vast loneliness as pure and cruel as the sky. The women were talking to me. I wanted to grab my head and shake the cement out of it. They shouted as if to a deaf person or an idiot. They put the pen in my hands, indicating that I write and remember names – uncles, cousins, mother's sisters husbands – then a jab in the ribs.

'Ratti ben, cha pio.' Nakki was standing over me with a cup of tea in her hand. I must not sleep there. Scorpions. It was time to move camp.

I had not slept more than two hours a day for how many days? Ten? Twenty? I had lost all sense of time. I had a soaring temperature and could barely swallow. They taunted me constantly: 'If you're ill, you'd better go back to Bhuj . . . Aren't you tired yet? So tired that you'll have to go back to Bhuj?'

Do they really want me to leave? How must I behave? I do not understand what is going on around me. I hear them talking about me the whole time, turning my presence over like a rock. What are they saying?

I had set up my tent, hoping for sleep but the sheep spent all night jumping on it and two spent the night inside it. They rubbed their noses on it so that globs of anthrax green snot hung off it in the morning. Another night I dragged my swag about fifteen feet outside the flock and fell into unconsciousness. No one saw me as they had gone to an uncle's camp to sing. But I was woken by the women – black ghosts against a background of stars. They ordered me back to my cot. I seethed with rage. Didn't they understand that I could not keep going without sleep? They laughed, pecked at me. Their fingers dug, bony as witches.

'If you sleep out here, Phagu will send you back to Bhuj.' How I hated them. The sheep and goats chewed and digested and coughed. They were so full of disease they were barely alive, yet they chewed the country into dust. The great grinding stomach of India, everything feeding off everything else.

When I woke each morning it was to dread. I must face them. I must sit and eat with them. Sometimes they smiled at me or laughed but I could not read their faces. They looked at me sideways and thought their own thoughts. They had no inkling what torture it was to be unable to speak, unable to order the world in any way, exposed and wretched in a place where even the sky was strange. My other life was unimaginable to them and so therefore was the degree of stress — solitary confinement and sleep deprivation combined.

The country was butchered, nothing but rubble and dust. Nothing invited the eye or the soul. The light beat the colour out of everything. Blue became white. Green, a dull grey or dun. Only the women's black withstood the domination of sun, like tiny rents in the sheet of light. The men in white merged with sheep or rocks and became invisible. In the evening the flocks poured out of the ravines. When they arrived in camp, the dust was unendurable. Throughout the night the animals, packed close around me, scraped themselves against my cot. I whipped at them with a rope in fury. I damaged my elbows and hands by punching them.

Sometimes it happened that I could not get water for myself as my companions had not told me we were to break camp early. I had no way of finding out how far I might have to walk without a drink. I was as helpless as an infant. I went by myself to a nearby train siding, nameless to anyone but its occupants. Perhaps there would be a shop. Something cool. Maybe even ice. To step out of the shade was to feel nausea. It was already autumn. How do they survive the summer? How does anything? Just a five-mile walk and at the end of it something cool. Something different. And I could be on my own during that five miles if I could avoid being seen. I approached the siding, pulled an orni over my face. A rutted street, dusty trees, a few sick dogs with ribs like piano keys, panting in the shade. A line of track ran one way to nothing and lost itself in nothing in the other direction. Along that line, from one end of north India to the other, I imagined identical clusters of huts, the same cows nosing garbage, the same children in rags and silver, eyes filled with flies. In either direction there was nowhere to go.

There was a shop, the usual shack distributing goods from tins and sacks, even here tricked out to entice with cheap little geegaws. No ice, but orange soda the temperature and consistency of blood. I drank four bottles. People began to collect. Hastily I bought sweets – hardened, spun sugar covered in grey dirt – and hurried back to camp.

Sometimes we passed the outskirts of villages, which to me were defined by whether they might have a telephone and if so how I might get there. If I could hear Narendra's voice, if I could express even one fluent thought, I could keep going. I could ring for Koju and the jeep. An interpreter from somewhere. The village might be so close you could see its detail. Why did they refuse to let me go? It would take an hour and a half to walk there, an hour and a half to walk back, and by then it would be nightfall and too dangerous to be out alone. Was that it? Perhaps they knew that particular village had no phone? Or were they keeping me here out of sheer spite? Sometimes Nakki would announce that we were all going to a village the following day and I would go to bed curling around the idea of tomorrow as if it were my child. Then, when it was time to break camp in the morning, we would leave the vicinity of the village altogether and walk in the opposite direction. The desire to talk was like some fantastic hunger; they were my torturers, keeping the food just beyond reach.

Malaria began to fell the shepherds where they stood. My own body was slimy with fever. I must not get ill. I *must* not . . . One afternoon, at last, the women directed me to get ready; we were heading into town for injections and supplies. Three miles along a path, then on to the road, all the while imagining Narendra's voice – like being alone on a boat at night, tossing in a stormy sea but seeing the steady blink of the port beacon.

The doctor called me into his office and as usual the Rabari trooped in behind me. He laughed and sat them down, ordering tea and water.

'I, too, admire these people. Their lives are very hard.'

'You're telling me,' I said.

'Now you will go to my home next door and meet my wife. There you will have a hot shower.' I turned to check with Nakki. 'It's all right,' said the doctor. 'They will wait out under the shade once I have attended to them.'

I do not even remember his name. But to that doctor I owe a portion of my sanity. Nor did I care that I abandoned my friends for the comforts of my class. I scrubbed and scrubbed in that shower and I think I probably sang. Half an hour later we were back in the streets, pushing upstream against the river of souls. I bought a box of sweets to take to the doctor on the way home and as many vegetables as I could carry for the dang. Then I told Nakki that I must find an STD booth to ring Jodhpur. Yes, I could go but I must be quick. (This she indicated by snapping her fingers.) They would wait for me here. I hurried off.

It took a long time to find the booth. Everyone I asked seemed to point in a different direction. Then, as usual, someone from the crowd I had gathered, about thirty people by now, took command and led me up narrow alleys and behind bazaars. Ten people crowded into a room the size of a lavatory. Breathing was difficult. Sweat saturated clothes. My head was bursting. The booth wallah couldn't get Jodhpur. (Oh please, please.) After ten minutes or so, he handed the phone to me.

'Madam, the line is very bad. You must shout.'

I shouted, 'Narendra . . .' and there was his faint, infinitely longed for voice.

'Are you all right? Where are you? Should I come?'

'I can't talk now,' I yelled. 'Too difficult. Yes, I'm all right . . .'

'What? I can't hear you.'

'*I'm all right . . .*' But the line had gone dead. I tried to reach Dr Rama Krishna but could not get through. I put the receiver down and to my shame, in front of thirty people, whose staring faces crammed the doorway and pressed up against the window, I hid my eyes with my hand and cried.

I almost ran back to our meeting place to find that a shepherd had come from the flocks to tell us to wait in town, which we did for four hours. As we did not know when we would be leaving I could not go back to the telephone nor could I deliver the sweets.

Four hours. We sat on the scorching pavement or took turns lying on a narrow wooden plank half shaded by a wall, next to an open latrine whose stench mixed with the smells of rotting garbage, cooking oil and spice. Fifty yards down our gully was the meat market. People sipped tea beside a mound of steaming offal – chickens' heads and feet, goats' stomachs, other less recognizable pieces of anatomy being shovelled into wooden carts by thin, glistening men up to their knees in blood and muck, naked to the waist, the sunlight pounding down on them like a hammer ringing on a metal lid screwed down tight. Heat and light, flies which whirled around the piles of sticky sweets, the teacups, the children's eyes, the running pigs, the woman in crisp white sari stepping daintily amidst the shit.

Along came a man carrying a large python. He wore rags; there were weeping sores up and down his legs. He extracted money from passers-by by thrusting the snake into their faces. He saw mine and bounded over. From up close I saw that the snake's lips were stitched together crudely with string and its mouth was bloody and deformed. It had no limbs with which to struggle, no mouth to protest its fate. All its suffering was condensed in its eyes which, in memory, are humanly expressive. From a comfortable distance – let's say twenty feet, that is to say the distance money can buy you – the sight of the man with the snake is marvellous, something to capture in a lens. Up close it is merely terrible.

How one longed for the poor to say, just once, 'War on the palaces, peace to the cottages!' Yet whenever a look of fury replaced the self-control on the faces around me, fear would creep up my back and I would repeal the instinct for revolution. Because here would be no vertical eruption – the bottom layer forcing its way to the top – only a lateral one in which everyone turned on everyone else, a war of all against all. Sometimes I thought the conflagration must be imminent and all that was needed to ignite it was just one more crooked official, one more lorry, one more decibel, one more stitched-up snake thrust into one more face by one more hungry man.

The shepherd came to fetch us. I don't remember how many we were, ten perhaps, crammed into a tin rickshaw. At the end of the ride we had a couple of miles still to walk, cross-country. But now there was an altercation. The driver was waving his arms around, demanding more money. It was a matter of five rupees. I took a woman aside and said I would pay. But Nakki's sense of injustice overwhelmed her greed. It went on and on. Ten minutes, twenty minutes. Why didn't I just hand five rupees to the man, twenty, a hundred? I don't know. I did as the group did. We had two sick children with us and one very sick man. I stood at the back of the group and turning saw, for just one moment in the face of the woman next to me, beneath the Indian forbearance, a despair as old as the continent itself. I pushed through the women, handed the man five rupees and we set off across the fields. Nakki muttered to herself about crooks and thieves.

Arjun was weaving from side to side as he walked. Down he went. We picked him up. Another hundred yards, down again, mumbling to himself in delirium. Two women shouldered him for a while, distributing their heavy head bundles among the rest of us. Down again. We waited with him for five minutes as he lay moaning on the ground. Another hundred yards. Another five-minute wait. And thus to the dang. It was time to pack up and move, quickly. Arjun was shoved on to the camel with the sick and newborn lambs. We walked twelve miles.

There was no more open country now; we camped always on dark, ploughed fields. Black dust, as thick as pitch. Some days we passed other groups of Rabari with their strings of camels. Every-one seemed to know who they were and where they were from. There were many dangs behind and many in front, wave after wave of sheep spilling out of Kutch into the fertile farmlands of Saurashtra.

Every now and then the hazy outline of a castle would appear on the horizon, a small town clinging to its skirts. We seemed to be circling it like the ribbons of a maypole. Eventually we pulled into camp just a couple of miles away from it. I could see its Victorian gothic towers on the other side of the hill. When I asked passers-by about it, they told me it had been turned into a guest-house. In any case where there is a palace, there is usually a telephone. There would be time to walk in to ring Dr Rama Krishna to send my jeep and a translator. To be able to speak was now more important to me than food. I did not let myself hope to get through to Jodhpur.

I crossed the fields to an empty road. Before long a young man pulled up beside me on a bicycle. 'Where are you going?' I pointed up the steep stretch of gravel and rocks to the castle on its summit. He beckoned me up behind him.

As it was clear to me that I had fallen through a rabbit hole some time before and was living in a reality in which I found myself, without much surprise, doing curiouser and curiouser things, I perched side-saddle behind him, careful not to offend him by touching him, but in danger, therefore, of capsizing us both. 'Where am I? Why am I doing this?'

My chauffeur puffed and wheezed until we reached the castle gates beyond which he refused to go. 'Hotel,' I said, pointing, then added, 'Come in for tea.' But he shook his head. I offered him some money and saw that I had offended him. (Would I never get this right?) But he said I must do something for him. For the life of me I couldn't make out what it was. Something about 'Charmanni' and writing.

'Don't understand. Come morning Rabari on hill.' I turned to enter the gates but he would not let me go. There was urgency in his voice; I had no idea what he was saying. 'Tomorrow,' I said, controlling hysteria and pointing again down the road. He opened his mouth to speak. 'Go away,' I said, less viciously than I felt.

The palace did not look like a hotel. It looked like something out of *Grimm's Fairy Tales*. But then I did not look like a guest. A man was shifting furniture about in an annexe, a graceful veran-dah'd row of rooms. I crunched across the weed-infested gravel of the drive, conscious of my unspeakably filthy kurta and even filth-ier chunni around my head. I looked down at my feet and hoped he would not do the same.

'Excuse me, I've been told this is a guest-house. I wonder, would it be possible to . . .?'

'Please wait. I'll be with you in a moment.'

Thankfully he did not seem to notice that he was dealing with a heat-, thirst- and fatigue-crazed, possibly dangerous, person and greeted my arrival as if we were about to continue a conversation begun the day before. Soon enough this gentleman (for he was certainly that), came out, rolled down his linen shirtsleeves and led me to the 'house'.

'Um, you see I wondered if this was a hotel because . . .'

I was guided to a cane table in the vast stone atrium, asked to wait, and left alone. I thought of the seconds ticking by, minutes wasted before I had to go back to the dang. A long time later a servant brought me a glass of water on a tray. I downed it in one gulp. He brought another.

'*Is* this a hotel?'

'Rajah sahib will be back shortly.'

Eventually my host returned in crisp white kurta and freshly combed hair. He smelt of expensive soap, sandalwood and mothballs. He composed himself in the chair opposite and said, 'Livingstone, I presume.'

I got the joke and asked Stanley if this were a hotel. But the maharajah wanted to talk about the fate of the Rajput rulers after Independence. About how difficult it had been for them. He wanted to know why more wasn't written about the Rajput rulers after Independence. He wanted to know why the rest of the world was not as interested as it should be in the Rajput rulers after Independence. (The image of a steaming teacup and a bucket of water was fading like the Cheshire cat's smile.)

'Hmm,' I said.

'You see,' he said, 'we were greater than the kings of Europe because we actually owned the lives of thousands of people.'

I thought that owning the lives of thousands of people was perhaps not something to boast about in these times. But then it struck me that whatever times we were in, they were not these ones so I said nothing. Occasionally he would ask me a question but the answer seemed not to penetrate very far. He suggested I write about the Rajput rulers after Independence. I did manage to ask if he had a telephone. This seemed to bemuse him for a moment, as if the mention of telephones was dragging him back from the kinds of places where nobody of any consequence asked about telephones. He answered with a vague wave of the hand. (A translator faded, along with the tea and the wash.) At last I asked if I might have some more water. Two glasses of green cordial were brought. I downed mine as a footballer might at half-time. If the maharajah noticed he was too well bred to show it.

Trying to bring the conversation around to something in which I might be able to make an appearance and in which I could at least say out loud the name of my friend for whom I found myself longing in a serious kind of way, I asked him if he knew Narendra.

'Of course. Who does not?' He paused. 'But he's not a *real* prince, you know.'

The sun was sinking. The maharajah excused himself. He had some Rajput pujas to perform. He would have his peon drive me back to the dang. I thanked him. He said, not at all.

'But tell me is this a hotel or not?'

'Hmm. Perhaps.' Then he was gone, swallowed up by lost time.

Despite my disappointment I could not focus any deep resentment on the maharajah. The function of a prince is not to imagine another's state but to be imagined. I had noticed this odd disengagement before in many of the erstwhile kings – their inability to hear what you say, the assumption that their needs are paramount and that everyone will automatically fulfil those needs. The narcissism is not insulting. It is too deep a belief to be insulting. And it is not personal, it is functional. A prince is only given meaning by the reverent gaze of others. His own eyes look beyond and above.

No one was present at the table but Stanley. Livingstone melted back into the jungle.

A new state of acceptance descended on me that night on the dang. I would not augment difficulties by protesting against them, as this only led to failure and wasted energy. I could not affect external events, all I could change was my own response to them. A morsel of Hinduism penetrated my soul that evening.

In the morning a bicycle made its slow progress across the fields. The women greeted the stranger with polite reserve. Nakki cast me looks.

It now became clear (I had a pocket Hindi dictionary with me) what my bicyclist wanted. He was a Muslim. He had lost his job

143

here. He was broke and he was frightened. I must help him by writing a letter to a German tourist whom he had driven around for a short time because that German tourist would surely send him a ticket to the west. He had pedalled ten miles from his village to make this request.

'I can't write in German.'

'Then in English.'

I tore out a page of my grimy notebook and, after experiencing some difficulty in focusing my thoughts, wrote the following: 'I am an Australian visitor to India. I am writing this letter on behalf of a friend – a young man from the village — whom you know. I understand he was your driver for some time here. He is in trouble and in need of a job. He hopes that perhaps you can offer him some sort of work in Germany. Please will you write to him at the above address. Even if you cannot help him, it would be most kind of you to write back.' I wanted to sign it Alice in Wonderland but thought it might lessen the bicyclist's chances.

He clutched the letter like a drowning man and took off. I went to collapse on my bunk. Something moved beneath me. I rose, horizontally, into the air, whipping the blanket out from under me at the same time. There was a spider the size of a hybrid clematis with hairy legs and chelated, serrated mouthparts so large they could cut through telephone cable in one chomp. It was looking at me. It wasn't pleased. I grabbed Jaivi by the orni and tugged her over. She looked at the spider, looked at me, and said what I can only suppose was the Kutchi equivalent of 'So?' It was, in fact, a rather fine specimen of what is known as a camel spider. I clubbed it to death.

My enlightened acceptance of things as they are lasted until we reached the outskirts of yet another village, a day or two, or possibly three or four, later (time, here, had the tensile capacities of chewing gum). I explained to Phagu that I must, now, walk to that village to ring for the jeep. Nothing would deter me. He seemed to understand. He watched as I packed a little knapsack and water, watched my excitement and hope building and, as I was about to set off with my stick and a jaunty wave to my friends who were looking at me in a dead sort of way, he stopped me, saying, 'You go tomorrow, not today.' I stared at him, then, without a word, packed away my things and sat, smouldering, on my cot. Something terrible happens to your innards when you suppress that much anger. They turn into snakes and bite each other.

That night I dreamt that our camp was surrounded by dacoits, each with six enormous penises. The heads of those penises took the form of the mouthparts of a camel spider. I slaughtered the dacoits in various ways until the whole dang was awash with blood.

In the morning I again packed up my things. Phagu was reluctant to let me go. 'I can't come with you,' he said by way of explanation and, I saw now, apology. I shook his hand, laughed and said, 'I am going. It is necessary.'

He walked a little way with me across the stubble looking concerned, hesitated and eventually said, 'Jao' (go). As I turned, there, charging across the fields, was a funnel of dust. Oh noble jeep. Oh blessed contact with the outside world. I would have gone down on my knees and wept with gratitude if Phagu had not been watching. And behind the wheel, like a cavalry flag, Koju's proud moustache, Koju's smile. He had brought mail, back issues of *The New York Review of Books* and a letter from Narendra. And he had brought Praveen Singh ji from the Bhuj department who wanted to see how I was getting along. Words, words, beautiful words. An avalanche of words.

Through Praveen Singh who spoke Hindi, and Koju whose mumbles and sign language I had deciphered long ago, we were able to communicate at last. Everyday speech, even at its most basic, is a subliminal trimming device, keeping thoughts from straying too far off centre. Without it you can find yourself in some fairly peculiar mental places, especially when you have developed a kind of hostage syndrome in relation to the people around you. Now I saw, in the enthusiasm with which they spoke to me through Praveen Singh, that the inability to communicate had been frustrating for them as well.

They had only joked about my going back to Bhuj because they thought I needed cheering up. I did not look happy; they were worried for me. They felt better if they could make me laugh but lately I had not been laughing at all. They liked having me with them and they wanted me to stay, but I must not sleep outside the dang unless I had a pistol. They were responsible for my safety.

'But I cannot sleep,' I said, 'and I would rather die of dacoits than of exhaustion.' A compromise was reached. I could sleep inside the tent, just on the outskirts of the flock. But if I could not get a pistol, at least I must keep a stick with me.

There was a kind of party that night. Other families came by happy to have the chance to ask questions, make jokes, but above all to explain to me how the dang operated, its deep structure.

'You see, this is why we could not let you go into town.'

'Yes, yes, Ratti ben. Now you understand why we had to leave the camp so early.'

'That's right, when you saw the shepherd waving his turban from the hill he was indicating where the flocks were.'

'No, Ratti, Phagu is not paid anything to be a mukki but his expenses are shared by everyone on the dang.'

The most satisfying piece of information, as far as I was concerned, was that Pala bhai, having heard on the grapevine (a far more effective communication network that the STD booths) that I was proving an asset rather than a liability, had sent word with Praveen Singh that I should leave Phagu's dang and join his own.

'But *this* is her dang,' said Parma indignantly and I assured her I had no intention of leaving.

Phagu filled in the details of his work. Usually two men scouted ahead, including himself. The night before he would tell everyone where the following day's route and camp would be, where the water, where the grazing. If there was any change to the plan he would come back to inform the women. Otherwise they would head in the direction of the agreed place and either catch up with the flocks or inquire. The shepherds would leave special markers to show which way they had gone or to indicate which track not to take. Phagu himself might have to travel many miles ahead and if a bus was available he sometimes took one. Most often he walked.

The main income along the way was from sheep droppings.

Phagu would negotiate with a farmer to camp on a particular field. The sheep would eat the stubble (actually they would converge on the field rather like vacuum cleaners) and out the other end came ready-made fertilizer, the payment for which would be distributed proportionately among members of the dang, according to the number of sheep each family had. Once Phagu had negotiated the deal for the sheep shit, he would leave his cloth with the owner of the field to confirm to the graziers that this field was booked.

'If the head of a family of, say, four brothers and one sister decides that only one member of that family should go on the dang, then the brothers and sister will give that one a fixed wage for grazing the sheep, whether or not there is any profit from fertilizer, meat or wool sales. If there is a profit, it will later be distributed among the members of the family.'

'But surely this must lead to confusion sometimes. What do you do if there are disagreements among yourselves, or with outsiders?'

'There are never fights between or among dangs. No, never. Perhaps a mukki might chastise a younger fellow if he doesn't follow the code and grazes where he shouldn't. But that's all. If ever there is a police case involving one person of the dang who has, say, beaten up a thief, then the money paid to the police to avoid the case, or any legal fees, will be paid by all members of the dang.'

Everyone was fired up by these questions. They loved talking about themselves and were justifiably proud of their expertise. It had been a good excuse to stay up late, to share prashad and drink tea; now people began to drift away to their camps to the sound of grating knees and 'Eeeh, Bhagwans'. A few chuckles and snatches of song could be heard drifting across the sea of sheep, then silence.

Phagu lay back on the bed, puffing his chillum and staring up at the sky.

'Do you know the stars, Phagu?'

'Oh, yes. In times past we Rabari navigated entirely by the stars. We were the pathfinders, which is what our name means. Certain configurations gave the time and place to a very accurate degree.

147

But these days there are watches and the country is closely settled, so that degree of knowledge is lost . . .'

'Already there are so many changes. I wonder what your grandchildren will be like? How will they live?'

'People tell me there is no future in what I am doing and that I should sell my flocks. But how can I worry about these things now? Grazing the sheep takes all my time and effort and concentration. I'm too concerned with survival, Ratti ben, to answer your deep questions.'

In the morning there was a collection around, under and within the jeep. People climbed over the bonnet or sat on the roof rack. Parma pretended to drive it and the children demanded to have their breakfast inside it. Young men lined up at the rear-view mirror to preen.

I drove the women into the nearby village for provisions, which completely turned their heads. On the way back my sisters sat in the front with me, heaping scorn on mere pedestrians. Parma, thinking I couldn't understand her, announced, 'This is our taxi and Ratti ben is our driver.'

I sent Koju back to Bhuj with Praveen Singh, saying that he should bring the jeep again in ten days' time. There had been some broad hints about keeping the 'taxi' with me and, although in some ways it was tempting, instinct told me it would create more problems than it would solve.

That night, too, a few women from the other camps came by. Nakki began to tell me why they wore black. (They are certainly the only Rabari and as far as I know, the only group in India to do so.) They were so determined that I should understand, the story was repeated by one, then another, each making a tremendous effort to bridge the language gap by making me write down sentences, cross them out, rewrite them.

'Long ago, when the Rabari lived in Jaisalmer, the rajah fell in love with a young Rabari woman whose beauty was famous for miles around. But her family said, "Even though you are our king, our daughter cannot be married outside caste." This did not please the king who was used to getting his own way. The Rabari knew they would have to flee and, sitting together in a circle, they threw salt into a cup of water and drank it, vowing never again to taste

148

the salt of Jaisalmer. Off they went into the setting sun, the rajah's soldiers in pursuit. There was a massacre. Rather than succumb to the king, the young girl prayed to the goddess to save her. Her prayer was answered; mother earth opened and swallowed her up. Ever since then, we Rabari who made it to Kutch have worn black as a sign of mourning and the place where the woman died is sacred to us. There are no marriages now between Rajasthani Raika and Kutchi Rabari. Once you have left a place that hurt you, you sever connections.' Perhaps, they said, one day they would take me to see that place. Or, better still, we would travel together as far as the Himalayas to see the home of the gods.

When it was time to turn in Phagu looked out at me from under his eyebrows. 'So, after Divali, I suppose you had better go back to Bhuj.' Everyone paused in mid-motion; there was a hush. I took a deep breath, screwed my fists into my face like a child and yelled, 'Please, please, don't send me back to Bhuj.' When they had stopped laughing, Phagu wiped his eyes with the end of his turban and said, 'Ratti ben, you can stay with us as long as you like.'

12

'Tell us about the time you had to leave your luggage . . .' Phagu
began deadpan but couldn't get the rest of the sentence out. Duti-
fully I charaded, for the umpteenth time, sorting through suitcases,
throwing clothes and tins of biscoot to the four winds.

'Tell us again your father's name.' Antil Guildford Montgomerie
Nugent Davidson.

'Show us how Arjun walked back from the doctor.' One two
three four five six blaagggh – and I fell backwards in a dramatic
faint.

If my contribution to the morale of the dang was to be Phagu's
straightman, I didn't mind too much. When the reality outside our
group was so threatening, harmony and light-heartedness within
it were essential and it was here that Phagu's genius as a mukki
made itself most apparent. He kept them all laughing, knowing
that if they let life's problems weigh them down they'd be six feet
under since their lives were nothing but problems.

I discovered something about my own culture, at least that of
the post-war generation: our assumption that life is not *meant* to
be difficult, that someone or something will always be there to
catch a fall – a belief that is lodged in our core, just beneath
consciousness. The Rabari suffered no such delusion. I had
thought of myself as resilient, as having ingenuity and self-reliance
in my genes. Now I knew how soft I was, how querulous, like
those old women in nursing homes whom you hope to hell you
won't become.

Unlike my hosts I had to learn how to be cheerful in the face of
adversity. It did not come naturally. Sometimes I seemed to be
nothing but grievance and distress, like a human storm looking for

something to deluge. At such times I thought their laughter callous and hated them. Then, when I thought I could bear neither them nor myself a moment longer, their public toughness would peel away like a warty skin, revealing sweetnesses, kindnesses and reaches of compassion. Rammi, walking an extra mile to show me a well, then carrying home my water on her head. Jaivi, hiding away some prashad she had made until I returned. Nakki, tiptoeing over to my bunk at night and whispering to Phagu, 'She is sleeping. She is tired. Tomorrow she must eat more.'

The goodwill in particular kinds of smiles, the ability to extend themselves for others without any expectation of gratitude: these aspects of their humanity had the power to haul me out of the pit. I would find myself chuckling with them, almost against my will, until affection returned like fresh air behind a storm.

It was for this, their use of laughter as a survival tactic, that I most admired them. Especially Phagu, on whom responsibility lay like a cement overcoat. He had to think ahead, plan and worry for them all, knowing that one wrong decision could mean the end of everyone's income. He had to be diplomat, psychologist, hard man, soft man, entrepreneur, spiritual leader, general and peacekeeper. Sometimes, when he thought no one was looking, his face set into lines of anxiety, yet in his demeanour there was not a trace of self-pity, not even the thought of it.

A mukki's position is not a hereditary one. When Phagu began losing his edge or became too old for the job, he would be replaced by a more able man and there would be no loss of face in this. He might continue going on migration under another's leadership or he might stay at home and send his sons and daughters. But while he was mukki, the community granted him and his family absolute respect, though I felt sure that in this case the respect spilled over into adulation because men of Phagu's calibre were rare in any place, any time. There was a subtle power emanating from our camp. Others gravitated to it because here was always to be found the happiest singing, the best prashad, the wittiest jokes, the cleverest talk.

At night when Phagu came in from his wanderings (sometimes he would be away for days), his eyes sunk in exhaustion, it was clear how highly they regarded him. Once I saw Parma, whom I'd secretly christened the Iron Virgin, adjusting the folds of his smock without his knowing; all her concern and love for him allowed a fleeting expression in that most tender of gestures, recognizable across cultures, across aeons.

One day Phagu's joke was handing me his long stick, a roti in a sack, a tin for water and ordering me to head out with the flocks. I played my part. Everyone giggled on cue. Phagu hauled me back, retrieved the props, put his arm around me and said, 'When are you going back to Bhuj?'

'I'll *never* go back to Bhuj . . . But I want to come with you, scouting.'

'You'll get tired,' said Phagu.

'No, I won't.'

I got tired. We walked into a village, out to a farm, across some fields, around a talab (dam), back to the village, across more fields to another dang, up hills, through ravines, made a deal with a farmer, met up with our shepherds and walked back to another farm. That was in the morning. When we were alone together, we were rather shy with each other, tacitly agreeing to abandon the stand-up routine. The frustrations of struggling to understand each other only added to our burdens, so we lapsed into silences made eloquent, if no more comfortable, by grins and sideways glances. But even if I had been able to speak his language, how much of Phagu's world would I have comprehended? Real travel would be to see the world, for even an instant, with another's eyes.

I knew that migration leaders often met up to discuss overall tactics, knew that shepherds gathered and disseminated news, but I could not see how it all fitted together to produce these mighty movements of animals and men which, far from being chaotic affairs, had more the quality of German machinery. Now I had a chance to witness how it was done. Whenever we came across another grazier, of whatever caste or religion, whether in the bazaar or on a lonely hillside, Phagu would first shake hands with him, then plug in the lakri o tar, the walking-stick telegraph.

No shepherd would be seen dead without his stick for leaning on (one leg raised), hitting sheep, fighting gundahs (thugs) or, as one shepherd demonstrated to me, knocking the revolvers out of policemen's hands. It is a symbol for pastoralists everywhere and has given its name to the miraculous networking without which the organizational feat of migration would be impossible. Two pastoralists meet. They shake hands. They swap information. How many sheep in that dang, where is it going, what are the farmers like in such and such a town, has a certain area been booked by any shepherds from elsewhere, how many sheep have passed through already, what happened on that camel dang, who died on that sheep dang, how much bribe was given to that forest officer, what is the state of the peanut crops in area A, when are the farms in area B harvesting, what did W say to X at village Y, how much did it cost to get shepherd Z out of that court case, and so on. There are some beautiful mathematics to be understood here, of the permutation, combination kind. So much travelling and meeting increases the chances of cross-fertilization of information and cross-checking of facts. However, it also increases the likelihood of error, that 'noise' which diminishes the effectiveness of any system of information, electronic or otherwise. But there is virtually no 'noise' in the pastoralist's system. Unlike the whispered message syndrome in which information passed from person to person is changed out of all recognition, the information disseminated by the nomads stays correct in the finest detail.

In the short term it would often be in an individual pastoralist's interest to fib to others who are competing for the same resources. Yet in a larger, overall pattern it is in everyone's interests to tell the truth. In other words, local, personal, short-term gain is sacrificed to community benefit with no one to punish you if you break the rule – and this among people who have turned dissimulation into an art form. Oh, admirable nomads. Oh, hope for humanity.

At last the dang lay spread out below us. Seated camels fringed the edge of the flock from which arose the mingling scents of urine, dust, incense and night and through which, like a string of lanterns, were little palaces of air and firelight. Above them Venus, Sirius and a slice of moon floated in purple space. The town we had come from was only an hour's walk away but it bore no relation to this movable world under the stars. We were far from everything, not just in space but in time.

Hatti belted me in the thigh in greeting. I raised my fist at her, sending her off into giggles.

'Eeeh, Bhagwan,' I said, creaking to the ground and leaning up against the leg of a charpoi.

'Take tea, Ratti ben.'

'After you.'

'No, no, you take.'

'No, you first . . .' Even though a cup of tea might bring you back from the dead, it was necessary to master greed, necessary to be human. Caffeine and sugar recharged the blood, the heads of goats protruded through curtains of darkness, sheep stared into the fire, the women's earrings swung back and forth from shadow to light, shadow to light, as fists pounded dough and the day's stories were told – weaving today into tomorrow, lives into Life.

Phagu lifted Hatti in his arms, kissed her palms and stretched himself out on the bed, his daughter snuggling into his side. He began to teach her the verses of a song, singing a phrase, which she repeated, over and over, until memorized. Other children came to join in, crawling up on the bed, curling like cats around Phagu who plaited black goat hair or smoked his chillum, occasionally handing it to the little boys to take a puff. The singing went on for an hour or more, occasionally interrupted by laughter and a hail of affectionate thumps if anyone got the words wrong. When it was time to eat, he handed me the goat hair he had been working on. It was a halter for Ram Rahim.

I went to my little camel, fitted the halter on him, tickled his lips and blew in his nostrils, then lay for a long time listening to ruminating, coughing animals, to the tink thunk of shepherds' sticks on the rocks, to lambs being born, schloop, beside my cot, and staring up at the darkness that covers us all. In the morning when we moved on, there would be nothing left behind to mark our camp but little black circles where the fires had been, and tracks dissolving in the wind.

I had been with the dang about a month when the jeep came bearing Dr Rama Krishna and his family. He had brought medicines for Phagu's flocks and, for me, what I needed most, friendship and the English language. Divali, the festival of lights, would soon be upon us and the village shops were stocked up with fireworks. I bought sparklers for the children and some firecrackers for myself, as the packaging sported a portrait of Chairman

154

Mao surrounded by exploding crackers and Indian gods. It was a prize of kitsch and I packed it carefully away with my luggage.

At the end of that weekend Phagu prevailed upon me to drive him back to Bhuj to see Rangka who had broken his leg in the home village, a couple of hundred miles away. The whole dang knew about the accident the day after it happened. We took sweets for Rangka that the women had cooked and a get well card from me, containing everyone's signature or thumbprint. Phagu could just as easily have taken the bus. That he insisted I drive him showed that my decision not to keep the jeep with me was prescient.

I had thought the heat would never end, that Indian winter would prove as fugitive as English summer. But on the night of my return from Bhuj, as greyness rimmed the east like a primitive sea creeping across lifeless littoral, marking the moment at which I usually fell asleep, a kind of queasy coolness crept under the sheet. Two hours later the flies and the sun's hot hand worried me awake as usual. Two things were different. The warmth around me was in motion. The shepherds were wearing blankets.

After Divali the winds had started, just as Phagu said they would. To me they were the offshore breezes of a Sydney summer. To the Rabari they were arctic blasts bringing disease. Soon a third of the dang was suffering not only malaria but influenza. If we were near a town or village, we would walk miles to see a doctor. If not, we simply kept going. The women no longer erected the tarpaulin in the morning, so we sat under a sky pitiless to my transparent skin. I hunkered down into the shadow cast by my cot like a worm exposed beneath a lifted rock. But the sun seldom came sideways, preferring instead to strike straight down from above. I felt ill and ate handfuls of antibiotics which had no effect, but I had learnt not to dwell on misery, to dismiss it as they did or to use it as material for comedy routines.

Boredom was more difficult to conquer. No one who has not sat for six, eight, ten hours on a black, ploughed field under a sienna sky, day after day, waiting, entirely dependent upon one's inner life, knows the true meaning of boredom. I did not have the nomad's talent for instant slumber as when, during those infinite afternoons, they put aside their embroidery and snored. One turns into a zombie in such circumstances. There is only enough of one's brain functioning to register pain, not enough to learn a language. Boredom allowed no relief from either fatigue or muteness.

I had long since used up Proust's prose as toilet paper. Those pages saved by fate, screwed up into little balls and distributed through my junk, I now retrieved and read like poetry, savouring phrases which formed a lifeline back to the shore of a more recognizable self. A receding shore.

The women had been promising to teach me how to make a gudio, but somehow I had never managed to buy the cloth during our forays into villages. I determined that the next one we visited I would do so and that I would give the finished product, which would take weeks to complete, to Narendra.

An opportunity soon presented itself. A five-mile walk to find a doctor. The tiny surgery, a blue cement hole with a light bulb, was filled with shivering grey-skinned figures in various Goyaesque poses around the floor. On one side was a trestle littered with old needles and a few bottles of antibiotic and chloroquinine. The doctor sat behind a rickety tin desk. He was neat as a new pin, his hair parted down the middle and brilliantined. He had a cheerful, efficient look and I liked him straight away. He was a real doctor he assured me. That is, he had studied western medicine and practised in a big city hospital. (Often the people who passed themselves off as doctors in these villages were ex-pill-wrappers from chemists' shops.)

Why had he decided to come to this place? He liked it here. It was quiet. He knew almost all his patients. He would have made more money in a city but what does one need money for if one is already content? Besides, 'The cities are made by man but the villages are made by God.' His treatments seldom varied. An injection followed by such advice as 'don't eat tomatoes for three days' or 'boil a little somf (fennel seed) each morning and drink the water'. He looked at me and winked. I was to understand that the prandial advice was for the benefit of the unlettered only. Then he said, 'They don't feel they've had their money's worth if I don't give a needle. People want to feel better in an hour, so we treat the symptoms I'm afraid, not the cause.' The doctor put the syringes into a sterilizer that looked like a Woolworth's toaster. Yes, of course, he was concerned about AIDS but there were 'more pressing problems in India'. Our sick ones received their injections, then off we went to do the shopping.

Stalls sold vegetables all along the street. A teashop puffed smoke merrily. I bought as much fresh produce as I could carry and little gifts – nail polish, sweets, ribbons. Then, my purchases stacked around me, I sat above a gutter, back propped against a mud wall, to watch life go by. The women would meet me there when their business was done, then we would head off together to buy the cloth. Inevitably the hordes began to gather. By the time my friends came back I was buried beneath them, my head hidden in my arms.

When the Rabari understood how much I hated these crowds, they used their skills to defend me from them. After all, they, too, were often greeted by children howling 'bhoot, bhoot' (ghost) when they entered a village.

'Why do you stare at her?' said Jaivi, making her way through the throng. 'Would you like it if someone stared at your sister like that?' Everyone agreed that they would not like it and continued to stare. I found it difficult not to compare the villagers unfavourably with the nomads, who are so respectful of another's humanity, so much more sophisticated and knowing. Whenever I saw any wandering castes in a village, they would watch me with frank curiosity and interest, but they would never crowd me.

The Rabari women made up lies on the spot to field the endless questions about me. Sometimes I was a government worker, at others a veterinary doctor. Once I was a policeman, which really shut everyone up. And they delivered these fibs with such facility that it was clear that shamming to outsiders was the habit of centuries. But they never lost their capacity for diplomacy no matter what the provocation. The terrible violence I felt towards the crowd appalled me. I wanted to take each face and screw it down in the gutter. Instead I entered that state of semi-catatonia in which you take in and give out nothing.

There was only one cloth shop – a forlorn little box lined with a few bolts of dusty cotton, a wooden bench along one side. We left our shoes on the step and spread ourselves importantly on the bench. Parma and Jaivi made the shopkeeper roll out, one by one, every bolt of cloth, even though we had already decided on the colours – white with a red border.

It was late. We had to hurry back. We hurled our way through the mass of humanity which followed us out of town, slowly thinning like a comet's tail, until just the core was left – my sisters and aunties hurrying single file along a footpath, through quiet hills. We paused to adjust our bundles. Parma smiled as she replaced the heavy load on my head. 'So, Ratti ben, now you are a bhoot like us.'

Eight women sat with me in a circle, the gudio stretched between us like a picnic blanket, needles and thread to the ready. It measured five feet by three feet and consisted of two outside layers of white cotton, and three inside layers of thin woollen rug, all clamped together with a few rough stitches which would later be pulled out. I understood why they helped each other begin their gudios. Imagine how depressing it would be to sit alone in front of fifteen square feet of cloth knowing that you had to make several hundred thousand stitches before it even began to look like a mat.

Parma studied the white space for a while, then, watched and approved by the older women, began to pencil in a design. She halved the rectangle. Inside each half she drew paisley swirls, large as palm leaves, locked together ingeniously within the two frames. She made the patterns in long continuous lines, so that one would not need to stop stitching until one ran out of thread or reached the outermost border. When it was done to everyone's satisfaction, we began. In tiny running stitches with thick red cotton we followed the lines of Parma's fancy. I noticed that this was only a guide, a theme if you like, and that when someone felt like it she added subtle variations – nothing so individualistic as to break the harmony of the pattern but enough to make it live.

Each woman had, as it were, a sewing signature and to this day, when I look closely into that gudio, I think I can remember who stitched what. Nakki stitched with the deftness of a fairy; Lakhma, with the lumpishness of a troll. Lakhma was, it had to be said, a woman of limited wit. She was always the slowest to get a joke, the quickest to take food, and when she wasn't eating her jaw hung open slightly. I rather hoped that she might stop helping me as I felt, already, rather possessive of my gudio, and her stitches looked like the tracks of vultures among the tracery of wrens. Nakki caught me frowning at those stitches and pulled her lips tight to stop herself from smiling. But it was no good. She caught Parma's eye, who caught Jaivi's, who caught Rammi's and so on until everyone was stifling laughter except poor Lakhma who smiled at us in a bovine sort of way. After ten minutes my hand was already cramped but if anyone slackened Nakki cried 'Karo!' (keep going) as if we were climbing a mountain. There was a tremendous feeling of solidarity, lots of laughter, story-telling, whispered tales. Women came by from other camps to lend a hand, bringing prashad. I never thought I'd enjoy a sewing circle.

'When is the taxi coming back, Ratti ben?'

'How far away is your country, Ratti ben?'

'How long would it take to walk there?'

'How is it possible that the stars in your sky are different from the stars in our sky?' (Try explaining that in sign language!)

Everything I told them in my halting Hindi, Gujarati and sign language, one of the women would turn into a song – or chant rather. Always the same notes and stanza, sung at walking pace with a strong emphasis on the last word. 'Ratti ben's taxi is coming, it is coming soon, coming *soon*.' Or 'Ratti ben's country is a long way away, long way *away*.' When I told them that in my country one small family might own an area as large as Kutch, and all the sheep and cattle thereon, they looked at me as if to say 'We, too, are good at telling whoppers but they have to be at least *credible*.'

Since they were helping me, it was expected that I provide the tea. I bumbled around with three rocks and jagged my skin on African thorn. Latchi cast me that look reserved by teenagers for particularly dense adults, took the matches and ordered me back to the gudio. It had taken this long for her to deign to notice me. Now she'd become my number one pal. Even that yellow-eyed brute of a dog had come out from under the bed recently and given me two psychotic wags before disappearing back under.

We had a break from our sewing for tea and the inevitable snuff to which the older women seemed addicted. Then they pulled out tiny glass phials of white crystal. A fragment was rubbed into the eyes, causing them to water copiously. Naturally I had to try. It was rather like having a heated dagger thrust into the eyeball and twisted, then caustic soda rubbed in the wound. Only out of sheer mastery of will did I not scream in agony. What was it for, I asked. To 'clean' the eyes. To tell the truth I think they had become addicted to the pain of the white powder, which had about it an orgastic quality. I asked them why they did not take other medicines with them on the dang and tried to say that injections might be dangerous as there was another disease passed by dirty needles. Wouldn't it be better, I suggested, to take quinine tablets for malaria or aspirin for fevers, as they were cheap and available anywhere. 'Oh, we will, Ratti ben, if you say so,' they lied, humouring me.

They were far more likely to take medicine for the sheep which suffered from anthrax, toxaemia and fluke. The shepherds injected their animals with Terramycin or drenched them, believing that the drugs were tonics because afterwards the animals miraculously put on weight.

I lay my head on Jaivi's lap. My legs stuck out in the sun. Baby goats pressed their sharp little shoes into my stomach or nibbled my ears. Later some Muslims arrived to buy a couple of sheep. The Rabari are not so much hypocritical in their attitudes to breaking the Hindu code of vegetarianism as low-key. Thus the selling of old or sick animals to Muslims along the way was done somewhat surreptitiously, despite the fact that the Rabari will, on occasion, eat their animals themselves. In any case the economic symbiosis between Rabari and Muslims militates, in a very practical way, against communal bigotry. But there is another reason, I think, for the comparative broadmindedness of nomads. They are constantly having to negotiate borders and deal with difference.

The gifts I gave them were accepted matter of factly. My own gushing gratitude when they did something for me, or gave me something, bemused them. Desert cultures seldom have a word for thank you because sharing is integral to survival and to social form. It is learnt young. Whenever sweets were given to children, they would automatically share them out.

Parma and Jaivi, Hatti and Latchi called me over to their bed to try out the nail polishes. I had bought four kinds – purple, pink, scarlet and maroon. The purple and pink were rejected out of hand. Was my taste in my sandals? What did purple match? And who would bother to wear insipid pink? Maroon was the best as it picked up the colours in their embroidered black, and the fiery red was best for Hatti who had not yet begun to wear black but was, instead, dressed like a Christmas tree – green skirt with acres of swish, lots of coloured stitching on her blouse, silver.

I had always enjoyed being in situations where I was free of the shackles of contrived good looks. I was more than happy to not give a damn whether my kurta matched my pajama or whether there was sheep shit in my hair. 'Who's to see or care after all?' The answer to that was the Rabari women, who might abandon their grooming out of necessity but never out of choice. Sometimes they would look askance at what I had thrown on. Reading those looks I would present myself to them and say, 'Is this all right?' and they would look at each other, mouths twitching, and say, 'Yes, yes, Ratti ben, it will do.' Later they would tactfully suggest that I add some kohl to my eyes or why not wear that pretty skirt they knew I carried. Perhaps I would like them to plait my hair? But it was easy to see, behind their solicitude, that they regarded me as a terminal case of sow's ear.

What was the vanity for? The dressing up, primping into little hand-mirrors tucked into bodices, the careful application of kohl, ribbons at the ends of plaits, bits of glass fixed with silk thread, the love of silver – and now this careful spread of nail polish on those work-battered, fire-scorched, thorn-torn hands which they held out and inspected like a bunch of Joan Crawfords in a boudoir? Who could they impress with it, since any sexual relations outside marriage were not just frowned upon but unheard of? At least so they said and I believed them.

I don't pretend to have entered the consciousness of a Rabari but where individuals have no meaning outside of their community, all possessions, even beauty, belong not just to the individual but to the group. A woman will adorn herself because she is a Rabari and Rabari women are famous for their beauty; to be beautiful reflects well on and within the community from which one derives one's identity and strength.

'When did you say our taxi was coming, Ratti?' Parma's tone did not escape me. Whenever the jeep came, it was difficult to resist the moral pressure to keep it with me. To them the taxi was a fantastic resource. But when it was there, distances and therefore times were transformed and this brought home to me the ersatz nature of my life with them. I was a tourist in pre-industrial time.

The dominant time in the world is my own – post-industrial technological time. Most people of my time are happy to sentimentalize an earlier one, yet unwilling to give up their comforts to participate in it. They would like some people to remain in those earlier times (whether the people wish to or not), so that they themselves may visit occasionally but always with the option of leaving when the going gets rough. I could decide to walk with the dang despite the hardships because I knew those hardships were temporary. They wanted to ride in the car because they were sick of hardships from which they had no possibility of escape.

'The taxi is coming soon.'

'Ah. And will "Kaajun" come also?'

'Yes, Koju will come.'

'And Sahib?'

'I do not know if Sahib will come.'

'When the taxi comes, we will all go to Junagadh.'

I refused to comment but accepted that a trip to Junagadh was a *fait accompli* whether I liked it or not, which I didn't. They knew by now that I could deny them nothing and they exploited me to exactly that moment when I baulked, at which point they turned on their irresistible charm. The last time the jeep visited, Phagu asked if the taxi would take him on a short reconnaissance of the area ahead. I left Koju behind and we set off at daybreak. By mid-morning I was wondering when we would head for home. I had no maps, so relied entirely on Phagu. I watched him out of the corner of my eyes. A man unused to sitting still, restless hands, darting eyes: looking for water, feed, camping places, villages for food and medicine; thinking when will the cotton here be harvested? should we risk this jungle area? – the paradigm of human intelligence.

Three hundred miles of dirt tracks, ploughed fields and rims of dams later, the snakes in my stomach were threatening to come out, crawl all over the car and fang Phagu to death. Every now and then he'd cast me one of those grins and the fury would lessen. This drive would save him miles and miles of bus travelling, incalculable amounts of walking, weeks of effort. It was not the recce I resented, it was his manipulation of me. If I had known I'd be driving that boneshaker all day, I could have prepared better.

'Are you tired, Ratti ben?'

'Of course I'm bloody tired.' (Said in English.)

He laughed. 'Stop here!' And what do you know, the old tight-wad shouted me as many cups of tea from the chai wallah as I could drink, and I defy anyone to drink more than five.

By the time we got back it was dark. The whole community welcomed me home with prashad and high praise but I was too fed up with them to be conned out of my mood and went straight to my tent. In my notes I wrote 'I am their milking cow'.

I slept flat on my back, palms up – the position of terminal exhaustion. Through the jelly walls of sleep I felt something cool and heavy on my left palm. I thought, To hell with them! I've had enough of their jokes. Putting a clod of earth on my hand in the middle of the night, it's just too much! I threw the weight off, burning with hate for my persecutors, and saw it change into the primeval shape of an S.

The snake landed somewhere around my feet among the baggage. In the torchlight it was a small innocuous-looking thing, staring at me in a trusting kind of way. I didn't want to hurt it but I had to get it out of my tent. I couldn't find my stick, so I called to one of the men patrolling the flock. Using sign language I indicated that he should hold the snake down with his stick while I picked it up behind the head and threw it into the cactus fence. He must have misunderstood because not a moment later blood, fangs and scales were spattered all over. I drew what was left of it, for identification. Weeks later I discovered that I had slept with a krait, the most deadly snake in India.

One morning, as I threw off my blankets and sat up, a full moon climbed into her western bed and pulled the clouds over her, while hundreds of cranes flew in watery formations above our camp – a Van Gogh painting, only in browns, blacks, greys and the luminous yellow of the sky.

I had been formed by Australian landscape, so spare, rigorous and pure, the earth itself sentient, untameable. But there was not a particle of India that had not serviced man: ploughed, thrown as pots, eaten, shat out, lifted as dust, ploughed again. Even babies had seen millennia. If the Australian horizon invited you to throw off your burdens and head for vanishing point, here the restrictions imposed by man dominated any impulse to move freely. Dogs and fences, forts and defensive walls, zinanas and spiked gates. Nose rings, leg-irons. Rules and codes bolting the social structure tightly into place. The shape of the country was defined by the safeguarding of property.

I met someone in Delhi who said 'I knew the Aborigines were very backward when I heard they had possessed Ayer's Rock for thousands of years yet never decorated it.' I imagined Uluru in India – smeared in saffron and silver, shit piled up in its caves, beggars and touts milling around its base, plucking at tourists – all the power and numinousness of the place buried under tat. What antithetical aesthetics they were.

When I first went to England, after living for years in the Australian deserts, I found the countryside domestic and merely pretty. Now I cannot imagine how I had not always been moved by its dignity and subtlety. What it required was a change in gaze. Not the Australian squint swallowing down vistas but a more myopic search in among the detail of the foreground where history is inscribed. English countryside had frames built in.

But India? How would I ever learn to decipher it, to be at home in it?

That morning marked some kind of beginning. Those colours, never seen elsewhere in such combination, the distinctive shape of fields and hills, the women in black – all those elements formed a place I could return to, something I could claim. Parma came to sit with me on the bed. We watched the cranes together for a while. She said, 'They are from across the sea, like you. Soon you'll go back to your country and forget about us.'

13

The plan had been to travel with the Rabari as far as the Gujarat border or, if the rains in Kutch failed and Phagu was forced to cross the border into Madhya Pradesh, I would certainly accompany them. Now, thanks to our jeep recce, he had decided there was no need to risk great distances and unknown territory this year: the dang would remain in Saurashtra.

What would the editors think of my circling around these benighted fields for six months? Hardly the epic stuff they had been led to expect. I was pretty sure Dilip would find the dang about as interesting as mud. I would have to think of something else to satisfy them.

And so that peculiar instability, concealed temporarily by the internal structuredness of the dang, now reinstated itself as the journey's dominant motif. No matter how much effort was expended, all intention was governed by the second law of thermodynamics. India is not a good place for people who, being chronically chaotic in themselves, need some semblance of external order.

My friendships with the Rabari had passed through phases: flirtatiousness, politeness, displays of best behaviour; then intimacies, misunderstandings, quarrels and making up. It had settled down now into a sort of ordinariness which, though less exciting, indicated a deeper acceptance. But just as couples begin to take advantage of each other's weaknesses, once mutual curiosity and the desire to please has gone, so the Rabari began to exploit mine.

A local woman had come to visit our camp; she had asked them whether I was wealthy. They answered, 'She is so rich, she stays in air-conditioned rooms.'

The woman puckered her lips, nodding slowly to some inner thought.

'She is so rich that she owns a jeep.'

The woman shot me a sideways look full of calculation and greed.

'An air-conditioned jeep!' They were all looking at me sideways.

I had made a huge mistake and was only now coming to understand the repercussions of my foolishness. I should have stuck to the letter of our contract as scrupulously as they had at the beginning, then given a gift of money at the end of our journey together. But how, in all conscience, could I deal in those unthinkably small amounts of money which meant nothing to me and so much to them. How could I hold back my hand when it came to paying a dollar for a taxi, or fifty cents for sweets, or the doctor's fees, or for medicine. But this was false reasoning. In my own world a paisa might be nothing; here it was a paisa and if there was one rule the nomads lived by it was that a fool and his paisa are soon parted.

It had begun innocently enough. In the distress of not being able to speak I wanted to demonstrate my goodwill by being spendthrift not just with gifts but with things it was their duty to provide for me. Imperceptibly at first, the avarice for which their caste is famous began to shine through like copper beneath worn silver-plating. It was done in good humour, with hints and references, never blatant requests, but even so it created a tension which I resented – another drain on energy. They had robbed me of the pleasure (and the power) of giving. Perhaps encoded in my largesse was a subtle insult – the barra sahib white woman so rich, she could cast her money at the lowly. And as a defence against feeling, or seeming, or agreeing to be lowly, as a way of retaining that pride for which they are also famous, they needed to exploit me for what I would have given freely anyway. Sometimes my exasperation showed and then they charmed me so subtly, so cleverly. When they couldn't tease me out of a mood, they would lay off, go quiet and then do some small thing – fix some piece of equipment, present me with some special food, bring tea to my bed. And when I did not give them what they asked for, which was rare, they laughed and hugged me anyway. It was like a game to them. I had bought a camel saddle from Nakki earlier in the journey. Now she was saying she had sold it at the wrong price and wanted another hundred rupees. At certain moments she was pure rapacity and I found it hard to stand up to her.

When Koju visited with the jeep, he noted this and he disliked them for it. Rajput pride was of a different order altogether. But my collusion in it baffled him. He had never asked for an extra paisa, as if our relationship had no economic aspects but was purely of the heart. I could hear him thinking, it doesn't pay to be noble. Dazzled as I was by his poise and natural grace, I did not always remember that Koju was not a sophisticated young man fresh from the excitements of big city life, out for a holiday romp around the countryside. He was a non-literate peasant whose experience of the world was limited to a cluster of huts in the middle of sand-dunes sixty miles from Jodhpur. Lately he had been as moody as an adolescent and about as helpful.

His great flaw was wanting to be the most popular boy around and in this he usually succeeded. But now he was in another country for the first time in his life, with strange people who spoke a different language and who were not as susceptible to his charms. He was lonely and out of his depth. And he lacked the equipment with which to untangle an immensely complex jealousy.

I had sent him back to Bhuj as often as possible as I knew he had found some Rajput friends there. But on the dang he would sit on his bottom all day, spinning yarns about his village while I lifted and hauled and loaded and unloaded. I wanted him to see it, wanted him to help me of his own accord, without being treated like a servant. Which behaviour was confusing for Koju who, if he wasn't a servant was – what? I found it difficult to give orders preferring either to do the work myself or wait until my need for assistance was so obvious that a cretin could not miss it. Either Koju was the latter or he was punishing me. Please, not now, Koju, I said to myself. Sulk later when I have some strength. Now I need you.

I was tired. I was tired between synapses and in the connective tissue of organs. The bone marrow was tired and the calcium around it bent with tiredness. Each cell screamed out I can't go on.

167

And the chemical reactions longed for their thankless work to end so they could melt down and become some other life form less tired than Robyn Davidson. And, another funny thing, I hadn't had a period in quite a while . . . but I could not think about that now.

The country here was so flat, so used, that the eye latched on to any distant shape and did not want to let go, as if vision itself could suffocate from so much Euclidean geometry. And on the horizon these days, sometimes in the south-east, sometimes swinging by us to the south-west, was a blue mountain − Junagadh, Mughal city of Hindu temples.

Had I known what Phagu must have known − that this holiday, so eagerly awaited and discussed, would mark the end of our happier times − I would, perhaps, have ignored the irritations of the drive to Junagadh and been more open-hearted. As it was, I left in a bad temper which grew with every difficulty along the way. The evening before, Phagu had taken my car with everything I needed and didn't come back till night. And what sort of an idiot was Koju that he allowed this to happen? Besides that (oh, heinous crime), I found that my carefully hidden packet of Chairman Mao firecrackers, that irreplaceable memento, had been discovered by Hatti, torn apart and the crackers used to terrorize sheep. *And*, on the morning of our departure, I was woken up before dawn by that authoritarian old bastard Phagu and told it was time to get moving.

'Koju,' I said. 'I absolutely refuse to have more than twelve people in or on this jeep. I'll leave it to you to make sure that no more than twelve people come with us, OK?' Koju seemed to think that was OK. I sat gripping the wheel. 'No more than . . .' I shouted but no one was listening because everyone was squealing, laughing, pushing and jostling, and very determined not to be left behind. There were children on the bonnet, a cluster of boys clinging to the sides like oysters, feet dangling around the roof like a surrey with a fringe on top. And the back of the jeep contained what looked like a hundred disembodied women's faces tied together with black wool. 'Let's go,' said Parma and dug me in the back. I folded my arms and sat, or rather crouched, in the driver's seat, waiting for the noise to die down. When it did I said, 'Twelve people, not *one* more.' Eventually I got it down to about seventeen. Koju sat next to me and there was a woman and two children next to him in the front seat. From behind, elbows and heads poked into my back so that I had to hunch over the wheel, then twist my body sideways to avoid the bodies crushing me into the driver's door. Just as I was about to start the engine, Koju opened the passenger door, pushed himself harder against me, lifted a knee over the gear stick and said, 'Room for one more in the front.'

You'll pay, Koju, I thought. You'll pay.

Phagu chuckled at me through the window and touched me on the shoulder. I glowered at him, then we were off, bump, crunch, grind, across the fields and on to the road. We made several chai stops along the way so that the women and children who had been sick in the back could wash and recover a little. Parma was whiter than me and had been using my window to vomit out of. The blokes were all right because they were sitting on the luggage rack keeping an eye out for policemen and occasionally dropping their heads between their feet to giggle at me upside down through the windscreen in such a way as to make seeing the road ahead impossible.

Why did I not ask Koju, my driver, to drive? I think it had something to do with a primitive response to sulk behaviour in which the sulkee counter-punishes the sulker by ostentatiously punishing herself so that the sulker will feel tremendous guilt and offer to drive the jeep. Koju did not offer to drive the jeep or perhaps he did offer and I said no in a long-suffering sort of way, because I was enjoying being miserable. I don't remember. I only remember arriving hours later at the base of a mountain and being confronted by the first of the nine thousand, nine hundred and ninety-nine steps leading to the summit and the ultimate temple Ambadji, where we could score points with God so that we might not come back as cockroaches or untouchables (or better still, not come back at all; the idea of which has always struck me as a deterrent to faith in the karmic system).

We parked the car and checked out an eating-house. Cooking pots bubbled on clay stoves at the front which was open to the street. Tin tables sat behind in a gloom pierced by shards of light from the roof. Little pigs ran up the front steps and under the tables from time to time, only to be kicked, squealing, back into the street. The walls and wooden struts of the restaurant were plastered with pictures of various gods, people who had climbed Ambadji and members of the restaurateur's family, of whom there seemed to be thousands. Nagji, my little friend, and I sat at a table and shared a cigarette; everyone had tea or food except Parma who lounged against the car. Beside the café was a blue 'hotel'. A few hawkers sold their vegetables in the lane but unlike so many other temples I had visited the atmosphere around Ambadji was peaceful. Here one could imagine God as a quiet, ruminative sort of fellow. The buildings gathered themselves into the rock which plunged straight into the ground, like an island into the sea. In a cleft, twenty yards away, cut into the mountain was the flight of steps, about ten feet wide and overhung by masses of dark granite. Little caves in the rock beside the steps contained a few shops selling temple offerings and paintings of the gods bedecked in tinsel.

The staircase beckoned up a modest rise, then disappeared around a bend. Secretive steps, snuggling into their mother stone, giving you a sense of entering something rather than ascending it. Perhaps the ancient masons had understood that if the mountain even hinted at what it would cost to reach its summit, no mortal would ever begin.

My tourist guide was written in Hindi, so at the time I did not know about the ten thousand minus one steps. Even if I had it would have made no difference. I, too, was smitten with summit fever though for less obviously religious reasons. Later I was told there were only six thousand, nine hundred and ninety-nine steps but deciding, finally, just how many steps there are to Ambadji would be like deciding how many angels dance on the head of a pin.

I waited for Dreamboat to take the camera bag from me as any well-brought-up young man would do, whether or not it was his job, but he was already disappearing up the cleft. Nakki, Gelo, Lakhma and Jaivi took the lead. Nagji held my hand. Parma called to me to wait for her. We began to climb.

The higher one went the lighter the heart became and the closer one felt to the spirit of the mountain and to the people who had fashioned these stairs. Winter sun sparkled on rock; altitude breezes lifted kurtas and swallowed sweat. Monkeys accosted us. Each bend turned, each plateau reached, presented something new – a shrine set in a niche, a minute chai shop shaded by rock, a stand of flowering shrubs and trees, a small temple with bells ringing and gods staring through glass eyes, a sadhu in saffron offering his prashad and taking our coins with a rapturous smile, vistas below, a looming mass above changing shape and weight with every turn of the stairs. Each turn revealed a new perspective on where you had been before – a metaphor for life.

The Rabari did not seem interested in any aesthetic pleasures the mountain might offer. For them the climb was a serious business. At every holy place they gave out their money or their gifts and were blessed, as if they were making up for all those godless days on the dang and all that were to come. Only the Iron Virgin seemed to harbour a romantic streak. Each time we stopped she lay down to look, dreamily, at the sky, the birds, the trees, a cliff charging through clouds piloted by an eagle.

'Ho, Ratti ben.' I turned around to see that she was still gazing upward. I went back to her. She tried to get up, fainted, came to, threw up, fainted again, then got up. 'Let's go,' she said. I was not to let anyone know how ill she was but by about the thousandth step, the others began to notice.

Nakki, though happy to wait with her until Parma recovered herself, was anything but soft-hearted. It was in Parma's interests to get to the top and mollycoddling would not help her to do that. Only will and determination would get her there, no matter how ill she was. 'Jai Ram ji ki (something) ho,' came her scourging voice and Parma responded to it like a foot soldier in Boadicea's army.

Not once did she complain. Not once did she think of giving up. She would drag herself out of a swoon, her face yellow and slimy, grin at me, vomit, dig me in the back as if I were the one holding everyone up and haul herself up the steps, a hand draped upon my shoulder to look like a gesture of intimacy rather than the life-support it really was. But if I looked overly concerned or made a big to-do of helping her, she'd give me that 'don't make me puke' look and struggle along on her own. Impossible not to love such people, even when you hated them.

Actually by the three thousandth but one step it was mostly Koju I hated. Whenever I caught up with him he would cast me a look in which conflicting emotions lay unsuccessfully concealed, like the wounded gaze of some half-wit lover. I handed him the camera bag. He took it. We did not speak.

Halfway up was a cluster of temples, their domes inlaid with blue mosaic. They looked like luscious fat cup-cakes stacked on the side of the mountain and the sight of them made you want to swallow down the sight and grab for more. Parma wore that quizzical, tolerant look as I oohed and aahed. To her they might as well have been built of breeze-block and it struck me as peculiar that the Rabari, who have such a fine aesthetic of their own, should be blind to the wonders that lay around them, apparently unable to tell the difference between the sublime and the kitsch.

It took us five hours to reach the penultimate peak. The closer we got to the top, the fewer the shops and the faithful, the slower and more agonizing the climb. But the air had a champagne quality and we were so close to our goal, we laughed away our exhaustion. Parma was feeling so much better that she could keep down water and no longer needed to lean on me. The path passed by the shrine of yet another Brahmin priest who waited like a spider in this choice position to 'give' water to the thirsty. When it came my turn he demanded a watch and a hundred rupees. Gelo said, shocked, 'But she's with us.' I said it didn't matter, I did not want water from such a man and poured it back into his lota.

At last we could see Ambadji on a pinnacle ahead of us. A few hundred steps down a gorge, then up the precipitous rock wall. I decided not to accompany them for this final leg. It was their day, their place, their gods. I sat against warm stone and watched sun on a patch of golden grass – a miniature Zen garden set in granite. When I was full up to the top with the bliss of the beautiful, I wandered back to the last chai shop on the mountain. It was the usual makeshift place open on two sides, the chai pots at the front, tables at the back in the dark. I was the only customer.

The shop owner continued to gaze out at the blue air which fell away below, just ten yards from his feet. A midget, dressed in red shirt and tiny sarong, scurried around in the dark, sweeping and muttering. All else was quiet. When I went to pay my bill I said, 'How do you get your provisions up here?' He smiled dreamily. 'Every day I walk down; every day I walk up.'

They were radiant when they returned. Even Koju looked happy. I fell in beside him and asked him to stick with me as I might want to take pictures. The Rabari skipped off ahead, saying we would meet up at the base. After half an hour there seemed to be no one left on the mountain. Dark was seeping out of the rock and it was difficult to see the steps ahead. Going up had been more exhausting but coming down was more painful. Knees creaked and complained. Calves cramped. Blisters formed. How I envied Koju his youth, that casual energy you do not realize you have until it's gone. Though he, too, let out little groans now and then. We tramped on in the darkness.

But at the base there were no ladies in black; the restaurant wallah had not seen them; they were still somewhere up the mountain. But where would they sleep? Second question, where would we sleep? Koju decided to sleep in the car. I asked him to get me a room in the blue hotel. It was fifty rupees.

Fifty rupees for a room empty of anything save a dozen jumbled quilts so greasy with use they had turned black, a light switch and bed bugs. I kept the light on and lay down gingerly on the filthy razais. The walls were thin. There was no lock on the door. A fat man in a white singlet barged in, then barged out again. For some hours I lay listening to truly awesome belching, farting and thirty-second throat clearings followed by a splat of spit, children wailing, a wife crying and to cap it, loudspeakers not twenty yards away, screeching bhajjans into the night. This is hell, I thought, and lay there, gnawed by bugs and by loathing for my species. At about three in the morning I went to sleep in the car with Koju.

When the ravens tap, tap, tapped on the window at daybreak I was not happy. They had spent a fine night under the stars on charpois up in that cool air. Why had I come down here? We breakfasted, then all piled in. But we did not head back to the dang, ah no. It was necessary that we stop at every temple in Junagadh. By mid-morning I had seen enough step wells and gonged enough bells to see me through lifetimes. In the centre of town I parked the car and left them to it. But the jeep was too hot to doze in, so I went looking for a tea shop where I could sleep sitting up. I wanted to be left alone. That was all.

I walked around the town looking for a den to crawl into. I was followed by men who hissed and giggled. I found a stone and sat on it. A crowd gathered. I put my head down into my hands and absented myself mentally. A few moments later I looked up and there, not a foot from my face, was a row of men's crotches. Above the crotches was a row of eyes looking at me in that dead way. A choking sensation filled my throat, burst behind my eyes. I began hurrying through the streets thinking I hate India, I hate India, I hate India.

I sat in a tea shop. Open drains full of grey slime ran beneath my feet. A little boy was washing plates and cups in a bowl of water glutinous with grease, food matter and drowned flies. Around the boy and the plates and the plate scrapings and the slime – a nimbus of flies. The child himself so thin you could have clasped your fingers around his waist. Beside us was a building that could have graced a street in Paris or upper west side New York. But it was broken down, the windows blinded by cardboard and tin – a slum of crumbling mortar and broken glass surrounded by garbage and the smell of shit.

What did other people see that I could not see? Or what was I seeing that others apparently did not see? The well-off westerners who came here for enlightenment, what did they see? This repression and corruption, spiritual? This worship of the rupee, non-materialistic? This stasis, this dead end, a goal to be reached by humanity?

I looked down the street and I saw an entirely naked man walking along, smeared in ash. I saw a figure in black and red, also smeared with ash, carrying a thrishool with which to pick out bits of burnt human flesh to eat from the cremation grounds – high tantric practice. I saw a dwarf selling plastic combs, hair-bands and bobby-pins from a wooden trolley. He was the ugliest little man I'd ever seen and on his head was an enormous toupee. Yet no one was looking at these tributes to human diversity, they were looking at me. And their eyes were peeling my flesh away. I went to hide in a car.

By mid-afternoon we were heading out of town. As we passed through the city wall, a great shout went up from the occupants of the car. They had been to so many temples and doused themselves with so much holy water, their souls were transparent. They carried bottles of water from the step wells of various temples to take home to loved ones and temple junk blessed by Brahmins; they had eaten all their stomachs could carry and they were being driven home in 'their' taxi by 'their' driver.

We arrived back in the evening but no one rushed immediately into camp. There was to be a ritual welcoming and exchange of the sacred water. I should have remained with the returning group but was allowed to go to take pictures of Hatti being dressed up for the occasion. It was she who would accept the water. Two older women made her up – kohl and lipstick, an antique, heavily beaded and embroidered headdress consisting of two discs covering the ears. On her head was placed a small pot. She began to tremble, just as if she were about to deliver Portia's mercy speech before an audience of thousands. When everything was ready, the two parties faced each other across the field and began to sing. They walked slowly towards each other. Hatti was in the midst of her party, being held and aided by the older women. Then she moved a little in front, quietly confident now, the Rabari genius embodied in her. And the venom that had collected in my blood that day was neutralized by the sight of her.

After that it was back to normal life. My rendition of Parma climbing to Ambadji was to become a popular set-piece for evening entertainment.

But at night now, as I punched sheep, it was clear that the pressures of the last couple of months had taken their toll. Again and again I would return to the rage that had assailed me in Junagadh, and the fear of that rage. It bubbled up from somewhere deep and was too strong to staunch. The words 'I hate India' did not fit with the person I thought I was. Everything enraged me but what enraged me most was the sense of hopelessness, that whatever one might try to do to change things would be crushed by the vast weight of this country, a weight measured not just by mass but by time. You could not fight India. It taught you passivity or it drove you mad.

14

Dilip was about the least passive person I'd ever come across. Where I could let most things ride over me, Dilip took issue on every point. If a beggar demanded two rupees instead of the one given, Dilip grabbed the first rupee back. When people gathered around me in the street, he shouted at them, 'Let's go to your house and leer at *your* mothers and sisters.' If a government wallah sat doing nothing while supplicants waited, Dilip thumped the desk and demanded attention. Nothing escaped his furious scrutiny. Or, perhaps, nothing allowed him to escape.

Working with a photographer on a project such as this is bound to have its frustrations. But when every step taken is confounded by difficulties, then it is good to find some common ground. And now that I finally admitted to being unhinged by this country, we had found just that – India-bashing.

There was something else Dilip offered me, the seductions of relative comfort. He needed to stay in a hotel because of his equipment and also because he could not see the point of doing anything else. I had found him the best one in Rajkot – a modern vertical warren in such a state of dilapidation that it had an organic look about it. Electrical cables draped it like jungle vines; cement peeled from its facade like slabs of granite from Junagadh mountain. Dilip said, 'Why aren't you staying here as well?'

A whole room to myself in which to write up notes, wash my clothes, sleep on a horizontal surface. In this room I could be the other Robyn Davidson for a while. Why punish myself? I could come to a town each week for a day or so, take a bath, have a decent sleep and drive the jeep back out to the dang afterwards.

Why, the Rabari themselves would think me a fool for staying with them when I could be in an air-conditioned hotel.

By the end of that shoot my room was no longer a luxury but as necessary to me as a snail's shell is to a snail. On the last day when I thought I must surely crack along the many fault lines appearing in my character, a beggar, coming through the crowds already surrounding me and blocking my way, accosted me as I was getting into Dilip's car. I did not want her to tug at my clothes like that, persisting, snatching at my sleeve now, aggressively, whining and scratching, but with an edge of anger. The more she persisted, the deeper my resolve to give her nothing. I felt my stomach tighten, unreason bubbling, rising. I got into the car and tried to roll the window up. Her arm came through, poking and jabbing. I turned and looked her in the eyes and between us passed pure hatred. I grabbed her arm and flung it out of the window. Dilip drove off honking his horn and threatening to run down those who were slow to get out of his way.

We went to an air-conditioned restaurant. There were waiters with trays and starched cloths. We sat by a plate-glass window which separated us from the life of the street. Its discomforts. Its desperations.

'I wanted to hit that woman.'

Dilip looked at me and registered that I was trembling. With genuine concern he said, 'When it gets that bad, it's time to leave.'

When he had gone back to Delhi, I decided to recuperate in the hotel for a couple more days. After propping myself under the shower for an hour, I turned on the television to dunk my psyche in a stream in English. I did not want to know what was going on in the world. It was too far away and it had nothing to do with where I was. I just wanted to be embraced by my language. It was like homesickness. Then I rang Narendra and my thin spirit trickled gratefully into the ocean of his.

'I don't know what to do. Dilip asked me, "Where's the story?" and I honestly don't know.'

'Hmm.'

'So I'm thinking of walking back to Jodhpur with my camels, travelling with other dangs along the way. Dilip can get his pictures and at least there'd be a kind of shape to the thing.'

'But are you up to it?'

'No. But I don't think I have a choice.'

'I'll do whatever you want me to.'

What I wanted him, or anyone else, to do was to tell me that I had done enough and could go home now. But of course that was not his style. For some unaccountable reason he believed there was value in what I was doing; believed in it even when I did not. Especially when I did not.

I made a drama of the problems with Koju, who was staying in another room of the hotel, as a way of letting off steam, little thinking what the repercussions would be. Narendra rang him. I do not know what was said but the end result was that Koju went back in tears to Jodhpur on the bus, and was replaced by someone from the Sheep and Wool Department in Bhuj.

'But Narendra, I didn't mean you to do that.'

'Listen, yaar. You're under pressure. You've got to have someone with you you can rely on and who is of use to you. If Koju's going to be a prima donna, a few weeks back here will sort him out one way or the other. He has to work out what sort of person he wants to be.'

As it turned out, Ramesh, my new driver, was multilingual and a thousand times more helpful than Koju. But Koju and I had been through things together. I had led him to believe that he was not so much a servant as a comrade. And I had betrayed him.

In order not to think of what I had done, I turned my attention to the television. I kept switching channels, trying to fit what I was seeing – the spiritual desolation of modernity – with where I had been. Gorgeous women in fabulous saris floated through kitsch marble bathrooms with gold taps, trailing pink toilet paper behind them like veils. Or poured Harpic into western-style toilets, leaving a trail of little stars. Or gave their suited husbands Nestlé noodles when they came home from work. Advertisements of the grossest, most manipulative kind, insinuating their poison into every cranny of the country. And those groomed BBC women announcing the world's most recent disasters. How alien they were. And how secure. How did those images fit with what existed on the other side of my door – the sweepers, as faceless as furniture, listlessly shifting dust from one corner to another? The next day I returned to the hardships and humanity of the dang.

It was mid–December. I had been with the Rabari for almost three months and my time with them was coming to an end. No one spoke of it but it was there, like a little moat between us, widening each day. I had the jeep with me most of the time now. It seemed unnecessarily puritanical not to enjoy the modest luxuries it afforded, such as driving to decaying dak bungalows (government resthouses) once a week for hot bucket-baths in the privacy of a cement cubicle; a bed in a room bare of anything but broken punkah and a mosquito net full of dust and holes. Whenever I returned, they greeted me just as warmly but it was as if they did so from the deck of a ship which would soon be leaving. We were cutting off from each other, streamer by streamer.

It was winter at last and a cool breeze blew at night. The Rabari huddled against it in their woollen shawls, like Inuit outside their igloos. Above, there were mackerel clouds. Outside the dust of the dang, the evening air was crystalline. Each day now Phagu went scouting in the jeep, Ramesh driving, he and I perched up on the luggage rack. That almost forgotten good-weather feeling – sensuous air making the world lovely again. We drove through undulating farmland and it was as if the light were refracted through amethyst. The ploughed fields were purple and Ambadji, larger now but still riding the horizon, was blue on pale pink.

While life was easier for me during these last weeks, it was growing more difficult for the Rabari. The way ahead was constricting, darkening. And despite their efforts at good cheer, the atmosphere in the dang now was sombre. One day we had just made camp when a local caste of herders came and began shouting and threatening us. The women placated them. Yes, we would move on. No need for trouble. Afterwards everyone joked with me about 'war' being imminent and I'd better learn how to use a sling. (We kept our sticks handy now, just in case.) But there was an edge to the humour. The situation was serious. Phagu drove off to scout another place; the rest of us packed up and walked an extra six miles.

Every day farmers told us to move on, threatening both graziers and women with sticks or knives. A gundah came to camp and intimated that he would bring his mates and make trouble. Phagu gave him five rupees and tea. The mukki of a local Rabari dang came to visit and there was a heated exchange in which Phagu pointed to the other man's stomach and then to his own. But it all ended amicably and by the afternoon they were gossiping together like old hens. Nevertheless we must move on.

I had driven to Gondal, the nearest town, to make phone calls and have a wash. When I returned, everyone was packing up and a cloud of tension hung over the whole camp.

'Parma, what's the matter?'

'Pack up, Ratti ben. We've got to go.'

Blood had been spilt this time despite all the evasive tactics and diplomacy. Phagu had decided that the dang must break up into three groups. Smaller flocks would be less threatening to the locals. And so we loaded in silence and, after walking a few miles down the road, the line of camels began to split up. Devshi bhai took his group along a dirt track to our left. We lifted our arms to them once, then concentrated on the road ahead. A little later Pala bhai's family and several others peeled off in the same way. Again, the silent farewell. I had only just memorized everyone's names.

That night the dang was miserably reduced – about fifteen of us, in each of the three camps. The sadness was palpable and enveloped us like the dark. We would not see our friends for a long time. From now on, travelling would not only be more physically demanding, it would be lonelier as well. With so few people, the work increased threefold. The most sleep the shepherds could hope for was three hours a night, sometimes less. The little boys worked like men and came in at night with grey faces. As for Phagu, sometimes I don't think he slept at all.

Nakki, Jaivi, Parma and I went to do some shopping. (No one even thought of walking any more.) Like a multitude of other little Indian villages, a line of shops opened to a dirt street, a tree and a well at one end (where we washed our feet), nothingness at the other. The local schoolteacher was notified of my presence. He invited us into his house where we sat in the cool of his courtyard – the women in their black robes sitting in a semi-circle, backs straight, conscious of their distinction and style. I thought how sad I would be to leave them.

The teacher said, 'These are poor people but good people.

They don't angry anyone. The oldest people in India. You must do something for them.'

Nakki and the others preened themselves under his praise. 'Yes,' they agreed, 'we are liberal people. We do not judge others but let everyone be.' They strove to look long-suffering, as befitted down-trodden masses, but it didn't work. The twitch of Rabari cheek broke through, quite spoiling their act.

The teacher gave them grain, saying, 'Mother Teresa gives. I too give.'

I asked him if he was a Christian.

'No, Madam. I am an Indian.' He handed the women ten rupees each, which they graciously accepted, Nakki's eyes luminous with greed. Then the women of the house brought tea. Days like this didn't happen often to the Rabari.

Out in the street Nakki said seriously, 'He was a good man.' But everyone erupted into giggles and bolted down the street as free of deference as the wind. Back at the dang, when the story was told, Phagu laughed, put his arm around my shoulders and said, 'You can stay with us for five years if you want.'

The next day I hopped on Ram Rahim for the first time since leaving Bhuj and paced him to the field where I knew Phagu was sitting with some local Patels. I think it tickled him, seeing me speeding along. 'She is with us,' he said grinning to the farmers whose eyes widened at the sight. I dismounted and we walked together to the other end of a field to tie Ram Rahim to a tree he could eat. It was then I told Phagu that I would, after all, be leaving them and had decided to walk back to Jodhpur. We sat together for a while. He said that they would miss me but I think he probably meant the jeep. I would so like to have been able to say, 'You are a most remarkable man.'

I had friends arriving from Australia for Christmas. We would have a couple of weeks' holiday together at Narendra's house in the Himalayas, during which, I felt sure, my old self would be reinstated and my energy returned. I would have Momal, Sumal and Chutra Ram Raika sent here. Chutra could scout around for any dangs travelling in the direction of Jodhpur and when I returned we would set off together.

I told myself that I resented having to fulfil my obligations in this way. But weren't there, in this new plan, shreds of dreams hanging around like tattered prayer flags months after the cremation? And that old sunset and dune picture, which I had thought long lost, was still there – blotched, faded and curling at the edges, but romantic still. In my imagination I saw a country road winding through granite hills or threading the sides of dunes. Here and there, people on bicycles or bullock carts came along, paying little attention to the Raika, the woman and the three camels. With this image went a sense of inner freedom, a kind of expansiveness in the chest as if a tight band had been loosened. I would be able to 'see' at last what was around me, able to engage with it. I would be allowed 'in'. I would find some way of camouflaging myself – wearing a black wig or a Muslim burqa.

There was a deeper motive for the prolonging of self-punishment: the quest for meaning, of which, so far, this curious journey had remained void.

Chutra arrived with the camels and an index finger the size of a canteloup – snake bite. He unravelled the dirty white bandage to show what looked like gangrene to me. Had he seen a doctor? Once, weeks ago, but he had run out of medicine. He had however performed the appropriate puja. We unloaded Momal and Sumal near Gondal. It would not do to take them to the dang as they were females and the dang camels were bulls. We found a farm on which to leave them, then headed off for the dang. Chutra, naturally, boasted all afternoon and treated my Kutchi friends with barely concealed disdain. I sent him back to the Patel farm with his snake bite and his elaborate complaints. Phagu's lips moved, just the merest hint of a twitch, and he gave me a look. Oh, those eloquent looks, so discerning, so rich with meaning. How I would miss them. If looks can be read, then Phagu's were Gogol and Sterne. And Chutra's were *Reader's Digest*.

On my last evening on the dang, the Berlin Wall of language collapsed and I had my first more or less fluent conversation. Phagu's son wanted to be my driver.

'But I already have a driver and anyway you can't drive.'

'You can teach me.'

'But why do you want to leave your profession? Is it the money?' It was not the money.

'Well then, is it the difficulty and danger of the work?' No, he did not mind hard work.

'It is the constant fights and trouble. There is no peace for us, night or day. Once we were like kings. Now we are treated like dogs.'

In the morning the women came to say goodbye carrying ceremonial pots on their heads and singing. I was close to tears. They teased me of course. They are the most unsentimental of people. All morning Phagu had been leading me around by the hand. He wanted to buy Ram Rahim (at a good price, naturally) but I managed to refuse. They wanted to extract as much as they could from the old milking cow before she left, but it was also true that their fondness was genuine. After all, hadn't I provided them with some good laughs? A vehicle? Money? And wasn't I, in the end, almost as tough as they? The yellow-eyed dog, who had taken such a shine to me he had ended up sleeping in my tent, came to say goodbye, giving me two perfunctory tail wags and even allowing me to touch his head. Phagu said, 'Take the dog and leave us the taxi.'

Then there were hugs all round, clasped hands and more hugs. I drove away to the sound of singing.

I have never done anything in my life as demanding as travelling with the Rabari. But I could go back to comfort and security; for them this was real life.

My admiration for them was boundless and while I hated them sometimes, I never disliked them. They endured everything without complaint, singing themselves drunk at night or walking twenty extra miles to a temple in order to thank the gods for life. I never saw any one perform an act of cruelty. And there was *nothing* servile about them. They asked for neither charity nor an easy life, only the same kinds of support that other Indians automatically received and a recognition of the value of their expertise. As Dr Rama Krishna said, 'The government gives compensation for all kinds of animals lost during drought or flood but not for sheep and goats. We have tried to explain to the government that by moving, the Rabari are relieving it of a burden. But no one listens.'

I do not wish to glorify them. They are as capable of underhandedness as anyone in their quest for survival; they are often the bane of peasants trying to protect meagre resources; and their herds and flocks do untold damage. But no more so than the ploughs and poisons of the farmers and not as much as the venality of the people who exploit them. Perhaps in a place as desperate as India, it is absurd to single out one group for better treatment. Yet something invaluable will be lost if their migrations cease. Because it is the fact of their mobility which strengthens the qualities which so distinguish them – tolerance, wiliness, independence, courage, wit.

Sometimes, when it was particularly hard for me, they would pause in their work to smile, knowingly and kindly, or to whisper into the darkness, 'Go to sleep, Ratti ben' or to call, 'Ho, Ratti. Come drink tea', words with which they might convey an ambiguous and difficult affection. It was at those moments that the shadow of something infinitely remote touched us, fleetingly uniting me with them from across the abyss so that I too could hear the faint echo from our common, immeasurably distant past: 'It is all right. We are all here. There is no such thing as alone.'

PART THREE

Eternal Return

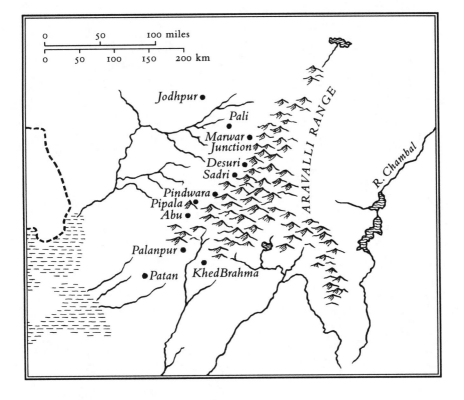

15

I stood on the rim of the Little Rann of Kutch, the smaller of two expanses of sand, mud and salt, thousands of miles square. During the annual north-west monsoon they are inundated by floods from the Aravalli Ranges in the east and tides from the Arabian ocean in the west, thus detaching Kutch from the rest of India during the wet, and providing a lot of nothingness between Kutch and the rest of India in the dry. The Little Rann of Kutch lies below and to the east of its big sister; the Great Rann is transected by the Pakistan border, which means that it is impossible to get a permit to go there. These days only smugglers and the Border Security Forces travel across it, which seems a waste of some splendid geography. The most exciting thing about both the Ranns — apart from miniature forests of crystalline salt, poison-blue and jade-green brine held in cut-glass ponds, herds of white asses and clouds made of flamingo wings — is that they are empty.

Stretching from the shore to the horizon lay brown, white and blue emptiness. Somewhere inside my chest, a sail was unfurling. My face, I know, wore the hungry look common to people who find in earth's vacant places the primeval garden. I glanced at Chutra. He wore the look of a man condemned by the caprice of a lunatic who, that being the upside-down way of things, was his boss.

'Kitna sundar,' I said, squaring my shoulders and taking a deep breath in such a way as to indicate that only people of heightened sensibility would recognize the loveliness in what lay before us, as flat and blank as earth's end. Chutra peered into it, scratched beneath his turban and said, 'There's nothing there.'

According to my map, which was a rough-drawn thing eight

inches square purchased from the local pan wallah, it was less than twenty miles across this slim section of the Rann. No need to take anything other than water, a couple of roti and a few oranges. Everything else was loaded in the jeep which would cross the Rann by the more conventional method – a bridge.

Our intelligence reports varied.

1. Yes, there was quite a good track across the Rann and it was as easy to find as the map said it was. (There were several dotted lines like running stitch which the legend described as footpaths.)

2. There was no track and never had been and we might never be seen again if we didn't use the perfectly good bridge which had been built so that people could cross the Rann without dying of heat exhaustion.

3. There was no track exactly but sheep and shepherds crossed every now and then, some recently, so there should be no problem for us.

The map contained a squiggle in the centre of the Rann, which was probably higher ground. In the middle of the squiggle, x marked a well. As we were heading due north, we would remain to the right, or east, of that squiggle.

Naturally I wanted to go alone and might have insisted upon it had I only my dear little Ram Rahim to handle, who was so good and patient, unlike the two maharanis who, during our two-day walk here from the dang, had shied at every truck or bus coming up behind them. Rickshaws and cars they treated with tolerant disregard, but trucks and buses made the one try to leap on top of the other or crawl all over the person leading her. In a pointed sort of way I had not remarked upon their behaviour to Chutra. Ram Rahim had not shied.

Everyone thought that my crossing the Rann by camel was a most peculiar idea. But going alone was a kind of subcontinental heresy: 'But there's no villages, no people!'

'Exactly,' I would say and feel the sail ruffle. At last, some moments when I could be as close to alone as it's possible in this country – that is, alone with someone else. I was not going to pass up this shard of pleasure, wedged, as it was, between the punishments of the previous year and the difficulties which, I knew, still lay ahead. So far I had prioritized everyone and everything before myself – the magazine, Dilip, the nomads, the people who worked for me or who offered their help. Now I was going to temper my spirit in the fiery wastes and if Chutra didn't like it – with his snake-bitten finger for which I still had not forgiven him, and upon which we had wasted much time hunting down doctors and pharmacists, and which I had to clean, dress and bandage for him thrice a day, and because of which he was useless at loading the camels – he could work for someone else. My own little medical problems – two small, suppurating holes in the ankle and the missing periods – were too insignificant to think about.

On the following morning I was the first to rise. An unusual event which cost me dear but it made the point to Chutra as to who was the leader around here. I was anxious to head off in the cool of the day but Chutra dawdled infuriatingly. I had asked him to check out the route the previous night but when we finally got going and were unable to find the track, it was clear he had not done so. It was easier for me to do things myself than delegate to Chutra. Yet, if I did so, he was deeply offended. He was not a lazy man – far from it. But he had his own way of doing things and his way and mine were several centuries and a couple of oceans apart.

Around the rim of the Rann were the hovels of the saltminers. Nothing protected them from the cruelty of that inferno or their skin from the salt which cut it like cat o' nine tails. The air did not move here. The salt mud stank and the children were juiceless, like scraps of cloth caught on sticks. They surprised you by moving. They worked all day in the mud; at night they slept on compacted mud under hessian lean-tos. Most of them were bonded labourers. Pay, if it came at all, was a pittance; work, neverending; hopes, nonexistent.

'Where is the track?' said Chutra to a scarecrow rooted in mud. He waved his arm listlessly in the direction we were going in and, despite Chutra's further volubility, would say not a word. The Little Rann had husked him.

Whenever we tried to head north, our camels began to slide around in mud. Eventually we came across a rope of animal tracks dropped across the pan, its wavy parallels disappearing into shimmer. The ground underfoot was harder, almost dry. Naturally the shepherds who had brought their flocks across must know the safest route. And, anyway, track or no track, all we had to do was head north and we couldn't very well help but bump into the northern shore. Then it was simply a matter of following footpaths to wells and villages. Heavens, I'd done this sort of thing hundreds of times. And in infinitely more treacherous terrain than this. Chutra was behaving as if this piddling little stroll was a ride across Lake Constance and he was making me nervous.

'Do you know in my country, Chutra, you can go for eight hundred miles without seeing another human being or coming across any water?' (Actually what I said was, 'Chutra, my country in, eight hundred miles in, people no, water no, see.')

'Achchha,' he said without shifting his gaze. I let him ride in front.

The 'rope' we were following unravelled after a while into three pieces. I assumed it would splice together further ahead. We kept to the middle strand. Something slightly less flat than the flatness surrounding it appeared on the horizon. It would hover for a moment, then deliquesce into the flatness again. This cheered up Chutra so much that he decided to talk to me. He relaxed into the saddle, tipped his turban over one eye with a stick and, half turning his body towards me, said, 'Madam Sahib camel very fiiiine camel; Chutra camel *not* fiiiine camel. Madam Sahib Ram Rahim beauuuutiful camel. Momal and Sumal sundar nahin, samajhdhar nahin (not beautiful, not intelligent).' He smirked and turned to the front. Sharp little incisors showed when he smiled, matching, in dainty repulsiveness, his naked shins.

I retorted, 'Momal and Sumal better camel is . . . er . . . are. All people this . . . understand . . . able. Ram Rahim not beautiful but me like because . . . him not criminal.'

These utterances did not come easily. They were costive, fatiguing utterances containing pauses during which a homunculus ran through miles of shelving in the brain, feverishly searching for vocabulary and grammatical rules. Often by the time this homunculus arrived, panting, at the speech centre, with the relevant material under its arm, the desire to say anything had left me, killed off by futility. At which point the homunculus would throw down its papers and threaten to strike.

Some hours later the 'shore' seemed barely closer and the ground beneath us was getting slipperier. Salt crust cracked, revealing squelch beneath into which the camels' feet sank, and pulling them up required a lot of muscle power to balance the laws of physics. We dismounted. Now the rope of animal tracks frayed in all directions, leaving us to our own devices and at the mercy of mud. If a camel slid and fell, it could easily break pelvis or limb and that would be the end of it. Momal and Sumal behaved like ladies who had just been thrown out of their zinana into a street which they had never before had to cross. Ladies who had forgotten how to use their bodies for anything other than reclining on couches, holding up mirrors and spreading spite. Imperious, fractious ladies who minced along, holding up their saris. To be fair, Ram Rahim's sure-footedness had a bit to do with the fact that his feet had been toughened by the stones of Kutch, whereas the princesses' feet had trodden only the sands of Jodhpur and were consequently like bald tyres. Even so, he struggled on gallantly, while the princesses snapped at each other and generally let it be known that, had they thought it was going to be like this, they would never have come.

About two hours later the mud was calf-deep and each step a little miracle of will. Not only were my feet bruised and swollen by the mud and the salt, not only was I feeling very nauseous indeed, not only was I expecting the fatties in front to fall at any moment but, having emptied my own water canteen, I found Chutra had brought only one extra, not all three as instructed.

'But Madam Sahib said five hours.'

'*Chutra, I say, said . . . Most important . . . Holding . . .* (Shit) *. . . Taking water . . . Everything . . .* (I mean . . . Goddamn it) *. . . Water important, five hours not important . . . Not . . .* (Oh, never mind!)'

Now, when you are on your own in deserty places and little things go wrong, you may feel dread (unreasonable in most cases because although you may get thirsty, or hungry or sick or fatigued, it is unlikely that you will die) and you may curse yourself for being a fool. However, water is the single most important resource standing between you and panic.

Every now and then I sat in the shade of my camel, head between knees and dry retched. At such times I said, between spasms, 'I am absolutely fine. Don't worry.' I lay on my back so that the Little Rann of Kutch would stop whirling like a top. It didn't. Chutra suggested I ride and he would lead Ram Rahim. This seemed like a good idea until we got moving. Diabolical though the walking was, it was better than ship-of-the-desert sea-sickness. The swelling on the horizon now seemed like dry land in the middle of an undulating ocean of light. We had been walking for five hours.

Chutra said, 'North side . . .' I didn't believe him, which was sensible of me because it wasn't the northern side, it was the squiggle – an island of sand, gibbers and skeletons which we reached long, long years later and which, I worked out, was about halfway to our destination. Night was falling.

At least we were out of the mud and I had started to feel alive enough to tackle a dry roti. We tied up our beasts, sat on the rocks and ate. After food and a swallow of water I felt positively chirpy. There is nothing likelier to give you a positive outlook on life than the cessation of nausea.

If I was on my own, I thought, I would be enjoying this moment. The place was stark yet intensely present. Wild horse and donkey tracks skirted the bases of red, sedimentary hills. Wind scuffed up dust and moaned in the sandstone. I led our little quintet along a dried watercourse, out to the other shore, then veered west, having decided to avoid as long as possible whatever wetness might lie on the other side of this island by following the 'beach' before striking out across the 'sea'. This tactic had the added advantage of lining us up with the village where the jeep would be waiting. Besides, we might be within striking distance of the well, a place to camp if necessary. Although the map had given wildly incorrect distances, surely it wouldn't show a well if there wasn't a well somewhere in the vicinity? But it was now dark. Moonless, starless, bottom of a mine-shaft dark. All day the clouds had remained in the wings, waiting for the footlights to go out so they could bustle on stage.

Luckily I always carried a small but reliable torch in my purse and this I shone on the ground ahead from time to time, looking for the animal pads that would lead us in to the well. The going now was easy, the ground flat and hard so that the sound of camel pads, softly susurrating, soothed like a lullaby. Ram Rahim was confident beneath me, a snug little boat on a big sea. So what if it took us fourteen hours rather than seven? So much the better.

I found tracks ahead. And beyond that, I thought I saw a twink of light. 'Chutra, dekho!' I urged Ram Rahim forward but Chutra called me back. He was very frightened. Nevertheless he followed me hesitantly towards that little glow in the night, which seemed close, then far away, then disappeared altogether.

No doubt about it – habitation. A tiny plot of tilled earth. There was a cooking fire and beside it a temporary dwelling. Chutra's camels were restive, picking up his nervousness. 'Ghosts!' he warned from back there in the dark. I called across a tall thorn fence towards the shelter. A dog went berserk. A man came out, looking as frightened as Chutra, who now overcame his dread enough to ask for directions. At first the man seemed reluctant to talk, no doubt fearing we were about to slit his throat and steal his dinner, or spirit him off to a cemetery. Eventually he told us to head due north from here, past the well (just as I had predicted), and we would soon see the lights of the village.

So relieved was my unth wallah that he twirled his princesses around and set them off at a fast pace, singing in his fork-on-plate falsetto. I followed, thinking this a reckless and unnecessary speed at such an hour but unwilling to humiliate Ram Rahim in front of the fatties by asking Chutra to slow down. He called over his shoulder that if he didn't have to slow down for Ram Rahim, he could reach the other side in an hour.

Ten minutes later, from somewhere ahead, I heard a little yelp and camel noises. I put on my torch and saw that Momal had run straight into a thorn tree and Chutra and she and the lead ropes and Sumal were entangled painfully in it. They gazed into my torch beam like cons caught in razor wire. We had come face to face with a forest of apparently impenetrable *Prosopis juliflora* and with the discovery that Momal and Sumal were night-blind. I gave Ram Rahim his head. He picked his way in one direction, turned, picked his way carefully in the other, until he found a way through the barrier. Apparently he could see as well at night as he could by day, thus scoring points for mongrels and touchéing the unth wallah who said crustily, 'Keep Ram Rahim in front. He can't keep up with *my* camels.'

It began to rain. Sometimes I cried. I cried when at last I saw the lights and realized that we would not reach them by 2 a.m. I had given myself that limit, 2 a.m. I had said to myself, I can make it to 2 a.m. but I cannot make it to 2.05 a.m. I could not get off Ram Rahim but to stay on was torture. My feet throbbed. The tendons in my groin pained all the way to the knees in one direction and to the teeth in the other. We arrived at approximately three-thirty. We were wet and cold and stiff, and the *Prosopis juliflora* had not been kind to us. Riding into that silent medieval village in the middle of the night remains, in memory, one of the most religious experiences of my life. Would there be room at the inn?

We saw the jeep and woke a very worried driver. We couched the camels and got off. The vertebrae in my neck had fused and my feet were approximately twice their normal size. Chutra walked like Pinocchio. We watered the camels. We led the camels to our hotel – an open air cement kitchen with a room at the back. We fed the camels. I saw to Chutra's sleeping arrangements, then collapsed in the room at the back on a filthy charpoi. I lay awake for a while, listening to the owner of this establishment – a fat man with fat gold rings on fat fingers, and gold medallions on his voluptuous breast – beating his twelve-year-old servant with a stick. The boy ended up whimpering on a mat in the corner of my room, for all the world like one of the cringing, diseased, vanquished pariah dogs that prowl the village lanes. An hour and a half later I was awakened by a truck stopping at the front of the hotel. From its cabin came Hindi filmi music screeching at enough volume to wake the dead then kill them again. I went to the window and shouted, 'Turn that fucking thing off!' Silence. I had never in my whole life yelled at anyone to turn anything off. I doubt if I had ever even asked anyone politely to turn anything off. I went back to the charpoi. I hate India, I thought and fell asleep.

At nine o'clock an angel transubstantiated at the side of my bed. I opened one eye and took the tea it offered. It was grinning. It was Koju.

★

And so, on a winter evening a few days before Christmas, after two days of driving, and burdened with deformed feet, fever and a sour soul, I arrived at last at Narendra's jhumpa, inside his aura of succour, to await the arrival of my friends and to consult a doctor. Chutra, I had left behind with instructions, an address where he should wait, and three camels. I would return to him inside a month and, with the camels, we would walk back here to Jodhpur and liberty. All he had to do was inquire of local people as to where the Rabari dangs were.

Narendra opened the jeep door and handed me a glass of Indian champagne. The servants popped heads out of windows, waved surreptitiously, then returned to the feast preparations. Behind the jhumpa, firelight was bouncing off rushes and thatching. There was the smell of frost falling and sandalwood burning. I handed Narendra his gudio and hobbled through the house out to the fireside. Mornat stood smiling in his grey gypsy coat and traveller's trousers, his hand at his chest, the other holding by a short chain the most beautiful dog I had ever seen. It was a Luria, a Jogi's hunting dog, which Mornat's ancestors had bred before there was history, which had travelled with the gypsies through Asia and Europe, spawning lurchers and whippets and greyhounds but remaining sturdier, silkier, more wild in the spirit. The Jogis never gave away their dogs, with whom they fiercely identified themselves. But Mornat had been prevailed upon, just this once, to sell one to Narendra to give to Memsahib as a Christmas present. His name was Seru (lion) but I decided to call him Zali, which means something like conman or vagabond. I offered the dog my hand. He held up his paw, kept his head down like a reined-in stallion and looked up at me.

'Zali, will you be my dog?' We shook hands on the deal.

My legs were propped on a stool. The feet at the end of them looked as if they belonged to someone who had spent the last few weeks on the bottom of the Thames. The left one was puffy; the right, elephantine. Serum flowed from the two ominous holes in the ankle. I did not care what was wrong with that ankle, as long as what was wrong with it wasn't Guinea worm.

'You have at least one balan (Guinea worm), possibly two,' pronounced Rana Khan the next day. 'The worm is curled up in the boil and soon it will want to come out. It exists in many segments, so that it will be necessary to go to a special balan wallah who will extract *all* of the segments so that reinfection will not occur. I know a good balan wallah in Jaisalmer, but no doubt we can find one here in Jodhpur too. Do not,' he continued, 'go to an ordinary western-type doctor. He'll mess it up. These deshi fellows know their job.' He went on to say that cobra skin ground up in jaggery was a fine cure – and there just happened to be a couple of big black cobras living around the jhumpa, but I couldn't see Narendra allowing to have them killed – and that a certain lizard, fairly rare, if ground up and made into a poultice, was guaranteed to suck out the most stubborn of Guinea worms. Mornat was consulted. Did he know of this lizard? Yes, he did. Could he find one? Yes, but he would have to go north of Jodhpur to the area around Koju's village.

In the meantime Rana Khan tied a black thread around my ankle and prayed to Maharajah Girda Singh of Jaisalmer (long dead) which, he assured me, was another effective remedy for worm-infestation. Rana Khan and his musicians had come to sing Marwari desert songs for us around the outside fire. Narendra and Rana were old friends; Narendra acting the traditional role of patron and the rather more modern one of trying to promote this music outside the borders of Rajasthan. In this he had had some success and these days Rana often played in the big capitals before audiences of thousands.

You simply could not be with Rana Khan and feel miserable. Music had cleansed him as a river cleans a gorge through which it tumbles. Every sweetness, sadness, foolishness, wickedness and wisdom that man had ever thought to record in ballads had flowed through him. He knew hundreds of ragas by heart, delivered them with his eyes fixed on your face, his free hand lifted toward you in entreaty, his buck teeth and rogue's features transformed into the face of love or of suffering or of saintliness. Funny songs, wise songs, romantic songs, epic songs, religious songs, Hindu songs, Muslim songs, Sufi love songs dense with meanings. When they played, the musicians and secondary singers seemed linked up with Rana Khan like nerves to a brain. If Rana became the embodiment of grief, the musicians too seemed barely able to restrain their tears. (Rana could make himself sob at will and real tears would flow.) His son, the most beautiful child on the face of the earth, played the wooden castanets; another man with a vast moustache and piano-key teeth played an empty clay pot; Rana played harmonium; and a white-bearded ancient, desiccated by too many nights sawing on his sarungi in the dunes of the Thar, radiated musical intelligence without moving a muscle in his face.

They all sat around the fire: a semicircle of turbans, moustaches, woollen shawls crafted deep in the desert, curious instruments and teeth. We listened enchanted for hours. Narendra got up from time to time to place money on the harmonium or to stop the singing and ask a question, challenge an interpretation of a raga or to cry 'va, va', at a particularly exquisite interpretation – all of which only increased the liveliness of the renditions, the laughter, argument and alcoholic high spirits. At last everyone stumbled away to bed, leaving us to savour in silence the moon sheen on blue-green cabbage fields, the sleepy bird calls, and the occasional and ever more swerving emergence of Mornat from the darkness, where he had been tucking into the bottle Narendra always provided, stoking the fire with a four-foot-long metal spoon, shooting up sparks to the heavens and reflecting light upon a golden dog with golden eyes who sat, paws crossed, considering the firelight.

Here, within a world constructed by the imagination and will of an exceptional person, under stars that seemed to shine especially for these evenings, that other India might not exist. Here, everyone was well fed, happy and secure. The trouble Narendra took with all things sensual meant that there was no discord or ugliness here. All was abundance and generosity. I had not come across anyone quite like him before – the self-containment, the seemingly inexhaustible well-spring of magnanimity and courtesy. How ironic that the qualities one might expect to find in a prince, and which had been so lacking in the ones I had met so far, should find, in a man who loathed royalty and all it stood for, its apotheosis. As much as he would have hated the word, I thought of him as a truly 'noble' human being.

Now that I knew something of his history and the world he had evolved from, knew the forces ranged against him, had an inkling into the reaches of his courage and how easy it would have been for him to remain safe and comfortable, my previous idea of him struck me as grotesque, as easy classifications are as soon as one gets close to another person. But in Narendra's case the difference between outward appearance and inner man was particularly easy to misinterpret. He was one of those people whom we only discover to be what they really are after we have come to know them well, and he allowed precious few people to know him at all. My admiration for him was in proportion to the effort that had been necessary to discover the truth. But what made him so different from most people I knew, not just in India but anywhere, was his lack of dependence upon the opinion of others.

The next afternoon Mornat returned with two fat and sleepy lizards. They had the faces of little old ladies who habitually attack policemen. I would not hear of them being killed. 'Mornat,' I said when no one could hear me, 'do I have a balan or not?' Quietly Mornat opined that I did not. I gave the lizards back to him to let go but I have a suspicion they ended up in the Jogi cooking-pot.

There was another opinion as to my state of health from a real estate agent in jeans and T-shirt who doubled as a palmist. He was one of the torrent of constituents who came to the jhumpa to sit under the shade for a few hours petitioning Narendra. He scrutinized my palm and then, in front of four or five men, asked me if my breasts had ever been bitten hard by a man. Poor Narendra had to translate. I said that I could not remember whether such a thing had ever occurred and managed to stifle a blush. He explained that if I had been so bitten, then I would have had difficulty carrying children to full term which would explain the fact that although there were five offspring inscribed on my palm none existed in real life. He suggested I wear diamonds.

The balan turned out to be nothing more exotic than an infected blister. The fever fell before a firing squad of new antibiotics and that other little medical matter, which I kept locked in a box at the back of my mind, would just have to wait until after my holiday when I had the energy to ponder its implications. For now there were friends, and music, and food, and Christmas, and snow-capped mountains, and Zali. And no Chutra.

16

The higher the altitude, the headier and happier our little group became. Zali quivered and sniffed for leopards. The weight of the plains dropped away like haulage falling off the back of a Tata truck, barrel by barrel down the ravines. We parked the car in a tiny village, loaded ponies and after an hour and a half's walk up through oak forests came the sound, from Narendra's retreat, of hot water being sloshed into buckets, of champagne corks popping, of a log fire crackling and of Rana Khan welcoming us with music. Pleasures piled up thick and sweet as snow.

I had hoped that three weeks' rest in the midst of good company would reinstate the more or less balanced self that I remembered. But no. I had only to glimpse at the end of a long valley, through twenty receding shades of blue, a scrap of the plains capped with dust from which we had ascended, and I would set my eyes resolutely in the other direction, towards the Himalayan peaks, as if averting my gaze from something threatening. And when anyone asked me to describe the previous eighteen months, I found myself indulging in some fairly hysterical India-bashing.

Yet such are the enigmas of human nature that if I thought anyone else about to denigrate India, I leapt to its defence. And I did not think of this behaviour at the time as signalling the beginnings of a process of identification because when I caught a glimpse of those plains, I felt nothing but dread. But just as a woman cannot recall the specifics of pain during childbirth and can only say that it was excruciating, so I could not remember the singular sensations of being down there, struggling and suffocating under the murk.

I wrote up my notes deep into the night, furrowing pages with black underlinings and asterisks. Such things as: 'India is a *horrible* society but of course I cannot say this. Instead I have to say how marvellous it is because it continues; as if there hadn't, throughout that continuity, been moral and aesthetic decay. Because of past glories and never mind the inglorious present. The corruption from top to bottom and from right to left; the giants of the Independence movement now like the giants of fairy stories – a species lost to time; the poor enduring because so few are concerned with changing the conditions which they have to endure; the structure of society is like a pyramid in which each level exploits the level beneath it and grovels to the level above (and the pyramid is bottomless). Huge masses of people are born to no purpose other than to be perpetually hungry and Hinduism has degenerated into an institutionalized abnegation of responsibility to one's fellow man.'

It was a great relief to write these things. I'd *lived* the belief that just as one is unjudging towards other cultures, one has a duty to judge one's own. But where did cultural relativity stop? What morality could be universally applied? When I felt outrage was I simply a cipher for cultural prejudice? At what point would I be allowed to move from the role of uncritical guest to participant with a right to speak, the right to express anger?

If one sees a man, over-fed and crammed with gold, holding a cringing half-starved twelve-year-old by the arm and beating him with a large stick, then flinging him to the floor like a bunch of rags, then turning to the white guest and smiling, obsequiously but without shame, because what he has just done is in the order of things, is his right, while the bunch of rags crawls off to weep in the corner of a cement room on his blanket on the floor, and falls instantly asleep because he works for the fat man twenty hours a day and is malnourished and exhausted. And if no one says a word or makes any move to stop it (including oneself) because the servant belongs to the fat man and, anyway, it is the child's fate and, anyway, how would one's intervention change anything? Then?

If a highly educated and powerful Brahmin bureaucrat explains to you, seriously and passionately, why untouchables cannot be allowed into higher government positions because 'for centuries they have handled excrement and it has entered their minds'. Then?

Or the wife of a diplomat, who announced to her book-besotted sixteen-year-old niece, 'You must marry rather than educate yourself, because if you are educated you will not adjust to marriage.' Then?

There had been no therapeutic yelling, no bursting of the laces. And on those numberless occasions when a stranger had said, 'And what do you think of our great country?', with that particular self-satisfaction, as if only a lunatic would find in it anything but greatness, I had never said, 'Well, as a matter of fact . . .' because I knew that it was fruitless to engage in such a conversation as what was conspicuous to me was invisible to him and vice versa.

At night, these toxic scribblings; but in the morning when I rose into bright alpine sun, the warmth of friends, of Narendra, the abundance of breakfast, the effervescent air, the affection of Koju and Hanuman and Chandrawallab and Bishan – in short, into the comforts of my class – I could gaze down to the plains and feel only admiration and wonder. Instead of muttering, 'I loathe this country,' I would think, No, I *love* it. I love India. Everything is contained in it. Because from this height, I could focus on the crowd and was safe from the lives of the individuals who comprised it. From this height, the words 'India will continue' made sense because one saw that great river as a god might, without risking submersion, free of hope, anger or compassion, without any desire to change it.

In such a state of mind I might visit Bishan's people down in the nearby village and experience only that unique Indian warmth and sweetness, hear only the laughter, and be able to say, as an American acquaintance said after a two-week holiday in India by air-conditioned bus, that 'the poor looked so . . . happy' and be able, conveniently, to forget that in this 'happy' village suicide is extremely common and that only last month a woman had hanged herself in the forest. Her family, to avoid being charged with murder, had paid many thousands of rupees in bribes to the police, and many thousands of rupees in bribes to the doctor signing the death certificate, and was now entirely destitute, tripped by one twist of fate over the abyss of which every Indian, rich or poor, is acutely aware. In such a state of mind I might describe the look on Bishan's face when he says, 'This always happens. Yes, every time. Kya karen? Yaha Bharat hai' (What to do? This is India), as an example of that enduring wisdom and acceptance of fate for which India's poor are so revered, rather than an absolute loss of faith in his country's ability to deliver justice. It was not a matter simply of corrupt police, corrupt doctors (as if it were possible for the majority of police and doctors not to be corrupt), but that the village people themselves, when given a chance, also participate in various forms of extortion on the principle that if the rich and privileged can get away with it, and the politicians and the judges and the police and the forest officers and the administrators and their own sarpanch, then why shouldn't we? And this moral corruption has spread so deeply and widely that there seems no way to get rid of it by any means other than a conflagration. It is not enough now to find a group to blame – the British or the politicians (vile and craven though they often are) or the industrialists or the bureaucrats – because everyone participates at some level.

When I paid the cop at the side of the road his two hundred rupee bribe, even though I had broken no law whatsoever, because I just didn't want to waste a day sweltering in a police hut at the side of the road filling out forms (or indeed risking being beaten up or raped because they were drunk and crazy), because I was already exhausted and hot and uncomfortable and fed up and fretful and harassed and there were still another eight hours of traffic and fumes and din before I could begin to breathe, to relax, to regain myself up here in the clean air of the privilege of my class, from which vantage point I would be able to discern the marvel and wonder of the crowd and of India's perpetuity, and be able to sentimentalize Indian rural life because I didn't have to live it, didn't have to notice the meanness and fear that lay beneath its 'happiness' – then I, too, was guilty.

If one cannot muster a godlike detachment, a sense of impotence is the next best protection from despair. India is too big. The problems too immense. What vanity to think one's own actions could make any difference to that swelling flood. The sheer volume of it suffocated every good intention. Here, Life mattered, lives did not and to achieve that famous serenity, which is now India's principal export (the frightening, vaporous serenity of the New Age movement), one needed to view individual lives as insignificant, mere vehicles for DNA.

To achieve the long view, one steps further and further back from lives as they are lived to that more tranquil position from which one sees only the crowd. From that perspective human beings become a species, worth preserving. But take another step back and it is no longer necessary to preserve the species. There will be another following us, after all. Until the view lengthens to such an extent that the world disappears and one is left with only the cold reaches of space, in a private *pas de deux* with God. Was it possible to accommodate the contradiction between action and being, to incorporate both long view and short view in one's attitude to life, to be both reflective and active, detached and involved?

There was an odd anomaly in my attitude to India. Here I had met the best people, the best *kinds* of people I had ever known. People whose depth, warmth and dignity, whose spread and reach, made westerners seem pinched by comparison (pinched between the finger of God and the thumb of Satan). The capacity for joy here, the gratitude to life no matter what hand it had dealt you. The openness to and respect for the beingness of another, as if all the souls of the world had met many times before. In that sense I felt more at home here, more in love with life than I ever had in England. Whatever I thought about India, I would find myself, a minute later, thinking the opposite with equal conviction. Not for a moment did it allow relief from the discomforts of paradox. Not for a moment did it allow indifference.

Narendra left a day before us. Some trouble in Jodhpur with Mornat. When I joined him there, we sat out by the fire and I pestered him for the story. He said in English that Mornat's son had almost died and that he, Narendra, had rushed him to a private hospital. Mornat did not speak English but understood what was being said. He became very emotional, started crying and kept putting his hands together in that way of his. I continued asking questions such as, 'But why didn't he send the boy himself? Why did he wait for you to come? Surely he knew you would pay for it? . . . Didn't he?' Until Narendra asked me pointedly to drop it. When Mornat went home, I asked why. 'Because it was making me sad and Mornat sad,' and he would say no more. I just could not fathom the master–servant relationship. I knew that of all the people who worked for him, Narendra probably felt the deepest affection and respect for Mornat. But what did that mean when the formal distance between them was so rigid that Mornat would risk his son's life rather than risk offending his patron? Before sending Mornat home that night, Narendra had said to him, 'That dog is eating my brains.' (He felt that I spoiled Zali.) Mornat had laughed genuinely and warmly and replied, 'He is young, he'll improve.' And I saw the complicity and understanding between them, an understanding from which I was excluded.

Previously Narendra had referred to his servants as his family and I had scoffed at such obfuscating language. They are your workers I had said, your serfs. But now I saw that family was the truer analogy. A hierarchical family perhaps, with a patriarch perched firmly at the top, but a family, with a family's responsibilities and duties to each other. It would be impossible, for example, for me to fire Chutra simply because he drove me crazy. If he was honest, which he was, scrupulously; if he did not shirk his work, which, it had to be said, he did not, then he was my unth wallah for eternity and his problems became my problems.

Narendra was the centrifugal point in the middle of my whirling. He was the interpreter of where I was. He had, in a way, *become* India to me. But to truly understand someone you have to understand his inner dialogue – that perpetual discussion with what formed him – his culture. When I had to accept that in this person I loved there were areas of foreignness which could never be mapped, and that this was mutual, I felt as if I had set myself adrift in this baffling place and would never find my way home. Once he had begged me not to ride a bicycle because it was 'the easiest way for someone to murder you'.

'But no one's trying to murder me,' I had said, aghast.

'How do you know?' he had countered and I had searched the horizon for something familiar on which to rest my eyes. Usually there was no sense of strangeness between us and the unlikeliness of our friendship was obscured by its strength. But so remote did he sometimes seem from anything I could comprehend, it was as if I had lost my footing and was falling. It was not that our thoughts were different, that was to be expected, but that the ways in which we thought were different. But inevitably a gear would shift and I would be back with my friend in the warmth of a deeper, human understanding.

When I said goodbye to him, it was a little like setting off from an island on which one has been entirely happy and safe but, once through the reef (the farm gates), turning to face an uncharted sea.

17

'Isn't forty-one a little . . .?'

'Not at all,' said the gynaecologist, beaming. By the look on her face she might have added, 'Congratulations.' It struck me that a western doctor would probably have tried at this moment of truth to arrange a look of sympathy on her face. It also struck me that I could not have chosen a better culture in which to experience this event.

Menopause. The very word has a funereal, dead-end tone. Grey women, sunk in obscurity, leeched of vitality, reaching for bottles of blue hair-rinse and packets of Valium, invisible at parties, husbands bedding secretaries, vaginas of sandpaper, any lingering sexual desires a joke for the cruel-hearted. Dear God, who would want to go there? Yet every Indian woman I spoke to, across the social spectrum, either experienced none of the physical and mental distress that so plagued her western sisters or, if she did, dismissed it as negligible. In the west the cessation of egg-laying signalled the end of female power, in India its beginning.

As it happened I had far too much on my plate to be worrying about such trivialities as 'the change of life', but it did strike me as typically perverse of fate to change it now, just when I needed my strength.

Chutra was not where he was supposed to be. When my friends and I found him, on a farm near the Rajasthan–Gujarat border, he had gathered no information as to the location of Rabari dangs with which we might hitch a passage back, more or less, to Jodhpur, nor had he made any adjustments to our saddles and gear as I had asked him to do. His excuse for not ringing me was that he could not guard the camels and use a phone at the same time. I suggested that he might have asked someone else to ring me, since his failure to find out where any dangs were did rather muck up my plans. That is to say I no longer had any. And his being at a place other than the agreed meeting-place had meant an extra day of driving and anxiety for me. He countered that looking after three camels was too much work for one man and he needed assistants. I made the point that if I could walk alone with three and a half camels across seventeen hundred miles of desert, he could surely manage a hundred kilometres through settled country, where feed could be purchased and kindly people were a rupee a dozen. This was a little unfair on my part because in Australia I did not have to worry about thieves, there being so few human beings to do the thieving.

Inside five minutes my best intentions of being authoritative with him, of not allowing myself to be either irritated or bullied by him, were rubble. Happily my friends could now validate everything I had said. Yes, Chutra Ram Raika did appear to be a total arsehole.

If it should seem that one gets used to the constant tearing up and tossing away of one's plans, I am here to tell you that one does not. One chases after the scraps which malicious winds lift up and away, out of reach. And it's not so much the despair one can't cope with, it's the hope. Eventually one returns to the sitting and thinking position.

There are movements of Rabari, swirls and swoops apparently random but fractal in nature. However, to plug into this pattern, one needed to be in many places at once, collecting and collating information, sifting out incorrect details, driving many hours to arrive at the office of a person who might have an overview of the local pattern to find that the person is away, dead or unheard of. If one could have fifty scouts, say, all of them at the very least bilingual, and if one had a central office where all fifty scouts could collate their material all at the same time, and if one then found a dang, or a series of dangs travelling in one's general direction, and if the mukki of each dang could be prevailed upon to risk the inclusion of oneself, and if, then, the plans of those mukkis did not change at the last second, well, then, one might get somewhere. But as it was, I would have to set off on my own, blindly striking in the direction of Jodhpur. At least this plan had the advantage of taking me through parts of the Aravalli Ranges, where a soul might take a breath before plunging back down into these malarial plains.

It was time to leave. In the loading-up process, I had tied a sirsingle knot in my own way, a knot I had used often and to good effect. Chutra checked everything I had done. When he came to the knot, he called for the attention of the entire gathering – farm owners, farm workers, relatives, neighbours, visitors, children and friends – and declaimed loudly that Madam Sahib would be lost without him because look, ha ha, at this crazy knot. Affectionate pity spread over his face. Still addressing the gathering he continued, 'Madam Sahib, I will now show you the correct way to tie a knot.' With exaggeratedly slowed down gestures he demonstrated the tying of the knot as if to someone with frontal lobe damage.

Arsehole. Unquestionably.

'Chutra ji, look, maybe bora no OK. Bora . . . (homunculus unable to find the words for length or breadth) . . . wrong, not right . . . This way?' I had asked him to stitch the bora the night before – a large rectangle of goat and camel hair which, when thrown over the saddle, forms a pocket on either side in which goods are carried. Instead of stitching the bora along the horizontal, he had stitched it along the vertical. The centre of gravity of the load was therefore so high that it rolled like a badly ballasted ship whenever the camel moved.

Chutra informed me that he knew how to stitch a bora.

'Oh,' I said. Why did I not say, 'Stitch it this way and that's that'? Why did I not bypass his ego by doing it myself? I have no excuses other than fatigue of the will.

I hugged my friends goodbye on the Deesa–Mount Abu road. I would have sat right down and wept there, if I hadn't been so worried about the camels, the gear, the magazine, Dilip, Chutra, the camels, the magazine, Chutra, the magazine. And the humanity clustered around us, shoving, staring, smothering.

Chutra seemed ambivalent about the perpetually gathering crowds. Sometimes they so annoyed him that he shouted and waved his stick at them, describing them to me as 'very half-mind' and tapping his forehead. On the other hand, they did provide an audience. He took charge of the princesses straight away, leaving me to lead Ram Rahim. Thinking I could not understand him, he informed everyone in convoluted but still decipherable language that the two Jaisalmer pure-breds belonged to himself while the undistinguished Kutchi bull belonged to me. He was also fond of boasting that he was contracted to be my bodyguard by the Royal House of Jodhpur. I doubt if anyone believed this because Madam Sahib, despite her paleness of skin, looked about as important as a pariah dog.

There was quite a large population of Rabari in this area. They had sold their herds and bought land and were better off than their travelling cousins. But the wilderness had left their spirit and they were just like anyone else. Once this land had been thickly wooded, ripe with bluebulls and big cats, rich with grasses for the nomads' herds. Now it was bare as picked-clean bone. The track wound beside a village which surely could support no more than fifty people.

All was quiet behind the broken wall; outside it a few chickens clucked around in the dungheaps. Then a sound which was chilling to me. Children. Avalanches of children, thousands it seemed, drawn out through gaps in the rubble as if by a piper, each with his own little face, her own little fate, beautiful, loved, unique and futureless. Because there is nothing left for them. Not enough land, or trees, or animals, or jobs; not enough money for education, or medicine, or the guarantee of a full stomach. Yet they will produce the same number of children again — and again and again — and the physical understanding of that mathematics, of the geometric progression of ever more indigent life, made the heart shrink in fear. I knew the statistics — that the resources spent on a single American child could support twenty-five Indian children. I loathed the moralism which demanded that the third world accept (and pay for) a version of environmental protection in which trees were more important than people. Anyone who used electricity or drove a car had no right to tell peasants to stop felling trees. Nevertheless it was the children of India who illuminated the obvious — unjust disparity and movements of world capital notwithstanding — *there are too many of us*. It was difficult, when I heard the cacophony of that stream of life pouring out of the most impoverished of villages, not to abhor human kind – its mindless replication. Any lingering grief at my own childlessness was assuaged by that sound, which now gradually died away as the river of life emptied back into the village, the further we moved on.

The nomads I had known tended to limit their children. But within one generation of settlement the women lose their independence, move further behind the veil and begin producing babies as fast as their wombs can manufacture them. I do not believe this is because more children are an economic advantage to settled people. Nor that children have a better survival rate in villages (rather the opposite). I think it is to do with the diminishing status of women when the wandering life ceases, to the point where they no longer have control over their own reproduction.

Everyone we passed on the road drew from Chutra the following questions: 'Where are you from? What is your caste?' Depending upon their answers, he was either friendly or dismissive. (The further down the caste scale, alas, the more dismissive he became.) Yet how well I understood this ordering of the chaos when, a little further on, we saw a travelling Kutchi Rabari. My heart leapt out to greet that woman in black – my sister, my family, my *jaat*.

But her eyes were like two striking snakes. She was alone with her little flock of sheep, her companions a long way behind. I knew enough about dang life to know that this was unusual and dangerous. Perhaps her dang had had to split into smaller flocks, so that now there were not enough shepherds to go around. Or perhaps the shepherd of this flock was too ill to walk, leaving the responsibility for the animals' safety up to this lone and unprotected woman. If she lost the animals, it would mean destitution for her and her family. This was not a place in which trust and survival went together. I did not frighten her further by going over to her but lifted my hand and continued on my way.

Zali was proving to be a high-calibre companion. The long association with Jogis had bred out canine slavishness. He had an aristocratic demeanour, mitigated by terrific street cred. Survival was his first priority and his best chance of securing that, on this journey, lay with the Memsahib whom, he had quickly worked out, he could twist around his little paw. Chutra did not signify. Chutra was inaudible and invisible.

Brave Zali. Beauuutiful Zali. Intellllligent Zali.

This perspicacity regarding the way things were communicated itself from the first night when he slept outside the front door, only to move over successive nights to sleeping outside the door of my room, to sleeping inside the door of my room, to sleeping beneath my bed, to sleeping on a corner at the bottom of my bed, to sleeping on the bottom half of my bed, to sleeping under the covers, my arm curled around him, his nose peeping out of the blankets. When Narendra condemned this behaviour, I pointed out that Zali had picked up an English vocabulary of at least a dozen commands and he obeyed all of them, which was more than could be said of the unth wallah.

But even with Zali's fine company, the first day was not as light-hearted as the first day of a long journey ought to be. Perhaps there were moments when there were no people clustered around, when there were no village dogs salivating at my ankles or threatening to rip out Zali's throat, when the infinite potential of a road beneath one's feet entered the spirit, so that it fearlessly called to the future around the bend, 'Here I am. I am coming to you.' But I do not remember them.

Being thus disappointed, I now set great store by what the first night might bring. Sleeping under the stars, camel bells tinkling in a cool breeze, perhaps some interesting roadside companions with whom to while away an hour or two, no trucks hurtling up the backsides of camels and scaring them out of their wits, no diesel fumes, no gawpers. Hope again, you see. Damned hope.

I left the finding of a camping spot up to Chutra as only he knew how to read the countryside. The place he chose was not salubrious but the pumping of a well muffled the thunder of trucks on the road and the mali (a field worker employed by farm owners) seemed a sweet man. He was very excited at the prospect of such unusual guests near his well and offered to help with everything. Alas, he had no milk. He would run to the dudh wallah to buy some while we set ourselves up. I mimed that this was not necessary but he insisted. I pulled out my purse and gave him some money. Chutra took the three camels off to feed. I set up my cot, laid my luggage on top, stashed my purse under it, built the bed on top of the luggage, perched upon it, invited Zali to perch upon it with me and proceeded to write by the last rays of the sun. When the mali came back with the milk, I would make tea on the little Primus stove. That would bring home to Chutra (towards whom I was mellowing in direct proportion as the weather was cooling) that I was not at all helpless or stupid and that he could allow me some independence without fretting.

'Madam Sahib does not understand,' he had said. 'India is full of crooks. Madam Sahib is too trusting.' Dear old Chutra, I thought, and smiled.

The mali returned. He said, or rather mimed, 'The stove will not light in this wind. You must bring it into the pumphouse away from the wind.' How very helpful, I thought. How can one not be in love with this country after all? So unlike his two companions, leering and unpleasant fellows, who had asked in a leading sort of way whether I drank alcohol. I hinted, with some very loud body language, that I was a Baptist missionary with a loaded pistol under her kurta. But the mali was harmless and I have never been one to panic over the presence of suspect men, having dealt with enough of them to know that fearlessness is usually the best defence. I handed out tea to the three men, took my own cup and went to sit on my luggage.

When Chutra came back we cooked roti and dal, then collapsed. However I soon saw that if I wanted to sleep *at all*, I would not be able to share my cot with Zali.

Steam rose off the underground water being pumped into the well, forming a thick wet shroud around us so that I could not say whether I was stifling hot or shivering cold. Somehow, I managed to be both. Zali whimpered and pushed his long nose under the covers. I reminded him that Jogi dogs were for hunting and for tearing strangers to shreds. Not for cuddling up to in the night. Neither the dog nor I slept more than three hours.

Chutra snored.

In the morning two things became apparent very quickly. Both Zali and I were ill, and my purse was missing. Had my purse contained only money, I might have neglected to tell Chutra of its disappearance, thereby hiding that inch which would lead to a mile of proof of my stupidity. But my purse contained torch, mosquito repellent, passport and all the papers needed to subdue bureaucrats from here to Delhi.

Chutra demanded an exact reconstruction of the movements of the previous night while he paced in front of me, hands clasped behind his back. He deduced that the mali had enticed me into making tea in the pumphouse away from the wind, then gone out to take the purse from under the luggage on the bed. Yes, perhaps I did remember him leaving while I made the tea. Yes, perhaps I had broken a cardinal rule by displaying money in my purse when I gave the mali some paisa for milk. And, yes, it was possible that he was watching when I buried my purse in the luggage.

The mali who had been so friendly the night before could not be found this morning. Chutra confronted his wife and daughter instead. He said, 'As I cannot find your husband, in order to clear up this little matter of the missing purse, I'm afraid I must go to the police in Sidpur, and bring them here.' The mali appeared shortly afterwards.

Chutra said to the mali, 'As you know nothing about the missing purse, you will not mind coming with me to the police station to help me explain to them what has happened.' But it seemed that the mali did mind. He would like to help us find this accursed and abominable thief but, regretfully, he had to go to work. 'Ah,' said Chutra, 'in that case you must take me to your master and I will explain everything to him. Perhaps I will take *him* to the police.' At this the mali shrank further into his rags and began to look far from innocent. I waited with the camels while Chutra prepared the *coup de grâce*.

There seemed to be lots of arm-waving and head-shaking going on. Eventually I called to Chutra and suggested that, if we gave them some time, we would most likely find the bag abandoned somewhere as they were now obviously frightened. The important things were the papers rather than the money, so perhaps we should make tea and wait. He agreed.

Less than half an hour later, the mali's daughter happened to spot the purse ditched in a perfectly invisible place. Everyone gasped and rhubarbed at such phenomenal good luck and looked so painfully guilty that I felt sorry for them and doubly angry at myself. But Clouseau was relentless. He paced to and fro in front of the gaping purse, twirled his moustache with one hand and lifted his other in a gesture for silence.

'Don't touch anything,' he commanded. 'We will now call the police to see if the money is inside because it is rather strange that the mali's daughter should have craned her neck over here, when in fact she should have been walking on the path over there.' The mali's daughter began to cry.

'How much was in the purse?' hissed Chutra in an aside.

'I don't remember. Probably fifteen hundred or so.'

'How can you not remember? It was your money. Madam Sahib is very forgetful.'

'. . . About one thousand.'

There followed several hours of horse-trading. By mid-afternoon the drama had reached its denouement. The mali was routed, I was handed eight hundred rupees and we loaded up to leave. The mali's wife was wailing; his daughter had fled. Public humiliation, public shame. But Chutra had no pity. A thief is a thief no matter what his circumstance and it was the woman's bad fortune to be married to one.

I, too, was covered in shame. How could I have been so thoughtless as to leave such temptation around for a man immured in poverty, whose only knowledge of Europeans is that they are unimaginably rich? Chutra chastised me for being too trusting (read stupid). And for being forgetful. Indeed I was forgetful, pathologically so, and for this too I felt nothing but remorse.

I had so forfeited any credibility that it was beyond me to make suggestions regarding the loading or the bora. Hadn't Chutra just proved himself infinitely more capable than I in this venture? And shouldn't a Raika camel man know, better than I, how to load three camels so that the luggage didn't fall off? In my view it looked very precarious but who was I to judge? A vague, gullible, idiotic 'phoren'.

We walked six miles to Sidpur. Chutra's victory over the mali had gone to his head and anyone who passed us, or indeed anyone who was five hundred yards away in a field minding his own business, would be called over and subjected to a rendition of the thief story in which our hero Chutra had, through wiliness and intelligence, retrieved for Madam Sahib (who came out of this story as a somewhat dim-witted figure, quite irrelevant to the plot except as paisa wallah) one thousand rupees, a sum which grew with every passing mile and every captured listener until, by the time we reached Sidpur, it had swelled to eight thousand rupees.

It was impossible not to enjoy these fabulations for the relief of hilarity they offered, but then I realized how vindictive Chutra's lying was. Everyone in the area would now know that the mali was a thief and that the mali's wife was a thief's wife. With each thousand rupee increase, with each increment of evil attributed to the mali, another shovelful of earth fell on his social grave.

Zali sloped along like an old tramp. Whenever we stopped to rest from the heat, he flopped down beside me so that I had to coax him back on to his feet when it was time to leave. Animals do not lie down constantly unless they are seriously ill.

'Zali sick,' I said to Chutra. He went over to the dog, filled his own clog with sand, passed this clog three times over Zali, muttered a mantra and announced that the dog would now be all right. Somehow this action overwhelmed me with futility. One might or might not survive but either way it was entirely out of one's own hands. In the streets of Sidpur I inquired about a vet. But it seemed there were no vets in Sidpur or, if there were, there was no way of penetrating the clamour, of finding a thread to follow.

On the other side of Sidpur, Momal shied at a bus. The bora toppled. The goods were scattered. It was hot. The road was tumultuous and full of fumes. The dog was ill. I did not know how to help the dog. I tried to lash him up on Sumal's saddle but he fell off, howling. My nose was streaming, my eyes itching, my throat raw. People stopped and stared, or laughed, or ran along beside us screaming.

Chutra found it impossible simply to do as I asked. I had to explain in my strained and exhausted Hindi, in my strained and exhausted voice, from the bottom of my strained and exhausted soul, *why* I wanted him to do it. Then, once I had got the words out, clumsily, foolishly, he would challenge what I had said or ask me to explain again, so that either I would have to struggle over the top of his will and back over the top of my exhaustion or let

him do as he thought best, which was usually right, but sometimes, infuriatingly, wrong because he was incapable of taking in
anything new. He had learnt one way of handling a camel, just as
his parents, grandparents, *ad infinitum* had learnt it and now when
the situation called for something different that tradition would
allow for no innovation.

I wanted two things more than anything I'd ever wanted. I
wanted Chutra to go away and this ludicrous project to end. At
the next STD booth I would ring Narendra and tell him I was
continuing alone. But the truth was that I could not do this kind
of travelling alone. It would be necessary to leave my luggage to
feed the camels. The luggage would disappear. Nor could I tie the
camels up somewhere to make a phone call or buy food for myself
and expect the camels to be there ten minutes later. This was the
reality. Chutra and I were stuck with each other like binary stars. I
knew this yet it gave me pleasure to imagine him disappearing. To
imagine the wording of the letter to the magazine describing my
own disappearance. To imagine myself disappearing.

We lost the luggage again. We struggled together with the loading – sweating, grunting. I indicated how the weight should be
realigned, how the luggage should be lashed. I said that the bora
needed restitching. But I was too tired now to force the issue. To
retain a semblance of composure I switched most of myself off –
that strange, ever-recurring necessity during the last two years, of
closing down vast landscapes, whole continents, of brain.

18

On the third day we pulled in to a roadside dabar. I sat and dropped my head into my hands. In the blackness behind them, I was composing variations on the theme of Chutra's disappearance. The rest of me was shut down. Someone arrived at my table. I did not raise my eyes for a long time. When I did, a young man in a suit said in Hinglish, 'I am a Raika. I am a teacher here.' I managed a smile and ventured that teaching was an unusual profession for a nomad.

'Yes, madam. But in this area we have become farmers. Madam, may I suggest that you spend tonight on Nagji bhai's farm? I will organize this. You need rest. And Nagji bhai will be able to answer many questions regarding the Raika, in fact about all the Rabari caste for hundreds of miles around. He is a knowledgeable and important man.'

Hang on. A Raika teacher speaking English? And this dabar. Not the low roofed lean-tos filled with spit and pariah dogs and flies, brewing chemical-strength tea on little mud stoves in infernal heat, but laminex tables and advertisements for Kwality ice-cream. Civilization. Vets.

'You are so kind, sir. But I must find a vet . . .'

'Nagji bhai will help you. Now I will give directions to your camel man. Please write well of our caste. Here we have been very fortunate but elsewhere . . . Well, you have seen for yourself.'

Hope. The dog could recuperate at Nagji's while I restitched the bora and organized the loading. The previous three days could be summed up as a false start. Even the policeman on the corner demanding money did not subdue the cheerfulness of hope. I refused to give him anything. I mentioned the superintendent of

217

the Rajasthan police, a friend of Narendra's, and wrote down the constable's name on a piece of paper. The constable let us pass. At this show of strength, Chutra was quite beside himself with happiness. Scraps of songs came out of his mouth as he skipped along, twirling his stick and tipping his turban to passers-by. He said, 'Look, Madam Sahib, that bird there. No, there. You see?' and pointed to something feathered sitting on an overhead wire.

It is easier to believe that one can control the course of events than it is to live with the thought that we are the impotent unfurlings of initial states, that even the setting of a direction on which chance might operate is itself an effect of multitudinous previous causes lying outside comprehension, separate from will, themselves reducible to infinitely remote first causes. We must behave *as if* we were the agents of outcomes, as if character contained within it a kernel of free will, enough, at least, to allow us to choose right or left when confronted with a fork in the road, yes or no when presented with a moral choice. If determinism rules, nothing can be predicted because causes are too multifarious ever to grasp. If free will rules, then wild cards enter the pack at every instant. Either way, in my world, the future was unfathomable.

But in Chutra's kingdom of consciousness the future was intelligible if one had the skills to decipher the codes of synchronicity – the shaguns. If a particular bird flew from the left of the road as we moved out of camp, or if another called from the right, we must pause a few minutes so that whatever bad luck was waiting for us would miss us (and perhaps strike someone else?), as if avian angels were forever resetting the clocks of chance. Chutra obtained proof of the veracity of these signs by ignoring those which, in retrospect, did not fit into the predictive scheme or by explaining anomalies as weaknesses in his own interpretative skills. From his point of view, there had been clear indications all the way along of our bad luck, which we had ignored out of ignorance and to our peril.

Just as, now, there were favourable shaguns leading us to Nagji bhai, like stars ushering kings across Sinai. The sun set, craypaz-pink. Cool air wafted from the irrigated crops; distant wells pumped like blood pulses; monkeys stole food from the fields, then leapt into the trees beside us.

13. *Hatti receiving the sacred water*

14. *Nagji smoking*

15. *Resting on the way up to Ambadji*

16. *Ambadji*

17. Jaivi

18. *Travelling*

19. *Chutra with my toy pistols*

20. *Zali*

21. *The Little Rann of Kutch*

22. *Chutra weeping*

Chutra hooted, bared his teeth, scratched his ribs. The monkeys jumped down from their perches, snarled at him, then sprang into branches above us to curse wildly at such effrontery. When Chutra saw that I was laughing, he redoubled his efforts until we were at war with hundreds of monkeys. We walked along for a couple of miles through a light as lovely as faded crêpe folded in an old woman's wardrobe.

By the time we reached Nagji's village the world was quiet beneath a gauze of moonlight. Buffalo were tethered and breathed warm air into the night. Outside houses old men sat silently, holding a great-grandchild or working at some craft by the shine of a lamp. Here and there a darker bundle and a glint of jewellery. Darkness threw a cloak over my strangeness, so that people let me pass with a nod or a softly called greeting. Houses, animals and people were part of one harmoniously integrated thing, like a carpet woven by gods who alone could perceive the pattern.

Come morning the gods would unravel their work, jumbling its elements into confusion, mess. And they would rip away my cloak, exposing me to the crowd. But, for the moment, the shuffling camels, the silhouetted dog, Chutra – silenced by tiredness – and myself were part of the weave.

I had not been able until a short time before to understand the Indian habit of staring. I had been wandering in the bazaars of Mount Abu and had seen a real freak. Even from the opposite end of the street, even when almost submerged beneath the swirl of people, she was the cynosure of all eyes, including my own. She wandered through the bazaar unaware of her monstrousness or perhaps inured to it. She was pale, larval and profoundly out of place. She too had tried to disguise herself in kurta pajama, had pulled her hair back as I had done. She too wore the expression I knew I wore in the streets, a kind of grim determination to deny being a European, to pretend that the people who pointed, stared and laughed must be pointing, staring and laughing at somebody else.

I had realized then, with an unpleasant little shock, that no matter how deep my identification with this country went, I would always be seen as alien. I would be like the fourth-generation Japanese American I knew whose spirit broke when he was a teenager and realized he could never be a credible Country & Western singer.

By now I was coaxing the dog along. He staggered sometimes, would lean against me, struggle on. I rode for a while, carrying Zali in front of me on the saddle until he pleaded so hard for his dignity, I let him down. Eventually in the darkness I, too, got down. The dog came to lean against my legs. 'Just a little further, my friend. Then you can rest as long as you want.'

But it wasn't just a little further.

The farms here were fertile. You could smell prosperity as you walked down the lanes. The scent of dense green growth, irrigation mist, massive trees not butchered for their fodder, fattened, passive cattle. How cruel to be so close to safety, in the midst of such abundance, while life eked out of a body with every step. Zali, most noble representative of his species, did not complain but kept on, sometimes touching his nose to my hand as if to give reassurance as much as seek it.

It was nearly midnight when we reached Nagji's farm. Among the faces looming out of the night, and through the fog of my exhaustion, my host was instantly recognizable. Authority radiated from him, touching and enfolding all, intimidating and protecting all. You could lean the weight of the world on Nagji and he would not bend.

I began to unload the camels. He commanded that I stop. What was Chutra for, if not to do his job? I was to sit on a charpoi and rest. I sat. Tea was brought by women who seemed to want to shrink under the patriarch's gaze. With the noise of hurrying skirts, they vanished behind the house. The offer of food was refused but food came anyway. Nagji said, 'While you are here, you do not open your food box.' I expressed my gratitude as best I could. Then, swallowing embarrassment at making a request after his kindness, I brought up the subject of the dog. Did Nagji have any antibiotics? From where and how soon could a vet be engaged? Could one be called now? I was not quite sure what Nagji said but eventually it penetrated that nothing could be done tonight, and nothing tomorrow, it being Sunday. I tried to keep the despair off my face but Nagji lowered his Old Testament head and stared right through me. 'I will send for a vet tomorrow. In the meantime God will be kind, or perhaps not, but there is nothing you can do.'

Chutra had been trying to big-note himself as usual. But he'd been silenced by a glance. I felt a strange protectiveness towards him. Could it be that, in spite of my wanting so desperately for him to vanish, there lurked some nascent affection for him? At last, at a lull in the conversation, during which I prepared my goodnight politenesses because I thought I might inconvenience everyone by dying if I couldn't get horizontal, Chutra found his voice. He stood up, spread his arms wide to indicate Nagji, his family, his farm, and all the people who had gathered to offer their hospitality, and declaimed, 'Madam Sahib. All this I have fixed for you.'

In the morning I took in my surroundings. An open farm-scape of hardpacked white earth, swept each day by the women and shaded by ancient trees. Three camels tethered to a ground peg; beside them two bullocks, sleek, gleaming, enormous, fit for Shiva to ride, nosing at fresh-cut lucerne. There were thatch-roofed stables and piles of hay the size of huts. Where dark roots penetrated the soil, charpois were stacked. A whitewashed veran-dah contained bags of wheat and well-oiled harnesses. Bordering the acre of whiteness and shade, blue fields burst with crops. To the Indian rural aesthetic, this was paradise. Here was security. Here one would not go hungry. Out there, beyond the fence, beyond the village compound, were bandits, wild beasts, lawless-ness, danger, hardships and death. Whatever beauty was in the world belonged to the villages, to domesticity, never to jungle where man was reduced to predator and prey.

One of Nagji's daughters, having swept the compound, was now wafting incense and burning coal around the farm to ward off dirt of another order. She shot a sideways smile at me, passed the incense over Zali, then indicated tea. I was to follow her.

Nagji had eight children, six girls and two boys. His wife was away, visiting her family, but the oldest daughter, a woman in her twenties, led me into the living quarters through a small wooden door cut high in the wall, which was bolted behind me. It was like entering a cage full of parakeets. Six women were upon me, asking questions, all at once, in the local dialect, each outdoing the other, one pulling me one way to see something, another pulling me the other – all of them laughing and looking into my face with wonder. I was in a small courtyard where the animals were kept at night. To the right was a door leading to a long room. To the left, a tiny cement cubicle, the kitchen.

They pushed me into the long room where everyone slept and in which the women lived when they weren't working, super-vised, in the fields or cooking in the sweat-box. The room was dark and cool. In one corner, illuminated by the only window, were some large clay matkis full of water and a small puja stand. I was to have a bath, it seemed. At the opposite end of the room, along the wall, were rows of brass and stainless steel cooking uten-sils which had been polished with mud until they could catch the faintest fall of light – a visual effect which, if translated into sound, would be an organ stopped at basso profondo. Hand-stitched quilts were folded along one wall; charpois were stacked against the opposite one.

The women indicated the water, gave me a low wooden stool, handed me some soap and sat in a semi-circle as if waiting for the curtain to go up. I had been told that one should not display one's fanny, even to other women, so I bared my breasts, wrapped the towel clumsily around my waist, dropped my pajama, placed soap and matkis on the stand and squatted. Sup-pressed giggles. Oldest daughter handed me a lungi (sarong) and bade me sit on the stool to have my wash and put the matki at my feet. The lungi did not quite cover my pubic hair so, once again, awkwardness crippled every movement. They watched, fas-cinated, as I bathed.

Once that was over, I was invited to sit with them in the kitchen while they prepared food. There was no chimney and smoke filled the room. Part of it was open to the sky, so that a wedge of scalding light fell into the gloom. How could they bear this in summer? How could they possibly bear to sit in this box in forty-five-degree heat, bending over fire with no air to breathe, hour after hour, pounding dough, boiling tea? What were they made of that they could endure torture without complaint? Al-ready I felt numbed by the heat and the smoke, queasy in the stomach. And yet, years before, I had lived in a stone ruin with half a roof, which I shared with snakes and fig trees, and it was so hot that cheese melted down off the shelves and candles disappeared into puddles without being lit. And associated with that time and place, there is not one memory of a moment of discomfort.

All the sisters were literate but only one spoke Hindi. She did the translating. They repeated questions over and over, louder and louder, closer and closer. The fire was crackling. Heavily spiced and oiled food was forced on me, which I ate to please them but felt ill. Guiltily I took some of my quota out to the dog. The women looked at each other. Waste this high-class guest food on a dog which will die anyway? Zali sniffed at the food, looked at me and lay down, leaving it untouched.

Back in the kitchen the ladies whispered together, then asked me how much I paid Chutra. I guessed immediately that he had been skiting to them, so I increased the amount by a third. The older woman turned triumphantly to her sisters and said, 'I told you so!' Silly Chutra had exaggerated so wildly that only an idiot could have believed him.

Suddenly there came the sound of the tread of the patriarch. Not so much an aviary now, more a hen-house when a hawk flies over. The women scattered to the four corners or concentrated on what they were doing with frozen attention. He came in and glowered at them. They did not look up.

'You have not given her enough to eat,' he bellowed, grabbing a plate and ladling yet more ghee on to a chapati.

'No, really,' I said, 'I cannot eat so much. They have fed me too well. Too well.' I grabbed my stomach and groaned.

Nagji harrumphed and cast one more threatening look over his flock before opening the door. 'Come to the front,' he said to me, 'when you are ready.'

The moment he left, the women flew back to me like naughty schoolgirls.

I almost always preferred being with women but Nagji's daughters exhausted me. One of the effects of being locked inside a room all your life is that the ability to imagine another's state is atrophied. They could not grasp what effort it required to communicate with six people without the words to do it in. And it upset me to see how far they had fallen in so short a time, a fall directly related to the family's rise in fortunes. Conforming to the more rigid traditions such as locking up women is a privilege only the upwardly mobile can afford.

Not that the women mourned their loss. How could they? They had nothing with which to compare their lives. And if you asked them, they would find nothing missing because, after all, wasn't their father an important man? Didn't he provide well for them? Hadn't he found them husbands from good families? Hadn't he married them off on the same day and provided a big feast for the occasion? Wasn't their little brother being educated at an English-medium school in distant Mount Abu? So what if they could not venture on their own to the front of the house and, if anyone came, must flee giggling to the shadows or hide in their long cell, like moles.

But I could compare them with the women of Kutch whose men looked at them with affection, respect and not a little awe, who could stride out and laugh with their heads thrown back, crack jokes and sing, haggle with the shop wallahs, and fight with their slings beside their men. I missed those women. Missed the space in their souls. And I longed to leave the kitchen now for the openness of the front compound.

One of the younger girls came flying through the door, breathless. 'Ma has come! Ma has come!' The women rose as one. Their faces had been transformed. Gone was any coarseness. Only love was in them, shining from them. A lump came to my throat and I had to eat something to keep it down. Their mother had been away just two days, yet it was as if she had returned from a decade of travel. The daughters pressed around her, cooed to her, kissed her hands, hugged her, touched her hair. They adored her with a passion I had never before seen expressed with such intensity between mother and daughters. It was as if, in their imprisonment inside the long room, they had grown into one another, forming one organism. I did not discover Ma's history but I suspect she had had a relatively free life before her marriage. The air of empty spaces still lingered around her. How awful it must have been to be trapped in that room or watched every second as she laboured in the fields. How deeply she must have needed the tenderness of those daughters.

In the presence of their beloved Ma, I became invisible and could slip away to the front of the house, to the world of men.

Whether they came on foot or in polished Ambassadors, the stream of guests sat before Nagji like supplicants. Charpois would be brought, trays of water glasses, sometimes tea. I could not follow their conversation but the exercise of power was unmistakable. Nagji was rich, he was on the local council, even the sarpanch was deferential.

An old Rabari arrived, a skeleton in rags like all travelling pastoralists in this area. He was so shy, he hid his smile behind the rug he wore when I asked if he were a mukki. Nagji told me that he was the mukki of a group of people from Sirohi area – goat and sheep herders. Nagji had convinced the village that these people should be allowed to graze their animals for several months of the year on the communally held lands. It was quite common for villages to lease out these areas to pastoralists but usually at exorbitant rates.

Had it not been for Nagji, they would have had to pay anything up to twenty thousand rupees to stay here. As it was, they paid only a thousand per year to the village, then individually to local farmers for grazing rights. Usually Nagji gave this old man his grass for free but this year there had been very little rain. 'It is a hard year for everyone. I cannot give away my grass.'

When I asked if these people got any drought relief from the government, Nagji said, 'I am his relief and he is my relief. It is like that. We are the same jaat (community). Here, God is kind. There is good soil, good rain. Where he comes from, if there is no rain, then there is no food. All day there is trouble for him from the landowners, all night from the thieves. He must patrol by night and walk by day. For him there is too much trouble and too much danger.'

Nagji's grandfather had arrived in this area when the big drought decimated Rajasthan. It was at the time when land was being redistributed and made available to the ordinary man. But most Rabaris had not taken advantage of it, partly because the caste councils penalized members who gave up traditional ways of life. He said, 'My grandfather was wise. He saw in to the future and sold his camels and sheep and bought this land. We are a very strong caste, a gypsy caste. My people have been in India so long no one can remember or measure the time. Did you know that gypsies came from Australia to populate this country?' I said that I did not know.

At a little pause in our conversation, I cleared my throat and said, 'Nagji, you mentioned that a vet would be called. When will he come?'

Nagji looked at me a long time from beneath his brows. 'The vet could not be found today. He will come tomorrow.' In my mind's eye I saw the dog's life flicker out in the night and was overcome by such a sense of impotence that it was impossible to keep it from registering on my face. I turned away, so Nagji would not read what was there.

The next day was lost to me. I watched the dog dying. I fought with Chutra over restitching the bora until Nagji intervened and told Chutra that I was right and he was wrong. Chutra sulked. And still the vet did not come. I fretted over the dog and tried to hide my sentimentality from the women. They could not see why I should waste money on a dog. He was replaceable – any dog would warn me of danger. But Zali was not *any* dog, he was *my* dog.

At night I drove to town with the sarpanch to ask Narendra to please send replacements for Chutra. A dozen men watched my face as I shouted into the phone. Yes, came his voice brittle with static, he would send Koju in the jeep and try to find me a couple of other camel men. The following morning the vet came and injected Zali twice in the neck. But the dog could not stand up; it was surely too late.

Nagji was a man used to imposing his will on others. One trick he had for gaining control was to make a statement which did not make sense until something was added to it. He would make his pronouncement, then wait, glaring at you for as long as it took for you to drop your eyes, concede defeat and say, 'Yes, please go on . . .'

That night he said, 'What is it' – I waited, dropped my eyes before his, and said, 'Han ji, bolie' – 'you think about that gives you so much tension? You think too much.'

I laughed. 'Well, partly it's my habit and partly it's my . . . work.'

226

The eyes pierced and I had no choice but to venture further. 'But, also, I think about the problems I face and how best to deal with them. It is difficult for me for two main reasons. One is that I cannot really *talk*. Speaking in a language I don't know, struggling to understand and to express, takes great mental effort. There are often misunderstandings which I have to let go because I cannot speak properly. When you can't express yourself, especially when there are difficulties that require quick action, a kind of pressure builds up in the mind and there is no way to release it. So that makes me worry at night, for example, and lack of sleep adds to my appearance of tension. It is like being deaf or blind, yet having to react as if you were not.

'Secondly (here I took a risk), in my country people spend time by themselves. We are used to it. I, for example, spend most of my day alone, sometimes days, even weeks, on my own. It is my preference. Even in families most of us have rooms to go where we can be private. Here, the opposite is true. You are never alone and this is your preference. But for me this is very very hard. Also it's worse than it might be because people constantly gather around me, so there is never any peace. They do not let me sleep or rest or eat or even go to the latrine without following and looking.'

The strange thing about learning a language is that sometimes one achieves what almost amounts to fluency. The homunculus seems to remember where to go in the stacks. But even then, and especially if the conversation is at a more intense level than usual, it is heavy work, interrupted by the need to find a way of explaining abstract concepts using simple words or, if the words are not there, then using mime. When I couldn't understand something Nagji said, I would look to Chutra for assistance, which was strange given that Nagji spoke better Hindi than Chutra. But by now Chutra and I had developed a kind of moronic language of our own. Poor Chutra, both Nagji and I got cross with him when he couldn't translate but he tended to labour the obvious and gallop through the difficult. Nevertheless the conversation proceeded, sometimes at a broken trot, sometimes at a crawl, sometimes circling back on itself to retrieve a meaning, but proceeding.

'Yes,' Nagji rubbed his chin thoughtfully, 'the public here is very bad. And you are a woman, so it is worse. They think of you as a statue, a perfect white statue. But all women here are treated badly. My wife, for example, cannot go out on her own, ever . . .'

I expressed my surprise.

'No, never. If she went out alone, the whole world would say what, who, how, and they would tear her jewellery and beat her.' He mimed being hit across the face. The subtext of the conversation moved on to rape. Chutra said twenty per cent of men were bad men and that Madam Sahib was very trusting and innocent.

Nagji said, 'Nonsense, eighty per cent are bad and all are thieves.' Then he turned to me and said, 'It is very very dangerous for you. You must try to understand.' He furrowed his forehead and jutted his head forward like a bull.

'I do understand, Nagji bhai, and I appreciate your concern, but this is my work. We all must work and sometimes it is dangerous. It is true that I might meet with trouble but it is also true that I find people like you more often than I find bad people. Except the police. They are always bad.'

Nagji said, 'You must put that in your story. Everyone is angry that the police are corrupt. And that the poor man can find no justice.'

I said that I certainly would but doubted that it would make any difference.

And so the conversation went on, ending, at last, in the labyrinthine politenesses concerning how long I was to stay. I said I should leave the following day. Nagji said ten days. Eventually, and rather more quickly now that we had been so frank with each other, a sensible solution was reached. I would be taken to the Sirohi Rabari who were camped by Nagji's well. I could spend as long as I liked there and, when the dog was well enough, leave from there for the forest areas of the Aravallis, through which many Rabari villages and dangs were scattered.

We had been talking for over an hour and we were strained by it. Chutra chose this moment to make a long speech. On top of the effort of conversing, the accumulation of the day's worries and my own physical weakness, he placed the last straw. I grabbed my head and collapsed on the charpoi with a groan. At which, Nagji let out a lion's roar of laughter and said, 'Sleep now. Tomorrow you will have peace.'

Before sunrise the next morning, I found myself perched behind Nagji on a very fine cart pulled by two enormous oxen with blue horns – a form of transport originating in the steppes approximately five thousand years ago. I knew my friend was showing off as he lifted their tails, making them go faster, displaying their form, their strength – adjuncts to his own potency and power.

'You should have chosen a bullock cart,' he said. 'Bullocks eat anything and can go anywhere, much better than camels, and you could have had some comfort.' We thundered along beside a river-bed, shaded, cool. Zali had survived the night.

The further we moved towards the Rabari camp, the more desolate the terrain became. A thousand sheep and goats were held on 250 acres. A few shepherds whom you could mistake for stones had they not been topped by turbans sat motionless under the sun. The trees, too – what were left of them – looked post-nuclear, with just a tiny tuft of leaf left here and there.

'This area used to be very dangerous,' said Nagji. 'Thieves lived here and wild animals. But now that I have sunk the well,' he smiled and tapped his head, 'the thieves have had to go. They are afraid of me.'

The camp itself was a collection of grass huts lined up along a fence beneath Nagji's well. Behind them were grass pens which would hold the animals at night. A woman carried a huge bundle of lopped tree on her head. This year there were approximately fifty people from several different villages, all related.

Nagji had had flowers planted around his well – busy Lizzies and marigolds. The Rabari took off their shoes when they used it as a sign of respect and gratitude to him.

He showed me inside a hut – a cubby-house made of sticks and clumps of roly-poly grass. The earth floor had been swept so clean it was almost polished. Attached at the back was a straw room with a straw floor, the size of a double bed. This was where the mother and father slept. It was the house of the first of the three little pigs. Yet even this poverty was transformed by a veneration for beauty. Everything was neat and prettily made. Nagji told me that the people were infested with fleas and lice but the impression these huts gave was of cleanliness and order. A gorgeous woman – sexy snaggle teeth and long-boned gracility – glided over to us with tea. There were bone marriage bangles right up to her armpits, eight yards of cloth in her skirt which was red, red, red. When I returned the cup, she grabbed my hand and pulled me down beside her. She told me that on their way down here, they stopped near the foot of Mount Abu and each day carried up their milk through the jungle to the tourist hotels at the top. Ten miles straight up, at the mercy of bears, leopards and tigers. She laughed and said that, yes, it was very dangerous but what to do? She mimed carrying the deghras (milk cans) on her head, swaying her hips.

As usual the men were, by comparison, as plain as planks but they too, when they overcame an almost autistic shyness, were willing to talk. Because of drought and lack of feed, this year's wool was short and very coarse. It would not bring in much money. Already the people and animals were thin. If there were no rain again next year, most of the herd would die and some of the people.

When I had inspected the camp and asked my questions, it was time for Nagji to implement his Idea. He ordered three black goat-hair mats for me to sit on and food to eat (rancid goat milk and dry roti). He himself sat on another mat approximately fifteen yards away. When I was settled, a shepherd brought a handful of marigolds which he strewed around me, then backed away. A woman brought incense and placed it beside me. Another brought water.

I wanted to run over to the patriarch and thank him for his largeness of spirit, his effort of empathy. Instead I sat on my mat, surrounded by marigolds, notebooks, goat droppings and incense, by huts that kept out neither dust nor wind nor rats nor even sun, by scrawny, tottering sheep, by donkeys, heads hung low and ribs like washboards, while fifteen yards away Nagji acted as guard and fifty people, smiling, and with silent respect, watched the white guest being alone.

19

Chutra had two topics of conversation – nothing and himself – and he talked without cease about both. It was possible to tune out much of the pandemonium – the cars, buses, rickshaws, radios, ghetto blasters, loudspeakers and truck horns playing tuba tunes – but Chutra's voice dripped upon my consciousness like Chinese water torture. He would clear his sinus passages with a sound like a nearby avalanche, spit the contents to one side with a flourish and, if there were no victims on the road to harangue, would turn his attention to me.

'Madam Saaaahib . . . it . . . iss . . . whaaat . . . taaaiim?' If I did not respond, he would walk beside me to shout in my ear. 'It is *whaaat* taaaiim? It . . . is . . . thirty . . . minits . . . of . . . three . . . teen bajje teez minit.' This he would yell several times and point to his own watch.

'Teen bajje teez minit. Thank you, Chutra,' I would whisper and pull my lips back from my teeth. Relief from Chutra was all I could think of, the only need or desire I had. All mental processes were focused on this one necessity – that Chutra should be far, far, far away from me. It is a strange and hallucinatory thing to have just one thought circulating in your head for a couple of days and nights. A form of meditation, I suppose, at the end of which you have either reached nirvana or are completely mad. There was no sign of the white jeep or the white smile of Koju Singh. And we were nowhere near nirvana.

Chutra refused to camp with or even near the Takus, a caste which, he said, were notorious for their wickedness, but whom in fact he loathed because they were untouchables and he was a detestable little bigot. We had to walk many extra miles and finally found a patch of dust and prickles out of sight of the road on which to pitch the tent. Chutra went to the well to fetch water. The camels were hobbled out to graze in the paddock. When they appeared to be wandering too far, I went to lead them back closer to camp. First Momal and then Sumal, with eyes rolling in their heads, charged me in their loose hobbles, knocked me down with their necks and began to dance on my body. I crawled to the protection of a spindly tree and proceeded to play hide and seek with these two, thousand-pound psychopaths until, unhinged by fury, and uncertain whether any bones were broken because the adrenalin had numbed pain, but in any case not caring whether I lived or died, I raced to camp, took a hobble chain and a long stick, ran back to the camels and, feinting to right and to left, used the stick to grab Sumal's noseline from around her neck – though in fact Momal was the real culprit but Sumal was stupid enough and close enough to be caught – and when I got hold at last of that noseline and yanked at it so that Sumal came down on her knees with a bellow, and when I began bashing at the beast with the chain, and bellowing louder than the camel, and cursing in words that no memsahib should know, and when a voice said, 'Madam, Madam!' and a hand tried to take the hobble chain from me . . . Then . . . I could not stop and was in fact barely aware of Takat's handlebar moustache, blue safari suit and horrified expression because the orgy of rage was delicious and necessary, and there was murder in my heart and blood on my kurta, and at last I understood, from the inside as it were, the eruptions of violence in India, among these most evolved, long-suffering and tolerant of peoples, because a human being can't keep up the good manners and the forbearance forever, and when those give way, madness comes pouring out the hatches.

Takat Singh ushered me back to camp. I was trembling and my mouth was very dry. Bruises the shape of camels' feet were forming underneath my clothes. I said, 'They tried to kill me . . .'

'Certainly, certainly,' said Takat but as he did not understand English he was probably just being polite.

'They were trying to kill me . . .' I said to Koju, who smiled hugely but perhaps a little anxiously and made tea.

There were four other men present. Two were very thin and

dressed in rags. They dropped their faces shyly and hid smiles behind cloth or hands. Their names were Rupa and Dullah and they were, presumably, the replacements. There was a man called Lakshman Singh, who was a forest officer from somewhere ahead in the Aravallis, and there was Jaswant Singh Natharwat, controller of Udaipur Range forests, a Rajput in matters of style and honour, but it wouldn't have mattered to me what he was or where he came from because he spoke English and hearing it was like being raised from the dead.

'They were trying to kill me,' I said.

'Please, Robyn ji, sit and take tea.'

Reality had taken on that snap-shot form associated with shock. Suddenly Chutra was there, standing as if before a jury. I had enough presence of mind left to feel sorry for him and was ready to intercede on his behalf. But something very peculiar was happening. They weren't preparing to lynch him, they were pretending that they believed his lies. I knew enough Marwari to know he was saying that he had trained the camels to attack strangers and that as I was wearing white (I had been wearing exactly the same white kurta for the last six days), the camels must have thought I was a thief. Even if it had not been such transparent mendacity, the idea of training camels to kill people was not my idea of good camelmanship. But instead of admonishing him, they were handling his ego as if it were the most delicate of flowers. They were putting it in water and admiring it. For a second, their generosity towards him made me feel ashamed. But only for a second. They didn't have to live with him, they hadn't just felt the cloak of the grim reaper brush them and . . . they were men. When Chutra had gone off with Rupa and Dullah, I said to this circle of moustachioed faces, with a certain amount of incredulousness in my voice, 'But they were trying to *kill* me . . .'

When this was translated, Takat said, 'It would be best if you stay away from the camels.'

Stay away from my own camels! I had few enough fields of expertise. One was handling dromedaries. Nothing I would boast about at intellectual High Tables perhaps but an extra-curricular activity in which I had privately imagined myself more than proficient. I understood and appreciated that Takat's concern arose out of chivalry but I suddenly had the strangest sensation that I was the only female left on earth. It had been creeping up on me during the last couple of days. Everywhere there were men in jeeps, in rickshaws, on bicycles, on scooters, in shops, sitting drinking tea, smoking on doorsteps, waving thin brown arms out of truck windows. Yesterday at a roadside dabar, the men at their tables looked me up and down. One said, 'Where is your Sahib?' with a sneer and his companions laughed. Chutra had muttered something about half-minds. We were getting close to the Rajasthan border.

'Forget these small troubles,' said Jaswant wisely. 'You have three men to help you now. Concentrate on your Rabari research. That's what's important.'

He was right. I could see that. Here, camels were simply a means of transport; I employed men to look after them as I might employ mechanics. Besides, what did anything matter, as long as my prayer had been answered, Narendra had not let me down, the torture was going to stop, from now on I would be free of . . .

'. . . *Three* men? Oh, no. Please, Jaswant ji, you don't understand. I beg you, take him back with you. Please. *Please.*' But it was explained to me that if Chutra left, Rupa and Dullah would not stay. It was explained to me that Chutra was like the harmless frog who, when the snake passes, puffs himself up so the snake will think he is too big and dangerous to eat.

'Now he'll have two people under his command. He'll be a general,' said Takat.

'You'll just have to get used to him talking all the time. It's another north–south difference. You rest your minds with silence; these people with talk. They will talk about everything and nothing all day and night. Who else can they talk to?'

So, Chutra was staying. Only Koju sensed the extent of the devastation this news had wrought. To save my pride, he took me to the jeep to hand me a letter from Narendra and a discreetly administered slug of gin. I thanked him, went for a walk by myself and sobbed.

But human hope is a resilient beast. 'Do not crawl into this cactus fence to hide forever', it said. 'The important thing is that the loading will now be done efficiently and quickly, so you will be able to set out in the cool of the mornings', it said. 'Chutra will have two other people to talk at and will, ergo, leave you in peace', it said. 'You must rise above Chutra and focus on larger goals and in so doing the way ahead will become clear, the chaos will order itself', it said.

Thus fortified, I went back to camp and found myself spilling out tales of the journey so far. Oh, glorious fluency between brain and voice. Oh, happy homunculus. The words were delicious in my mouth, like food to the starving.

'Which hand?' said Takat.

'My left,' I said.

'Are you sure?'

I was sure.

'Ah,' he said and nodded to himself.

'Yes?' I said, when it seemed he would continue staring at his sandal forever. He assured me that the bad luck caused by the snake choosing to sleep in my *left* hand had very likely run its course, but he did not seem at all convinced himself. But that was just superstitious nonsense and nothing I needed to worry about because another plan was taking shape thanks to Jaswant ji and thanks to the superiority of the rational mode over the irrational, though I wished the krait had chosen my right hand.

Jaswant knew where the Rabari dangs were concentrated and suggested I push on towards that area and take what luck offered, as it would be almost impossible to organize a dang to travel with ahead of time. I was most interested now in the camel-breeding Raika but, as Jaswant said, the migration routes did not exist any more. They had broken up because some villages would not let herdsmen through. However, there were various small dangs scattered throughout the Aravallis whose mukkis waged a quiet and mutually unwinnable war with foresters like Jaswant.

'Like wolves, they look so harmless and quiet and blank in the eyes, but they are not like that at all. They survive by their wits, just like wolves, and when they fight, they fight like them too. One man, if pushed, can usually fight off ten. I've seen it happen. It's a hell of a life. All day, every day, they are harried by everyone they meet. You see, often there is no food left for the local herds after the migrants go through. But there is no land set aside and no government programmes to sort out the problem. When land was being distributed, the Rabari should have got some for themselves. But they didn't understand what was going to happen. Now, of course, they do, but it's too late.'

Almost the whole of Rajasthan has been cleared of forest. Those portions remaining are in constant threat of devastation by graziers, by locals gathering firewood, by illegal logging companies giving kickbacks to bureaucrats and politicians, and, ultimately, by the pressure of population. The dilemma is this: to protect what is left of forest resources, from which regeneration may occur, is usually at the expense of the people immediately dependent upon them. But when the forest is cleared, the land becomes ultimately non-productive and the social, economic and ecological catastrophe gathers further momentum.

When Jaswant first came to this job, the forest under his jurisdiction had been felled and overgrazed illegally for a long time because of corruption at all levels. Aware of the difficulties the Rabaris faced, and wishing to reach some fair agreement with them, he had gone to all the head men, explaining that some of the forest from now on would be closed to their herds so that it could have a chance to regenerate, but that the remaining forest would be made available to them for grazing. When the rested section was robust enough, it would be re-opened and another section closed, and so on. He promised to plant grasses on waste land. He promised to include them in all further planning. The mukkis shook his hand and guaranteed their support but then set about gathering, from the thousands in their community, a lakh or so of rupees with which to bribe local politicians into transferring Jaswant somewhere else. Narendra had interceded and Jaswant was reinstated. He said, 'I don't blame the Rabaris for what they do; they have to survive. But so does the forest.'

Previously I had not found Chutra's caution credible, mixed, as it was, with bigotry. But Jaswant, too, talked of danger in this area. Dacoits. Lawlessness. I began to see how vulnerable I was, and how visible, and it sobered me. Underlying the illusion of order created by metal roads, pretty little cottages on the outskirts of woods, was another reality altogether – a whole new way of understanding the word 'jungle'. Jaswant would prepare people ahead for my arrival and from now on I would be delivered, like a package, along a line of Rajput havellis (mansions) or forestry department sanctuaries, moving out of one sphere of safety into the next. I would be – had already been, without realizing it – a traveller in medieval time. And I understood that from Chutra's point of view if I would only let myself be Guinevere, he could fulfil his function as knight.

It is curious to enter a lawless place. That is, to enter and take on the state of mind necessary for surviving in a lawless place. We privileged ones are not even aware that we carry expectations of there being a law to which most people adhere most of the time. There may be discontinuities to the process of that law – a murder here, a robbery there – but by and large we expect such events to be anomalies or, at worst, breakdowns of an existing system. Of the *norm*. Here, lawlessness, poverty and desperation were the norm. Cunning and suspicion of motives were the qualities necessary for survival. Yet everything appeared benign. People went about their business. The sun shone. There was no eerie music playing. It was like walking in those summery fields in which battles had occurred and which give no clue as to how they had been transformed into hell. (Did dying men see flowers in front of their faces, bees buzzing amidst the blood?) And now the strangeness of a wood where trees burst with orange flowers, where nothing but picnics should happen, but where bandits and leopards hid and only fools ventured alone.

The next morning my knights took me to Badir Sahib's havelli, first in the line of Rajput safe-houses. As Jaswant said, 'There is still great respect and fear here for the Rajputs. We protected the people, cut heads for them, and if someone is in trouble and asks for help, it is in our instinct to give it.' My host was away but the gatekeeper welcomed us with a ringing 'Badir Sahib's name is symbol of safety' – his only English words.

One entered through an elephant-sized, brass-studded gate, which was locked at night. On the inside were two small rooms for wayfarers and, in the courtyard, a third guest room to which I was escorted. To the right was a second gate leading to a walled garden and the main house which included the zinana. The women would see me tomorrow, when I was rested.

As soon as I was settled, Koju had to take Jaswant Singh ji back to Udaipur. Jaswant leaned out of the window, waved and shouted, 'Old Marwari proverb. Trust everyone as your friend and guest but keep tight hold of your purse.' They were gone, leaving me once again deaf and blind, and wishing to God that it could be Koju walking with me instead of Chutra. But Koju was, immutably, a driver and Chutra, immutably, a camel man.

How often and how generously I had been accommodated, in every kind of household from palace to pauper's hut, and everywhere I had experienced the same largesse. But my hosts were sometimes anxious as to how to look after the foreign guest and I was excruciatingly aware that I might be a burden to them. And the rigours of politeness, when all I wanted was to crawl away into something dark, were often more of a drain on my resources than mere physical discomforts. But now I had all that I needed or desired in India – a room with a door that closed, something to read and earplugs.

Bang bang bang. 'Are you all right, Memsahib?'

'Yes, thank you, Chaukidaar ji. I will sleep now.'

'Can I bring you anything, Memsahib?'

'No thank you, Chaukidaar.'

'I will be right here, Memsahib.'

'Thank you, Chaukidaar, but there is no need.'

'Where do you come from, Memsahib?'

'I come from Australia.'

'Ah. That is a very long way.'

'Yes, Chaukidaar. Please do not trouble yourself over me. I think I will sleep now.'

'Very well, Memsahib. I shall be here to guard you while you sleep.'

'Thank you, Chaukidaar ji.'

(Thirty-second pause.)

'Memsahib, will you take tea?'

'No thank you, Chaukidaar. I will sleep now.'

'Water?'

'No thank you.'

'Water for bathing?'

'*No!* . . . Thank you.'

But a bucket of hot water was brought by a young girl who flashed smiles of luminous innocence, tried to press my legs and showed a great deal of interest in the little keepsakes inside my purse and in the two toy pistols Koju had brought, which looked suitably deadly under cover of darkness and made a most impressive bang when stuffed with a cork. 'Don't be frightened,' I said to her, 'they are not real guns.'

I bathed. I ate. I eventually made it clear to the servant girl and the chaukidaar that I did not need them to come in and out to check on my welfare every fifteen minutes, that I did not need the servant girl to sleep on the floor beside my cot, that I did not need the chaukidaar to stand guard and bang his stick outside my door. I read until my eyelids turned to lead. Then I placed my purse under my pillow, but as it was rather lumpy put it on a small table two feet from my head. The world disappeared. In the night I thought I saw an angel bending over me and in the morning my purse was entirely empty of money.

There were many reasons not to tell Chutra, not least of which was the fact that the beautiful young thief was an untouchable. After breakfast I took tea with the women of the zinana and asked them to call the servant girl. She sat at our feet in perfect composure, head high, her eyes never meeting my gaze. I could detect terror behind those eyes but no one else would have noticed a thing. I punished her by holding her in suspense. Surreptitiously I pointed to my purse and raised my eyebrows at her. She contrived a look of bewilderment, bordering on wounded pride. In the face of such talent, not to say courage, how could I expose her?

The Aravalli Ranges are like the petrified body of a giant half-buried in the plains. In the distance, the blue swell of a hip, and here, scattered bones of shin and toes protruding. Villages, simple and earth-coloured, surrounded by walls, were clamped on to the sides of low hills. And as the country got wilder, the population grew thinner and loveliness increased in direct proportion to danger. Gone the sense of being squashed into nothing by flatness and sameness. But the psychic suffocation continued.

What beckoned, one could not enter. There was no sense of

abandon, no possibility of dawdling, no pleasure to be gained by investigating something new, by indulging whim. To Chutra, this landscape was not scenery. It was an enemy, the equivalent, for him, of a slum in Rio de Janeiro. Once again, I was struck by the antithetical nature of Australian and Indian landscape. There, jungle is benign, haunted perhaps, and certainly powerful but, as long as you understand its signs, a garden in which all may enter as equals and be sure of sustenance. But here were fences not just of property but of the mind, fences of fear between those who possessed and those who thieved. Suspicion rose like a miasma from which it was impossible ever to take a breath. I could not see a Rajput fort gracing a line of hill without thinking of the human rapaciousness that had made such architecture necessary.

Contrary to mathematical expectation, the presence of Rupa and Dullah did not decrease the loading time by two thirds. The general had to explain to his soldiers what to do and, as they were simple to the point of idiocy, this took a long time. Chutra was a boss now and not a worker. Therefore the lifting of so much as a strap was unthinkably degrading. Even if Rupa was twenty feet away and a rope needed tying, tying the rope was Rupa's job and Chutra would call him to do it. Often I tied the rope myself in the vain hope of shaming Chutra but all I did was lower myself in my employees' eyes.

We missed the cool early light and set off in the heat of the day. It now took three men four hours to cook chapati and dal and load three camels. The camels had done some damage to my back. A kind of toothache shot down my spine and into my right leg whenever I took a step. Riding was intolerable. Zali was ill again. There was a small town ahead. I would leave the chaps outside it and walk in with the dog to look for a dark room for me and something more sustaining than roti for him.

My room at the Dreamland Hotel had pink, scrofulous walls, a charpoi and blanket, and cigarette butts on the floor. There was a colourful display of various spits in one corner. I bought the dog eggs and chicken biryani and I had half a bucket of plain hot water, no soap. There was only one thing wrong with my room in this Dreamland Hotel. It contained, in a corner of the shit-encrusted bathroom, a small cracked mirror. Who was that beaten-up old bag wearing my clothes? Now I knew what Jaswant meant when, on seeing photos of me in a magazine, he said, 'Ah, yes. Well, you were a lot younger then.'

I returned to camp early the next morning to find them still dithering around cooking this, arguing about that. Then came bathtime by the well. (Never let it be said that Raika don't wash. Every time I looked around at these three, suds were flying, though they didn't manage to look any sprucer.) Suddenly I gave up the struggle. There was no point in my trying to change anything. There was no point in trying to control my environment at all. I must appear to enjoy being waited on and I must accept their methods, their meanings, their time. I lay back on my pack. Chutra came over to me, smiling and holding out a lukewarm nimbu pani, the texture of boiled starch.

'Madam Sahib. I *untrained*. Koju *trained*.' Then, in Hindi, 'But is the nimbu pani OK?'

'Yes, Chutra ji. You have made it very well, though perhaps a little too much sugar.' I snoozed and was woken up by Rupa informing me it was time to move out.

But where was the general? I could hear singing from behind a rock. Chutra emerged moments later, his turban cocked at an even jauntier angle than usual, one hand placed on his hip, the other holding a long stick with an axe on top and, strapped across his miniature chest, in the style of a Mexican bandit, were my toy pistols. Sometimes you just couldn't help but love the little guy.

But most of the time you could.

20

'Ho ha, Rupa, Dullah. Ho ha.'

'Ho ha, Chutra ji. What is it?'

'The rocks. Look at those rocks. Aren't they big? Just like cinema halls.'

'Ho ha. Those rocks are really big. What do you think, Dullah?'

'I was just going to say how big those rocks were.'

'No rocks like that in Marwar, are there, Dullah?'

'Not big rocks like these.'

'These are really really big.'

'Have you ever seen rocks as big as these, Rupa?'

'Never. In Marwar there are no big rocks such as these.'

'Madam Sahib. Rupa and Dullah say there are no rocks as big as these in Marwar.'

When, at last, the rocks had been bled of the last ounce of notice they could inspire, there would be a twenty-second interval whereupon Chutra would demand to know how Rupa or Dullah were getting along, to which they would reply that, ho ha, they were getting along fine and how was *he* getting along . . .'

These were not meant to be conversations. These were noises to stave off the silence into which misery might seep, noises to throw against the hardness of life. Sometimes the noise was in the form of songs which would have been infinitely preferable to me if Chutra had had a sweet voice. Alas, he was the only Raika in the whole of India who had a voice like a sheep being quartered alive.

But it was impossible not to be touched by the way he treated his footsoldiers. For all the bragging he subjected them too, he also encouraged them, joked with them, elicited their opinions, forced them to address me across shyness wide as oceans. To them he was

Einstein crossed with Garibaldi and they were guileless enough to display their admiration naked.

'Madam Sahib?' said Chutra's lips. I smiled and nodded but he would not be put off. I took out the earplugs which I had taken to wearing permanently.

I was to notice, please, that Ram Rahim's tail had been lifted and tied to the saddle, so that his balls were prominently on display. (Ram Rahim was led forward and his exposed globes duly exhibited for my inspection and admiration.)

'Madam Sahib, it is because he is a young man. He looks at the other camels and says, "Ho ha, I am a man." Just as dogs do.' Chutra thrust out his chest and twirled one side of his moustache.

The country we passed through was once thick forest. Now, its degradation could be felt, as if it was an animal flayed and left to suffer under the sun. Grit blew off the granite outcroppings and the fields beneath grew nothing but rocks and dust. Nevertheless we were gaining altitude and, with it, good humour. Mamer sanctuary lay not far ahead where Lakshman Singh, Assistant Conservator of Forests, would be waiting to show us around and where we could rest and find medicine for Zali who seemed sometimes to be well and, at others, merely stoic.

We were entering the land of the Bhils, tribal people who had populated the hills of India before the Aryan invasion. They were quite different to look at – short, muscly people with flattish faces. Being Adivassis (that is, outside or beneath caste), they were the lowest of the low, which accounted for the boldness of the women who strode along the road in groups, their heads and sometimes breasts uncovered. They did not cluster around me but either nodded and passed on, or called out 'Burri ben' (white sister) and laughed. I liked them.

Chutra must have realized this because he tried, as he had many times before, to disabuse me of my ignorance in matters of class and degree, that is, in the natural order of the world of men. The Adivassis' function was to inspire loathing and Madam Sahib should understand that this had always been so.

Eventually, unable to contain my irritation, I said, 'You mean all Adivassis are bad? Adivassis are *born* bad? Why do you think such an ugly thing, Chutra? It is nonsense.'

'Why are they bad? Because they have dark skin and dirty clothes and filthy habits. They are uneducated and' – here he paused to prepare me for the irrefutability of the evidence he was about to give – 'they . . . eat . . . *buffalo!*'

'Rhubarb, rhubarb,' agreed Rupa and Dullah.

Chutra had already proved himself resistant to reason in such matters. The Kutchi Rabaris, for example, being a slightly lower subcaste of his own caste, aroused his disapproval. Why? Because they were not clean, inside or out. In the morning they did not wash and they did not say their prayers. I had pointed out that they had had no water. Anyway, members of his own group, the Raika, were hardly paragons of cleanliness, often going *years* without taking a wash. Ah no, he had said. If there were even a teacup of water, a Raika would use it to wash the face, arms and stomach in order to be ready for puja. And if there were not a teacup, a Raika would wash himself with sand so that God would say, 'Ah, here is a good man.'

'In almost all countries but India, people eat buffalo and cow and it is not considered bad.' I turned to look at him. 'I have eaten cow. As for colour,' I went on, ignoring the expression on his face, 'does the soul or the heart have a colour?'

This elicited a smile and an admission that I spoke the truth. But he addressed me as one would a precocious ten-year-old which so annoyed me that a little thrill of cruelty went through me and I delivered my *coup de grâce*. 'Did you know that Lord Krishna was an Adivassi? That is why his skin is always blue, to signify its darkness.' Chutra stopped in his tracks, then fell back to join his helpers, a visibly shaken man.

I was left in peace until we came to an enormous tree by the side of the road, whose trunk was as knobbled as a witch's nose and beneath which were hundreds of terracotta horses of various sizes, some broken and black with age, some fresh from the potter's wheel, all crowded together in ranks and facing inwards as if revering the piece of rock which could only just be discerned as a woman on horseback, so resolutely had time's hand erased the work of the sculptor. Each horse was, on close inspection, minutely varied but all had the same characteristics – perfectly round mouths with extruded tongues, women's curvaceous legs, heavy and fat, a round hole where the tail should be, but most disconcerting of all a hole, like a bullet wound, at the back of the head, as if to let a spirit escape. Each expressed the essence or magic of horse, horse as it might be dreamed. Chutra informed me that it was an Adivassi shrine, probably to the black goddess.

There had never been anything glamorous about poverty in the places I had lived. It diminished its victims, it was lucidly ugly. But here desperation and squalor could mask itself with the exquisite, which perhaps explained why many urban Indians and foreign visitors romanticized rural life and refused to see its attendant misery. In the cities and towns now, a hideous vulgarity reigned. But objects made by village people for village use were still energized by the ancient Indian artistic genius.

I looked at the horses and wondered how long it would be before they would be swept away and replaced with a McDonald's or a television. And whether the Indian genius was strong enough to resist the homogenizing and stupefying principle which has come to dominate the modern world, drowning us in inanity and stifling the desire to travel or investigate or criticize because everywhere will be the same – a global village of the dead.

I took my earplugs out so I could hear the songs of little honey-eating blackbirds with blue satin waistcoats and long dainty pipes in their mouths. We were entering Mamer – over three hundred square miles of forest – which was proclaimed a sanctuary in 1988. There were no large cities near by and no main roads; local thieves were small time and stole the wood only for their own use – mostly for making farm implements; which explained why the forest was still intact. But pressure on the park was growing from increasing numbers of animals and men, both inside and outside it.

Lakshman Singh had arranged to drive me to Ambassa, a small village where some cow-herding Rabari had settled permanently. After that I could stay in a series of forestry lodges where I would be under quasi-official protection until I had passed safely through the Aravalli Ranges.

'Many nomads came here thirty years ago, but still more continue to come and settle, while others pass through here on their way to Gujarat and Madhya Pradesh with their herds. It is impossible to keep a count on the numbers and anyway there is only one ranger per thirty square miles and only one car between the twelve rangers employed here. Really, there should be sixty guards because forest is open property; it can't be locked. When the park was established, the villagers who were already here were allowed grazing and use rights. But the migrant Rabari have formed villages too, so they also have grazing rights because those rights were never clearly formulated on an individual basis but on a village basis.'

Powdery white dust swirled through the jeep as we stopped at Ambassa – thirty little houses and a few shared fields. As usual I was treated courteously by the Rabari who pulled out a charpoi for me and Lakshman ji to sit on, while they squatted on the ground around us. However, they made it clear that while I was quite welcome to remain and ask questions, I would not be welcome to stay the night. Even though they knew Lakshman Singh well, they had developed a siege mentality after so many years of bad relations with the Bhils. I might be some kind of Trojan horse sent by their enemies to make it easier to steal their cows which they kept locked inside at night. I was warned not to camp anywhere but with the foresters.

'Very danger!' said the old mukki who had picked up a few words of English on his travels.

The Bhils were natives of this area. They were essentially hunting people (though now they farmed as well) and from their point of view these new arrivals were eating out their forest and threatening their subsistence. This protracted war had more to do with competition for dwindling resources than xenophobia, though the latter inspired its language.

I asked the mukki when he decided to change from herding goats to herding cows. About thirty years back, he said, because during the rainy season goats and sheep got foot rot. The people who still herded goats had to keep them in their houses during the wet season or walk them back to Sirohi, the ancestral village.

And what were their other sources of income? Eyes shifted from left to right and people shuffled a little in their places. The old mukki began. He himself owned fifteen cows and from them got four litres of milk in the morning and four in the evening.

The morning milk would be sold at four rupees per litre and in the evening it would be made into ghee and curd. In addition he might make two to three hundred rupees per truckload of cow shit, but that only twice a year or so. He might also sell a bullock every two to three years – or in an emergency even sell a cow. He made eight hundred rupees per month for a family of seven.

This was an underestimate of course. He thought we might be government representatives and if he diminished his income to us, we might provide relief. Even so, he was still a poor man.

These people only returned to Sirohi for deaths and marriages. Their society was still very tightly bound by their own panchaits (councils) whose ruling all individuals must obey or risk being outcast. Twelve villages came under one panchait, and from this village there were two representatives. I asked why women did not sit in the panchait. As usual this question raised lots of laughter and banter.

'We ladies are never in the panchait but we force the decisions from inside the houses before the men go to the meetings.'

'In our caste, ladies are much wiser. If you give me money, I won't know how to count it but if you give it to her, you won't fool her.' But this was said with typical Rabari disingenuousness. I couldn't imagine anyone outsmarting this old coot, especially in something as important as finances.

The conversation petered out; it was time to go. A young woman who had been butting into the conversation with the mukki got up to leave.

'Come, talk some more,' said Lakshman Singh to her, 'you are bright and intelligent.' To which she retorted, 'If I were so intelligent, I'd be the one sitting on the charpoi.'

Mamer forest guest-house, set beneath the hills, consisted of two simple rooms and a little verandah. At a respectful distance were the houses of Adivassis, scattered sparsely through woods and fields. I suggested to Chutra that we rest here a few days and, divested of our luggage, ride into the bush on our camels, looking for Rabari herds. Chutra did not like this idea but managed to indicate that if I was *determined* to do such an incomprehensibly stupid thing, then we should both ride Ram Rahim, leaving Momal and Sumal behind to eat. I insisted that we ride the fatties and leave Ram Rahim behind to eat, he being the thinnest of the three.

Some rangers were staying near the cottage and the only thing they and Chutra seemed to talk about was how vile the Adivassis were. In the morning I had gone for a walk by myself and an Adivassi man had showed me the path home. He resembled Mornat and I liked his presence very much. I invited him in for tea. But as we approached the cottage, I felt him grab my legs from the back. I spun around to find that he had prostrated himself on the ground and was clasping my feet. I pulled him up. He was almost in tears.

'What's the matter?'

He was too frightened to come closer to the house where he believed he would be punished for his temerity.

I had visited the little local school and talked with a teacher there. I commented on how earnest and attentive the students had seemed to me, poor and shoeless but all dressed up and pressed and oiled. This was at odds with everything the rangers had said about Adivassi laziness, Adivassi stupidity. The teacher told me the students worked hard and wanted to succeed but the schools had no equipment and hardly any books. Most teachers gave up after six months of these conditions and simply waited to be posted to a better area. Some teachers thought it beneath them to teach Adivassis and thought of this posting as a punishment, simply to be endured before something better was offered.

On the morning of our ride Chutra was looking smug. When he knew I was perfectly primed, he said, 'Madam Sahib? That story you told me about Lord Krishna. I have consulted the rangers. Alas, you were mistaken. The blue colour of Krishna's skin is for other reasons.' And off we went in a rush of morning air.

It was as if the landscape had been dipped in a purple rinse and hung out in the sun to fade. There were lavender tints in the acra plants, hills, castor stalks and under the clouds; the road was a strip of purple disappearing into lavender woods. At a clearing in the forest we found a tethered camel and her calf. Later, two herdsmen came in with about thirty camels. Chutra could read the brands. The camels belonged to two sub-castes – Bumalia and Aal. He also said that these days camels are only really sold for farm work –

carts and ploughs. They were not used for this purpose thirty years ago. The camels would be sold in Pushkar. It was hard to say which were skinnier and more gaunt, the men or the animals. The camels were diseased and almost bald with mange, the men half-starved, living on nothing but camel milk, roti and tea which, of course, they offered us as if we were kin. I took some camel milk in an acra leaf (the men were too poor to have a spare cup). We sat on the ground on a filthy piece of cloth beside a clump of tattered belongings. The men possessed only the barest minimum necessary for survival. Unth wallahs don't take women on the dang because there's no work for them – no buttermilk to make, or ghee, no lambs to look after, so it is better that they stay safely at home. But after travelling with the Kutchi Rabari whose women could create palaces around their cooking fires, whose job was also to bring joy and lightness to life on the dang, this sad little camp was the equivalent of a bachelor's bedsit on the Bowery.

These men came from a village near Udaipur and every few months they would change places with another two men from their home village. The camels, however, remained out for eight to nine months.

'This was my grandfather's and my father's work but these days it is a fool's work. When I go home I have a job as a truck driver. But the camels are my true work and I do not want to leave them. But it is becoming impossible for us.'

They told me that to use the forest they had to pay two rupees per year per camel to the government. They would receive receipts for the money but then would have to pay anything from a hundred to fifteen hundred rupees in bribes to local rangers.

And then there were the diseases. Please, please, could we get some medicine? Could we send that medicine to his village? His camels would die without it. There was no point asking why they did not use the local veterinary clinics. I already knew what they would face, having gone to one to buy some medicine for Zali. There had been no medicine whatsoever in stock. These clinics were run by the government to serve local people. Theoretically drugs were free but in practice money was paid either into the vet's pocket or to middlemen who sold the drugs on the black market. One anthrax injection for example might cost eighty rupees, far more than these men could afford to pay. Even if drugs could be found, they were seldom enough to cure a whole herd, so that the animals would re-infect each other immediately. The Raika were clinging to wreckage and, without properly organized assistance, they would go under.

After several days Chutra begged that we move on. Taking the camels out to graze was too dangerous for his men, he said. The first evening, we camped with a family by the side of the road. They owned camels, cows and buffalo and they lived for many months of the year beside an Adivassi house. 'There,' I said to Chutra. 'They seem to get on well with their neighbours.' To which he replied, 'They have no choice.' The women at first had shouted at us to go away. Chutra convinced them that we weren't bandits but even so the atmosphere was tense.

I asked how long they had been coming here. Three years, to this particular place but longer, many years, to this area. They did not like it here.

'Why did you come here? Because there was drought where you were?'

'No. It gets dry sometimes but it's because jagah jagah kheti' (literally place place fields, or everywhere farms, or nowhere left to graze). They used a little room of the Adivassi house and an outside camp surrounded by leaf fences. For this they let the Adivassis have the animal droppings for their fields. The milk they sold in town. No doubt one day they would settle here permanently. Where else could they go?

The two young women between them had nine children, all naked, filthy and sick. One woman carried her youngest child. It was bright yellow and shrunken, like a mummy. It was two years old and had never left her breast. She fed it now with a desultory kind of patience. It would die soon.

Other women came over; one was very pregnant. I said, 'Will you go to hospital?' They laughed bitterly. She answered, 'Of course not. I'll be having it out in the jungle just like an animal.'

'Who will be with you?'

'Her.' She pointed to another woman, slightly older.

The women's arms and legs were covered with lumps and sores, and infections had formed where the silver bracelets pressed into flesh. Then I noticed a most incongruous thing. They shaved their legs.

The men came over and the women shut up, covered their faces and went back to the house. The men talked about the gold I must own in my country, my house, my car, how many lakhs, how many lakhs, how many lakhs. The real wretchedness of poverty was here. Desperation, despair, boredom, helplessness, rage.

Later that day, Koju showed up. Drunken Adivassis had stoned his jeep the previous night as he came through the hills looking for us. They had thrown bottles at the windscreen and tried to stop him. I hopped in the jeep with him and when we passed some Adivassi schoolchildren on the road, he swerved the car at them to frighten them, and for the first time since I'd known him his face became ugly.

From Kukawas to Suaroopganj was the most beautiful country I'd seen in India but it was exactly here that we must not tarry; it was the worst area for dacoity in the whole of western Rajasthan. It was the Bhils, or rather a criminal element within the Bhils, who did the dacoity. Chutra and Koju mimed their technique. Two would fall in beside us, a few would emerge from the jungle and gather behind us, while others would be waiting up in the hills with their bows and arrows. We really were in danger. These men cut throats and ventilated people with arrows as easily as skinning rabbits. And there was no law to stop them.

I have to confess to a little thrill of excitement as I pulled out next morning. I had been so protected on this venture that any sense of risk had disappeared long ago. But safety did make for dull days without edges. Keeping your senses attuned to danger makes you feel less like a package and more like a postman.

Koju had had the presence of mind to bribe a local policeman into accompanying us. The policeman was suffering a hangover — his flies were undone and his shirt torn — but he was wearing his uniform which was all we required of him. Koju strapped on one of the pistols. On him it looked kind of low-slung and sexy while on Chutra it looked what it was — a toy gun on a miniature man.

We had only gone a mile when two men fell in beside us. They looked like villains. They looked like *caricatures* of villains. One had a scar across his face which terminated in an empty eye-socket. Both of them carried what might have been large knives under their shirts. Chutra came up beside me, Rupa and Dullah clustered behind us. Koju and the uniform revved the engine and drove belligerently in front of us. I could tell Chutra was terrified and I didn't feel too cocky myself. Several minutes passed before our dacoits thought better of it and vanished into the woods by the side of the road. We heard shouting. They were calling off their comrades who waited in ambush further ahead.

Oh joy, oh elation. Chutra had expanded to twice his size. Koju's grin took on ridiculous proportions. We congratulated each other on our brilliance and bravery. But really it was the men's moment and I let them have it – warriors all, and not so much as a scratch on the package.

Once out of the woods Koju drove ahead to set up camp while we stopped to feed the camels and eat a cold roti. It was such a pretty place – granite outcroppings with good trees clutching at the base. Two Adivassi shepherds were sitting on a rock. One began to play a flute and I was instantly transported to imagined times – Krishna with the Gopis, or the Mediterranean at the time of Christ. The sweetness and purity of the music, the simplicity and harmony of this tiny world filled me with – what? Happiness? On this trip? Could it be that for just a moment something beautiful and true penetrated the pervading cloud?

'You, what caste are you?' The music stopped.

'Adivassi.'

Chutra spat and demanded to be given the flute. The shy young shepherd brought it over, shrinking with terror of me and submissive to Chutra's rudeness. My camel man made a great show of washing the reed, then began to play very, very badly. The moment was as irredeemable as shattered glass.

21

Pipala village faced out from its hill like a threatened animal backed up against a wall. A high thornbush fence indicated a state of siege. But once inside the fence, there was the smell of clean earth and healthy animals, and there were people with attractive, intelligent faces who welcomed us with that open-heartedness which one can almost begin to take for granted in India.

Ma, a widow of indeterminate age and fabulous beauty, showed us our room – the other room of her two-room house which was made of mud and dung and fronted by a small, white-washed verandah containing a line of charpois where everyone slept at night, bathed in each other's snores. Inside, the floor was being swept by a tot in skirts, whose besom was bigger than she was. On seeing me, she abandoned her broom and climbed on to my hip where she was to spend much of the next two weeks. There was a tiny fireplace without a chimney, corn stored in sacks, bales of wool, a wok full of clipped goat hair, a clay water pitcher and a charpoi covered with one of the rugs these people made and which I coveted – thick brown camel wool with black goat-hair stripes. A stone stuck out of the wall and on it was a metal wick lamp which would throw a glimmer at night, as spectral as starlight. The roof could not have been rainproof as dots and lozenges of light fell through it to the floor. A girl in red and silver brought wood and stacked it in the corner in the shape of a Christmas tree, each stick placed just so. From the doorway opening to the verandah, a shaft of sun cut into the darkness, illuminating a wall painting of camel and rider. The camel was black, the rider, red, and out of the camel's cornucopian bum flowed a stream of khad.

Barju Ma and her eldest son Parabu bhai were my hosts. Shanti ben, Ma's daughter, had brought the wood. The enchanting creature on my hip was Ma's second son's child. Her head was shaved so she looked like a little punk with her rows of silver earrings. She was less than three years old, yet she could smoothe out her skirts, hold her head on one side, compress her lips and lift her gaze at you with the craft of a courtesan. Her name was Bubbli and between us it was love at first sight.

The camels were tethered to the verandah, our possessions stacked inside. Then there was time to talk and drink tea. Bubbli climbed on to the charpoi to sit in my lap but from time to time moved across to her great-great-grandfather to comb his long white beard which was split into halves.

The first topic of conversation was the Bhil thieves. How they would ambush the women and rip off their jewellery, hold up the men with bows and arrows and steal their sheep. It was not safe for women to go out alone, they must walk in groups of ten. Each accounted an incident that happened 'four days ago', 'two days ago'. Ma's husband had been a very important and respected man here. (There was a shrine to him outside where Ma prayed morning and evening.) When he died everyone had gathered at the front of the houses, in the courtyard, for the mourning ceremony. Some thieves chose that moment of distraction to climb over the back fence and steal everyone's possessions. The disgust on Koju's face at such a hitherto unimagined depth of human treachery was of such intensity that I thought he might drive off right now to skittle some villains. And Chutra took this opportunity to inform everyone present, 'Ha ha, Madam Sahib, you said the Adivassis were a very goood caste, a very sweeeet caste.' I ignored him.

'But why is nothing done officially to stop them?' The Bhils paid money for protection to the local cops plus a percentage of the take, a certain amount of which percolated all the way to the top to the Superintendent of Police in Sirohi. I said I would visit that SP and demand to know why, after all these years of exploitation and robbery, when everyone knew who and where the criminals were, no arrests had been made here, not one. Everyone thought this was an excellent idea but like many excellent ideas during this journey, the strength, moral and physical, one needed to bring them about gave out. I never did confront the SP because life whirled me off in another direction and I needed all my presence of mind just to hold on. Koju said, 'All police are rotten in India but the worst are in Rajasthan. In other states they take small bribes only.'

Ma's husband had obviously been as exceptional as she was. Where life was so close to death, so unprotected from it, one mistake sent you over the edge. But with cleverness you could build a small safe place for yourself and your family. Their ancestors had migrated from the north several generations ago. (Only the Rao would be able to tell me how many.) Compared with the Rabari up the road, they were rich but their wealth showed in a subtle confidence and well-being, their ease with laughter, rather than in anything concrete. As Chutra had remarked when we first came in, 'This is *not* poor man. He lives like poor man, no fancy clothes, but his money is much. This is intelligent caste, especially the women.' Soon their herds would be heading out to Idar area where I had recently been. Two or three women would go to do the cooking. Perhaps I would go with them?

That was the beginning of a fantasy that sustained me for days. I would take only Ram Rahim with me on the dang and send Chutra, Rupa and Dullah home with the princesses. Then, when it was time to leave the dang, I could hire a man and wife from this village to walk home with me. I would slink into my room, close the door, lie on the charpoi and drift into a world in which there was no Chutra and no cameras. Of course, even then, I did not allow myself to get too attached to this idea because by now I knew that any plan of mine was doomed to failure by the simple fact of it being what I wanted to do.

That night at about ten, like demons conjured from our conversation, the police arrived, drunk and demanding money. They had seen the jeep and whoever was wealthy enough to own a jeep was wealthy enough to pay big bribes. When they saw that the jeep's owner was white and had one large, quiet Rajput and one small, shrill Raika to protect her – because they had been hired, as Chutra pointed out several times, by the Royal House of Jodhpur for that purpose – and when certain high-up names were dropped like rocks on their heads, the policemen's faces became pasty. But they were in too deep now to back out, much to Koju's and

Chutra's delight, because they could play with these two mice as they liked. To save face, the police demanded passports and registration documents. It was obvious that they had never seen such things before and did not quite know which way to hold them. The next demand, therefore, was entirely predictable. Did I have a C form?

Chutra laughed operatically. 'Why, I do believe,' he said, wiping his eyes, 'that you cannot read English!' (As they did not speak English, this seemed credible. Their literary skills, even in Hindi, were probably on a par with Koju's.) 'Because if you could,' went on Chutra, 'you would see that this passport is not only valid for Jodhpur but for the whole of India!' Here, Chutra pushed the passport under the policeman's nose, jabbing his finger at a line of printing.

Eventually we were left to savour our victory. I asked all those gathered around to estimate how much per year they might pay in bribes. It was dependent on what happened in that year, they said, but even in a bountiful year it would be at least two thousand rupees from each family to police and to forest officers.

Chutra said, 'Forest officers say, "No, you can't enter here." Then you give them money and they say, "Oh, OK. Cello, cello!"' (move along, move along). Everyone began to chime in, 'That's it. "Cello, cello!"' and they waved their arms as a traffic cop might to let through a stream of traffic. Chutra was enjoying his audience.

He pointed to me and said in a mixture of Hindi and English, 'Madam Sahib not understand. Police big thief, government servant thief. All public in India big thief.' Then he added in Hindi, 'In India paisa is god. Paisa is mother and father.' There was a general murmur of agreement and everyone smiled the resigned, cynical, Indian kind of smile but I did not forget the Rabaris who had bribed an official to get rid of Jaswant ji.

It is mysterious to me why intimacies should form with some people so easily and quickly, yet with others, not at all. Perhaps it was simply the good humour here or the high fence keeping out the world. Whatever the reason, and despite the frustrations of language, bonds of affection grew with everyone in this family, especially the redoubtable Ma. As Zali was again ill and I had developed some sort of lung infection, I decided to base myself here for a while. Mount Abu was only two hours' drive away. I could zoom up there to find a vet, ring Dilip and grumble long-distance to Narendra.

The vet, who had worked specifically on the diseases passed from camel to man, explained to me what they were: Q fever from my home state in Australia, TB, brucellosis, rabies, tapeworm and trypanosomiasis (sleeping sickness). Now, I had always done a lot of kissing of Ram Rahim's lips and a lot of blowing into his nostrils. He had done a lot of blowing into my nostrils and nuzzling of my neck, ears and nose. We were fond of each other.

'And how are these diseases passed, Doctor?'

'Most of them through the breath,' he said.

So there it was. I had TB, brucellosis and tapeworm. What a relief it was to know that there were very good reasons for feeling as moribund as I did. How happy and well I felt, all of a sudden, because I wasn't a hypochondriac and could check into a hospital any old time where I would receive lots of sympathy and attention because everyone would be able to imagine how much I had been suffering (how did she keep going with all those diseases?) and how bravely. Zali received half a dozen injections and I received two.

Back in Pipala some family friction had developed over the sale of sheep manure. (In one month Parabu would earn two thousand rupees from the sale of khad, so it was major income.) Ma and her husband's brother's wife negotiated the price with the truck-driver who would take it to Jodhpur for sale – a lively interchange in which you would think murder was being threatened but which ended in smiles. The money would be divided according to the number of sheep owned. Ma controlled this distribution, while the role of the junior women was to cook, clean and accept her ascendancy without question.

Ma was upset. She came to sit with me, throwing glances over her shoulder and announcing loudly. 'My first daughter-in-law is good and simple but my younger son's wife, her habits are very bad. When I divide up the khad money, she wants more and more.' I thought I perceived a deeper reason for the friction between those two. Younger daughter-in-law was a Carmen kind of

257

character and number two son panted after her like a puppy. The older son's wife was also beautiful but Parabu was not besotted by her. He was a man aware of his responsibilities to his family and his community. It was to Ma he went for advice, Ma who was the first love in his life and with whom he shared his power. Despite her widow's weeds Ma was a sexually potent woman and there was something unsettling about the way she muttered so intimately with her grown-up son. As if the cord between them had never been broken. Number two son, on the other hand, had betrayed his mother by falling in love with his wife.

By the next day the surface of life had returned to calm, as if the ripple from some sub-aqueous disturbance had never occurred.

When I wasn't directly involved in the choreography of village life I would sit on my charpoi and watch the performance: Parabu's heavily pregnant wife carrying bales of hay out to the lambs in a pen, stacking grass in an earth shelter, lifting pots of water on to her head – as unencumbered by her great belly as a whale in the sea; ten boys coming home from school and immediately going out to the herds; Parabu getting feed for the animals with a forked stick and a rope; little girls grinding corn gathered from small fields at the back; two young women sewing in the sunshine; Bubbli tottering after her mother to the well, balancing a tiny pot on her head; Ma walking ten miles into town to buy goods, carrying bundles home as if they contained feathers not flour; men spinning wool and smoking; women sweeping, stirring chaach (buttermilk), medicating animals, boiling tea, clearing the courtyard of every last dropping and carrying headloads to heap outside the fence, washing clothes, grinding corn and wheat, plastering walls, restacking fences, grinding more corn, sweeping again, cooking again, and on and on like a slow, unending waltz.

Whenever I helped to make the chaach and ghee, or sat in a corner of the verandah grinding corn, I had to strain against aching muscles and tickling sweat, whereas they could go on for hours, knowing that rhythm and grace are the foundations of doing and that you must never think about working until the work is done.

Each afternoon during the hour or two of rest from the day's effort, the women took me as far into their confidence as language and propriety would allow. Or they would play with me, dressing me up in their clothes, decking me with their jewels. I asked them if bangles all the way to their armpits were a bother. 'At first it takes a little getting used to, but the bangles are useful when you fight with your husband.' It was also explained that a woman's plait, often increased in length by ribbons, was like the lead to a camel. A husband could control his wife by means of this lead and in a fight could grab hold of it and throw her down. 'But you can hit him back with your bangles like this,' said one, and she demonstrated on the wildly giggling girls around her. When I asked Ma if it was a relief when she broke hers, I realized I had asked a culturally uninterpretable question. I had meant was it a physical relief, a freeing up?

'Not at all. It was my husband's death and who was to be my companion and helper then? The responsibility came to me and I was full of grief.' She shifted her glance to the second daughter-in-law. 'Who would help me handle the wayward members of the family when he died? For daughters, the mother is indispensable. They will always love her. But for sons, the mother is often done away with when they marry. What can one do then, and who can give help if the husband is gone?'

Parabu's father's brother's wife came to say hello. Surprisingly, she was very young. And very, very poor. This was one of the main social problems here – impoverished widows. Men tended to die young, from accidents or murder while on migration or out with their sheep. But no matter how destitute the widows were, they were not allowed to work outside the village. This young widow had three sons – two babies and one who had passed ninth grade. The older son now worked in a shop for two hundred rupees a month and with that supported the family. She owned no sheep or animals. I asked if the rest of the family would help her financially if she was in trouble. It seemed not. And would she marry again? 'No. I have three children, so there is no need of another husband. If I had had no children, then, perhaps . . .'

There was a lot of affection displayed here, just as there had been with the Kutchis. But unlike the Kutchis, these women were

259

much more sexually frank with me. Ma would look down the front of my dress to see if I wore a 'blouse'. Then she would pull out my bra strap to display to everyone. She would tease her daughter by pinching at her budding breasts and talking about her marriage. They would fall about laughing, the girl embarrassed but rather proud. She would hit her mother a great affectionate wallop. There was talk, too, of the relief of menopause, of the climacteric being the happiest time of life, even if your husband had died and you had to shoulder the family burdens on your own.

Dilip arrived in time to photograph a wedding at a neighbouring village. It was to be a big show and I was to lend one of the bridegrooms my camel. If ever there were a little job for a camel to do, like going out at the end of the day to carry home cut feed, it was always Ram Rahim who copped it. This time I protested.

'Chutra,' I said, 'that disgracefully obese Momal has done nothing but eat for days and poor little Ram Rahim is as skinny as a bone. I *insist* that you use Momal for the wedding.' (Remember, please that what in fact I said was something like, 'Chutra, very-very-fat Momal, long time eating only. Sitting. Little Ram Rahim very-very-thin, sick-thin. OK better Momal take absolutely wedding for.')

Chutra got that long-suffering look and pointed out the obvious. 'A bridegroom cannot ride a female camel.' So Ram Rahim's tail was tied up to display his barely dropped balls and Momal's finery was draped over his puny hump.

By the time Dilip and I reached the village, the fire ceremony had been completed and the three bridegrooms sat on separate charpois, immobile under their regalia. They were surrounded by brothers, fathers, uncles – six or eight men crammed to a charpoi. The village itself burst at the seams with people. Men in their best laundered whites and blood-coloured turbans, their gold, beaten into heartshaped shields and studded with precious gems, on display around their necks. The women's clothes tinted pink to red, their metals scattering light. That rare thing – a Rabari public servant – fat and absurd in his caste gear which he would only wear for occasions like this. Everyone else rangy as wolves, their fat melted off by sun and work, their shrewdness showing in gold.

Until now I had judged child weddings, at least within this community, a sensible way of dealing with practical limitations. The girls returned to complete their pubescence at home and the various groups of Rabari I had met were united on this point: child brides were all right, child mothers were not. But now I wasn't so sure. One of the brides was four or five years old and her terror was so tremendous I thought she might pass out. A dozen men stood over her with swords drawn, her mother was nowhere in sight, there was banging and crashing and shouting and frenzy, and she herself was screaming. All she knew was that she was being sent from her home to stay in a strange place with strange people who paid no attention to her cries for her mother. Great gentleness would no doubt be shown her by her in-laws at this stage but, even so, the trauma would surely stay with her forever. And the mother? There she was outside, cut off from her child, weeping.

Jogis employed for the occasion were pounding heartbeats on skin drums. Someone said that the bride's bangles had been broken but I couldn't be sure what was going on. People were jostling each other. There was booze around. Excitement passed through the crowd like contagion. When I caught a glimpse of Dilip, he seemed to be involved in an altercation. I felt myself carried along with a mob past a dancing competition between the women of two castes. They faced off against each other as if at war. Two small stones landed on my back. They were thrown by children standing on a roof. The music and the frenzy had broken their restraint and it was as if the impulse to throw arose not from belligerence but from a desire to cause a reaction, to connect. Perhaps a lot of violence begins like that. In any case it was time to go.

With Dilip around, the days transformed. He found little to interest or occupy him in the village. He was impatient for a different India, where the electricity worked and the politicians did their jobs and people had fewer children and more material possessions. Not only did he not romanticize Indian village life, it seemed to grate against his soul, and he could find no beauty in it. When he suggested we book into a hotel in Mount Abu rather than twiddle our thumbs in this boring place, I agreed.

Narendra drove from Jodhpur to see me. I spent most of the time complaining about a certain unth wallah and threatening to send him home so I could head off with the shepherds on my own. This bid for autonomy disturbed my friend whose primary motivation in helping me, I was beginning to see, was to make sure I stayed alive. When we parted he said, 'You and Chutra are illustrations of the old Marwari proverb: Two one-eyed men cannot get on and yet cannot separate.' He laughed and repeated it to Koju, who turned away to hide his grin. I had my own proverb regarding Chutra: On a long journey, even a straw is heavy.

When I returned to Pipala, Parabu's wife had had her baby – a son. Parabu sat outside, grinning. Inside it was dark and dusty. His wife lay on a charpoi, behind a curtain, and beside her was the youngest life I'd ever seen. Ma was exhausted, having helped her daughter-in-law throughout the night and previous day. Ma indicated that it had been a breach birth and that the mother was badly torn. They had thought she would die, but God had pulled her through. She could hold nothing in her stomach, not even water, but she had no fever. I sat beside her and placed my hand on her forehead. She was still fully dressed in all her bangles and the plaits pulling her hair so tightly from the scalp were damp. She was the colour of corpses. Big tears squeezed out of my eyes. They were complicated tears. The horrible marvellous strangeness of life. Anger that Zali had received better medical attention than this woman. Grief, I suppose, that my own reproductive days were over, a fact that I had had no opportunity to assimilate but that waited for just such a moment to ambush me. The women watched me, commented and laughed gently. Ma patted my head as if to say, How sentimental these westerners are. As if birth isn't an everyday thing, like eating or working or dying. Besides, this is a woman's lot. Whoever heard of medicines for such a thing? Men die on migration; women in childbirth. Being alive is a dangerous business.

Three days later Parabu's wife was able to sit up on the side of the bed and smile wanly. She showed me the scrap of life which had almost killed her and with which she had entirely fallen in love.

The next day a baby camel died. It had been born in the courtyard two days earlier. The mother was desolate, called and called, and followed the men around. They cut off the dead calf's tail and hung it up for her to smell as they milked her. A little of the milk was given to Parabu's baby.

The flocks were leaving and I had still not made up my mind whether to travel with them or not. Certainly I would go out for a night or two so that Dilip could take photos, but to continue with them now seemed leeched of validity. Dilip had brought with him that other reality. Jodhpur was only a few hours' drive away, not a few weeks' walk. The world of cars, hotels, telephones, medicine and magazines superimposed itself upon the world of villages, walking, hunger, dacoits and deaths. Two worlds, two times, untouched by each other yet occupying equivalent space. To refuse to live in the safe one, the easy one, was mere stubbornness.

We headed out in the morning and despite the demands of the camera it was nice to be moving with people again. Bubbli ran to catch up with me for the first few hundred yards and that made everyone laugh. Ma took the lead with Parabu, leaning into him as if in conspiracy, her hips swinging, her son bending to catch her words. We walked about ten miles and camped in open ground. Two of my favourites, Shanti of the budding breasts, and Sina, her brother, came to sleep with me in the tent. They took off their shoes to enter, their voices dropped and their fingers grazed the orange nylon as if it were blown glass.

The following afternoon I left the dang so that I could be photographed walking through the Aravallis – a visual reconstruction of the previous weeks. I assured Ma that I would meet up with them on the way back but she was beside herself, insisting that I remain with them as far as Mount Abu road, that having met so fortuitously we should not part. We would be safer if we stayed together. (They were heading into dangerous hill tracts, where the odds of being robbed, kidnapped or murdered were uncomfortably high.)

Backwards and forwards for the photos. Stand still, turn, walk back the other way. The sun climbing, burning my nose, my brain. It was impossible for me to leave any part of myself open because out of that opening might come a flame of rage. We reached

263

Kukawas forest lodge in the evening and I went straight to bed. Fantasies of quitting and handing the noselines over to Dilip crowded the pillow. But of course I would go on, joylessly, angrily, propelled by the momentum of past decisions. Koju brought in the gin. I bade him sit and share a drink.

'No, Memsahib. Not while I'm on duty.' But he sat for a while and took a tiny sip. 'Are you all right, Memsahib?'

'I'm all right, Koju ji.'

On the way back to the dang, we passed one of the young shepherds on the road. When he learnt that I had decided not to continue with them, that this was in fact goodbye, he burst into tears and stood, unable to speak. We did our namashkars; he took my folded hands in his, then turned to tend his sheep.

When we entered the dang, everyone knew of my decision. Ma greeted me and threw down a camel-hair mat for me to sit on. I gave Shanti an embroidered purse which she had admired. She took it bemusedly and gave it back. 'It belongs to you now,' I said. It was as if I'd given her a pot of gold. I had one last cup of tea with all my friends sitting around me in silence. Ma tucked a strand of hair behind my ear and whispered something about Bhagwan. As I turned to go, she took my hand and kissed it twice on the top, twice on the palm, in the Rabari way.

22

Three days later we made camp at a well tucked under a banyan tree as full of worlds as the Quangle-Wangle's hat. A Rabari shrine – a little incense, some candleholders – was set into the knobbly bole around which was a mud-smoothed platform. A shepherd came twice every day to tend it. He was the great-grandson of the ancestor who, fifty years ago, chased an Adivassi who had stolen his buffalo to this very spot, where-upon the Adivassi had killed him with his bow and arrow. Beside the well was a vast talab (dam) and, behind that, the blue Aravalli hills.

The talab was empty but threaded through the green grass in its basin were strips of silver water. I took Zali for walks there. Cranes, spoonbills, ducks, dotterels, geese, plovers rose and sank as he dashed himself into the mud, skidded, flung himself backwards, leapt after a Saras crane twice his size, then turned flat out back to me, everything about him saying 'Look at me! Look at me!' I'd had one other dog who could match him for intelligence, cun-ning and charm. But none who could match him for beauty. I had not intended to fall for this dog as I knew when the journey was over, I would have to leave him. But Zali had never doubted that he could flirt his way into the Memsahib's heart. When the time came to leave him, I would miss him far more than he would miss me. And I liked him all the more for that. Zali was a survivor. A gypsy dog.

It was such a pretty place, we decided to rest there for a couple of days. Yet it was precisely in resting that I realized the extremity of my exhaustion, not just of body but of spirit. I had to keep going. I had to. But keeping going had no meaning.

On the second afternoon I noticed that Ram Rahim and Sumal were eating lantana.

'Don't let them eat it, Chutra,' I said. 'It is a noxious weed. I'm sure it can't be good for them.' But Chutra, as always, knew better.

That night I was woken by several men standing at the bottom of the cot. (Zali was sleeping under the blankets with me and continued to snore.) I could smell the grog on them from where I lay and they were very belligerent. 'Madam, madam, madam, madam!' shouted one until I could ignore them no longer. I sat up. There were about twenty of them, all carrying large heavy sticks. Suddenly little Chutra was there, puffed up like a frog and holding his stick with the axe on top. I decided to say nothing – it would be better that way – but I pulled the toy pistol out of my pack in an obvious sort of way. I was not even remotely frightened, just profoundly bored. Dilip came out of his tent looking like a B-52. He held a large stick behind his back. It was rather comic: the dumb princess sitting up in bed under the moonlight, the watchdog putting his nose into the cold air then pulling it back into the warmth, the chaps squaring off against each other. Comic and demeaning and ineffably stupid.

The first man said, 'I don't want any Christians here in India. We got rid of the Christians. They shouldn't live here.' After that he proceeded to poor scorn on the Rabari. They cut his trees, they stole his grass, they were dirty and cowardly and poor. We were to get out of this place if we knew what was good for us. Eventually, his steam released – and being frightened of Dilip who, bless him, would have scared the Devil – he left, taking his gundahs with him. I yawned loudly as he went, a pathetic revenge.

The next day we moved on to Pindwara, where the range forest officer, Mr Nayak Ali, offered us a cottage to stay in and to drive us around the forest under his jurisdiction. Nayak's job was not a happy one. There were fourteen grasslands under his care, the biggest of which was about two thousand acres. Keeping these available for pastoralists meant that the forest was under acute pressure. Some areas were closed for regeneration, which took five to ten years, and those were the areas most tempting to graziers: 'Illegal grazing is the main reason for the lack of success of regeneration and replanting. The problem is obvious. The cattle population is much too high for the available grassland.'

266

The regenerating areas were fenced or ditched in two-hundred-and-fifty-acre blocks. Each block had just one chaukidaar. If cattle were found in the grazing area, the department took the cattle to a compound and imposed fines on the owner. If the guard was a department employee and suspected of taking bribes, then a long process began, to fine him or take him to court. It was seldom worth it and the department chaukidaars knew they were fairly safe. However, most guards were local men who were paid very little, so they automatically took bribes as there was social pressure on them to do so from relatives or friends.

The graziers had to pay a small fee to the government to use the standing grass, then another for the cut grass. As this was an official drought year, the grass would not be contracted to outsiders but to departmental labourers, most of whom were Rabari and tribals, who would cut the grass for a set fee, then sell it at low cost to the graziers. There was no antagonism between Adivassis and Rabaris because each group had access to separate areas of the forest. Also the tribals here were fairly prosperous, whereas the Bhils in the hills through which we had just come were extremely poor. Their 'trade' was thieving because they had no other income.

Almost the whole population used wood from the forest for fire. By right locals could have as much dry wood as they could carry on their heads. But there was not enough for everyone, so people ring-barked trees or cut green wood and let it dry in the forest. Then they would come back a few weeks later and carry it out as dry wood.

All villages had access to certain areas for pasture but these had been open to grazing for a hundred years, so were not only barren, there was no seed left in the soil. The department took these areas for replanting but, understandably, this caused resistance. Where else could the people take their cattle in the meantime?

But the worst problem facing Nayak was corruption: 'If you get some profiteer cutting wood and putting it on a truck to sell, a political leader will want to settle it unofficially because the profiteer will either give money to him or promise vote banks. All the panchait and MLA members are involved. They have their own fieldworkers who tell them what's happening, then they come to

267

me or my men and say, "You do this or that and, if you don't, this or that will happen to you." If I try to prevent illegal woodcutting the political leaders will have me transferred and bring in their own puppet. Or they will make false complaints.' Had this happened to him in the past? Yes, he had been transferred from his previous position for just these reasons. I asked if it would be helpful for me to interview these men and to write about what they were doing, try to expose them. He smiled wryly, conferred with his officer, Balwan Singh, and said, 'It would be difficult just at the moment.' Nayak had learnt the hard way that he must compromise with power if he was to have any positive effect at all. I also suspected that this compromise had demoralized him. He worked eighteen-hour days but the frustration in him was souring into hopelessness: 'In front these politicians are very nice and clean, very white-clad people, but behind is something else. They are the main hurdle in our development in India. The corruption of politics has worsened in the last four to five years, along with communalism. I am a Muslim, so I know. There is none of it among my staff and very little from the Rabaris or the tribals, but from politicians, shopkeepers, traders – yes, there, communalism has taken root.'

On the way back Nayak took us to meet a Rabari bhopa who had a direct line to an ancestral deity Mama ji. This was a special day when people came to him with their problems to ask for intercession and advice. The bhopa was a most impressive-looking man – big, well-muscled and sleek, with wild grey hair and a psychoanalytic stare. His eyes were pale green. A handful of people clustered around the tiny temple. Men were allowed into the inner sanctum, an enclosure where the bhopa lit a fire in a little ghee lamp. Women remained just outside, looking in, and if we wanted to ask the bhopa something, we asked a man to intercede for us.

The bhopa began to shake and puff, hyperventilating himself into a trance. He snorted like a bull and the shaking looked epileptic. The old lady beside me murmured her reverence to the presence of Mami ji, who had entered the body of the bhopa. Suddenly he hit a cushion on to which he jumped from a cross-legged position, just as if he'd been thrown there by some mystic force. He banged himself on the back with a flat steel bar. In among the snorts, words began to form which people answered quietly, like a litany.

An old woman asked, 'My husband was ill and behaving strangely. He seemed to get better but last night he was worse. Will he become better?'

'I cannot answer you. You must bring this man to me, to my house.'

A man came forward with a gold necklace. The bhopa put grain in the man's hand, grunted a few words in between snorts. He then wheeled the gold around the ghee fire and again took a pinch of grain. 'Yes,' came the reply, 'the money you lost will be found. Don't worry.'

Our own guide, Balwan Singh, approached and touched the priest's legs. 'I want to leave my post and seek another. What should I do?'

The bhopa wafted peacock feathers over him and delivered the message. 'Wait for thirteen months. Then, if you still wish to go, you may do so.'

Nayak explained to me later. 'Balwan Singh works seven days a week and his job is not pleasant. There are no direct benefits that he can give to the people to convince them that our ideas are right and will help them in the end. I think a forest officer's job is the most difficult.'

I wanted to ask the bhopa's advice myself: Bhopa ji, tell me how I can get rid of this anger. But I did not. The bhopa went deeper into trance, then suddenly he was off his cushion and calmly winding on his turban as if nothing had happened.

When we returned Chutra informed me that Ram Rahim was refusing to eat. I feared my little favourite was poisoned but had no idea what I could give him other than a purgative. We hurried into Pindwara to buy drugs for him at a pharmacist's shop. But the shop wallah could not hear what I was saying to him because about two hundred schoolboys had gathered around my strangeness, and Chutra was threatening them with his stick and calling them half-minds. This only made the screeching more hysterical and Dilip, his veins standing out in his neck, chased and grabbed two of them and was tugging them towards me, yelling, 'Come on, touch her. See if she's real or a movie.' The woman next to me whispered through the window in her burqa that it was terrible and she was sorry. I shouted again to the shop owner but his attention was continually taken by the mob, or by the men who had begun to gather around, half-joining in the fun, half-scared of their own daring. Eventually I was given needles and some white viscous stuff but I could not bear to wait for the rest and, pulling my orni over my face, negotiated my way through the boys, who seemed not human but to constitute a pack, howling for my blood, tugging at my clothes. Dilip, realizing that protest was like petrol to the flames, waited till we got to the jeep before spitting out, 'You are monkeys, apes. You should all be shot!'

Inside the car Chutra said, 'Here public is very ignorant. Very half-mind. Rajasthan is a poor country. Not educated.'

I said nothing.

I was not looking forward to giving the injections to Ram Rahim. It would involve throwing the needle, thwack, into the animal's neck and he would not like it any more than I did. When we returned, he was sitting beside his food, munching. The entire incident at the pharmacist's had been unnecessary.

Perhaps, under different circumstances, I would have given the injections anyway. That would have been the sensible thing to do. But good sense requires its modicum of energy and when you have reached the dregs of your reserves, you tend to be abstemious. I crept into my room, closed shutters and door, lay down on the cot. The door opened. A young man simply stood there, staring as if I was a television set. I told him rudely to go away and instantly felt ashamed. I locked the door. I sank into the dark room where images of defeat swarmed inside my head like poisonous bees.

I kept returning to the rim of the talab where I had stood a couple of days before. It was evening. Below me, a thread of platinum wound through grass as short and lurid as poker-table baize and reached, in the far distance, to a white temple on the opposite rim. I waited there in the twilight and it was as if I were looking down on a miniature world. On the far side, the toy temple, and in the 'valley' toy oxen ploughing the green. Dotted here and there were tiny Rabari men with their sheep and goats. In the water, minute, exquisitely crafted birds. You could pick up the creatures below and inspect them on the palm of your hand.

The sun had set, leaving everything dusted in the soft pastel blues and pinks of Indian nights. To the left, a full yellow moon rose behind the mass of the Aravalli Ranges – blue collage against a violet sky. There were strange birdcalls, moonlight burnished the water. As the sky deepened, lights began to appear in the valley – the cooking fires of the Rabari. Slowly along the left-hand rim came a string of silhouetted bicycles. How impossibly beautiful it was.

Except that it was not beautiful at all. It was a lie.

Those fires, as romantic as fluttering candles from here, were in fact miserable and mean, made from a few bits of cow dung and whatever thorny sticks the men had scavenged from a landscape eaten down past dirt to stone. And those luminous clothes on the bicycle riders were really bits of grey rag hung on half-starved men stunted by work. The toy Rabaris with their toy animals, and their glowing red turbans, were lonely men living on goat milk and one roti a day, whose stomachs rumbled in the night, who would not see their families for months, who would be lucky to get their animals and themselves through the season. And the water, precious metal from here, in reality was poisonous with Guinea worm and disease, a malarial swamp. The mountain range beyond, dark voluptuous shapes, the holiest place in India some said, and I thought of the filth I had seen in its streams, of the Rabari women walking ten miles straight up with their urns on their heads, then ten miles back down to their village, every day of their lives, to supply milk to those vulgar and ugly hotels where people like Dilip and I might stay when we couldn't stand the discomfort any more.

The disgust I felt, the rage, was not at India but with humanity. If India was terrible, so was where I came from. Worse, because it was so spoilt, so comfortable, so oblivious and that comfort purchased at the expense of countries like this one. Each country leeching another and, within all the countries, groups of humans leeching other groups of humans down the pyramid, until you got to the very bottom, the little toy Rabari men. Fucked.

The anger chewed me up. I could not sleep at night with it.

There was nowhere to dump it. Everything I had done here was fraudulent and absurd. I knew nothing about the Rabaris and, even if I did, it would mean nothing to them, make no difference to them. I had understood nothing of where I was. And I would perpetuate the fraudulence by producing yet another useless artefact for western consumption, another bit of noise for a culture drowning in noise – an article for a glossy magazine with beautiful photos of beautiful India, beautiful noble Rabari, so that people could sit in comfort in their homes or doctors' waiting-rooms and not see. I loathed my initial romanticism more than my present incapacity to deal with reality. At least this had truth in it. At least, through the discomforts of my own body, through the exhaustion and illness and rage, I had an idea of how people really lived.

There is a theory dreamed up by some theoretical physicists that the universe spawns a multitude of new universes at every quantum decision. Sometimes it seemed as if I had made some wrong choice in my life and it had shunted me into one of these neighbouring universes, so that I was living in a world where I was not meant to be, which was eerily familiar but terribly wrong. Many elements were the same – camels, dog, photographer, journey. I was being condemned to repeat, but in a hellish distortion.

Next day we left Pindwara. Dilip and I scouted ahead for photo-sights and for a camping spot. There was a dry river-bed amidst boulders. At another time, in another place, I would have found it lovely, would have enjoyed sleeping in the sand, absorbing the warmth and goodness of earth, waking at dawn to birds and sky. But would we be protected from thieves? And if I were to go for a walk, wouldn't I, as always, be set upon by dogs or followed by the curious, or watched by suspicious, frightened faces, or stopped by a cactus fence and guarded gates, or ambushed by gundahs? The only duty left towards the magazine was getting some pictures of me with the camel-herding Rabari. We found a village where they lived, a week's walking distance away. Dilip could see no point in camping out meanwhile. Why didn't I drive back with him to Jodhpur, have a few days' rest, then ring him in Delhi and both return for the final shoot? The chaps could carry on without us to the meeting place.

On my previous journey through Australia, I absorbed the

rhythm of the world of walking, in which time and space are related to the human gait. Twenty miles is calculated by the movement of the sun, or the moon or the stars, or by how tired your legs have become, or by a mountain making its way towards you at a mountain's majestic pace, by increments of steps. On that journey there were no vehicles to remind me that, in the world I had left behind, twenty miles is equivalent to twenty minutes by car along a tarmac road. A world in which the landscape diminishes, recedes, becomes irrelevant to the same degree that the ancient human awareness of the relationship between space and time is broken.

This journey was reduced to kitsch, partly by the constant movement between the two worlds.

Dilip said, 'Rob, you look terrible. You look a hundred years old. For God's sake, come to Jodhpur with me. What difference would it make?' I could think of no difference that it would make. I climbed into the air-conditioned jeep and within four hours we were in Jodhpur. Four hours, or two weeks, depending on which world you inhabited.

The farm was pretty much deserted. I went to my little room, closed the door. Darkness, silence. In the morning I woke to find that I was deaf and there were lumps in my throat and armpits. And that there was a message for me. Ram Rahim was dead.

I waited for Koju and the jeep. The next afternoon, another message. Sumal was dead. Their deaths had been as agonizing as deaths could possibly be, the lantana poison spreading slowly through organs, culminating in the brain, causing fits of madness.

When we arrived, Dilip wanted to photograph me beside Sumal's body – a key picture, he said. I refused. Chutra had to pose instead. And crumpled into sobs. He had coaxed them, doctored them, watched them going mad, watched them die. Ram Rahim had died in a village compound. But the residents had refused to help him get rid of the carcass. It took another day to find some untouchables who would drag it away.

The following morning he and I walked together with Momal until the silence, which I had so often longed for, grew unbearable. I put my arm around his shoulder and told him it wasn't his fault.

273

Two one-eyed men, one deaf, the other weeping, leading a camel through nothing into nowhere.

By the time we reached Phalodi, Zali was listless and refusing to eat. Chutra and Koju both said it was nothing to worry about. Nevertheless, about this, I would finally assert myself. I would take him to Jodhpur to a vet, now, this minute. Dilip could stay and photograph the Holi festival without me.

Koju and I arrived in Jodhpur at four in the morning. We woke up a local vet who injected Zali half a dozen times. 'But will he survive?' I said. 'Oh, yes. He'll survive,' said the vet. 'No question.' The next morning the dog could barely walk. I took him to a veterinary hospital, where he once again received injections. Mornat came with me. When we got home to the farm, he said, 'I will give him some whisky. It is what we do with our dogs.' I knew it was the wrong thing to do and yet I let it happen. My will had run out. I watched as they held Zali on the ground, forced his mouth open and sent a shot of whisky into his stomach. I carried the dog into my room. He was unconscious. Two hours later he began convulsing. I yelled for Mornat and Koju. I ran to the jeep carrying the dog. But instead of driving out the gates, Koju took the track to the back paddock of the farm near Mornat's camp. 'What are you doing?' I screamed at them. 'We have to get him to the hospital.'

They dug the hole and inside it placed Zali's collar, lead, food bowl and blanket. Koju made me lower the dog. Mornat filled the hole. Koju lit some incense. Mornat tried to comfort me by saying that this was Bhagwan's will but I was hardly aware of him.

My hysteria had little to do with the dog's death. It was that the wretchedness, disgust and protest I had controlled for so long had found a vent.

The journey was over.

Coda

Three years have passed since then. I 'live' in England but whenever I'm there for too long I find myself longing for that other
place, those other people, and I return to India. I have mellowed
towards it in proportion to the new understandings I have gained
and, perhaps, as my life there has become more comfortable. I
remember the anger and distress but as if they belonged to someone else. And with the return of health I discovered that the
menopause had been a false alarm, so I still have that to look
forward to.

Koju has risen in the ranks and spends all his money on clothes.
His grin continues to delight my days. Chutra is working for
'Sahib' and has indeed built his mother a new house. Naturally, he
inherited Momal who terrorizes the whole village. We rarely see
each other which means that we can afford to like each other.
Mornat's people have begun working on the farm. They are
secure and making money. Khan ji, the genius, is hoping to
become a politician. I have made many new friends and through
them I have discovered a host of new Indias, Indias I had not
known existed. With each return I discover a new one which
contains memories of the previous ones, fixed, like props, from the
theatre of the past.

For a long time I could not see how to write about my experiences. They were nothing but a series of disconnected events,
without shape, without meaning. I had passed through India as a
knife does through ice and it had closed behind me at every step.
How does one write about failure?

And my inner censor was working overtime. The day after the
dog died, I had returned to Delhi and Narendra. I was more than a

little unbalanced and knew that above all I needed to talk, needed to find a sounding-board of like-minded people. From them I would be able to find a frame of understanding for what I was feeling. Because *they would understand*.

I invited an acquaintance to dinner and he brought a friend. Nice men – decent, liberal men. I had not had any alcohol in months and drank the Indian champagne like water. That was a mistake. I was bursting to speak but the politeness of the evening left no chinks. Narendra, as always, perceived my state of mind and every ten minutes or so endeavoured to bring me into the conversation. But the guests seemed to exist on a different wavelength. They were laughing, joking, as if the world outside the gates were not hell. They viewed that world, they had intellectual and political opinions about it, but they did not live in it. I do not remember what I said, or how I said it, but it soon became apparent to them that they had a madwoman on their hands and they were bewildered. In my incoherence I chose the example of the woman of Pipala who had almost died in childbirth with which to express my anger.

The second guest took immediate offence. He spat out, 'Our Indian women have been having their children in villages forever. We don't need your Christian compassion.' To which I might have replied that I did not think the capacity to imagine another's state was limited to Christianity, but was rather a universal human phenomenon. In any case, it wasn't compassion I felt but white hot rage. But I did not say so. I shut up because I understood, with sudden and appalling clarity, that what he saw when he looked at me was my whiteness. I was north, he was south. I was white, he was black. I was the colonizer, he the colonized. And what I saw, when I looked at him, was an example *par excellence* of the effete Delhi intellectual who had never walked more than fifty yards in his life, who had servants to cater to his every need, and whose wife did not bear her children on the floors of huts without midwife or doctor. This man was as alien to Pipala as I was. But at least I had been there.

When the second guest left, he said, with all the haughtiness of wounded pride, 'Please accept my apologies on behalf of my country.'

Failure.

The ethical imperative of siding with the powerless was all very well but who *were* the powerless? The doubts and self-questionings concerning my own prejudices, my own beliefs, meant that in the end I felt I had no right to say anything. I had been deconstructed. But dead or not the 'subject' had to write — and as truthfully as the distortions of memory would allow.

About two years afterwards, Narendra and I went back to Kutch to visit my Rabari friends. I had promised them a holiday and had planned to take them to Mount Abu for a feast. Koju would be there and Mornat, and Chutra too, and as many of the new friends I had made as could come.

First we went to Rangka bhai's village. He and Jasu were tending the flocks a few miles outside it. Jasu had had a son and Rangka was now a man of importance. In my memory of our first meeting, they were strong, powerful, good-looking people. Now I saw, with a shock, how thin they were, how little they had — and the desolation surrounding them. I had edited the hardship out of memory.

Rangka came with us in the jeep to look for Phagu's dang. But first we stopped at Parma's house. The Iron Virgin's hands shook as she pulled me to the floor beside her and there were tears in those unsentimental eyes.

'Ratti ben, you came all the way from Delhi just to visit *us*? You came from across the *sea* just to visit us? We thought you would leave us and never think of us again.'

'How could I forget you? Come with me in the taxi to the dang.'

'I cannot come, Ratti ben, but after you've seen Phagu, come back here and live with me.'

I mentioned the proposed trip to Mount Abu which delighted her, but then she looked hesitant. That would be a community decision.

It took a couple of days to find the dang — about fifteen camps spread out over gibber stones. Phagu's first words to me were, 'You're only a year and a half late!' And there we were, as tongue-tied, shy and grinning as teenagers. I had brought presents and piles of photographs. At first they were bemused by the

277

photographs, turning them upside down or sideways. But when I pointed out who was who, there was great excitement. I was taken from camp to camp and at every one I was greeted by hugs and the inevitable tea. I must have drunk forty bowls of the stuff that morning. Gelo said that if they'd known I was coming, they would have provided Coca-Cola to which they had become addicted. He laughed. 'When you travelled with us, we were unsophisticated people. Now we drink Coca-Cola just as the phoren do.' We spent the rest of the day reminiscing about my days on the dang. Everyone repeated the joke over and over of how, each time Phagu had asked me if I were tired, I would reply, 'Thori si, thori si' (Just a little, just a little). And they held their stomachs, laughing, or gave me one of those affectionate wallops.

That night I slept on Nakki's cot. I had forgotten what it was like to sleep, or rather not sleep, on a cot. With me were three women and a child. I had a Z-shaped depression in which to wedge my body. It was impossible to move. My feet stuck out the end. The women snored and threw their arms and legs across me. Goats jumped on me. I found myself punching them, just as I had always done; the patrolling shepherds giggled at me, just as they had always done.

The next morning Phagu explained that they would not be able to come to Mount Abu for the holiday because, 'All my sons, and so many other young men, have had to find other work. There is no future for them here. So there are only us old men left to guard the flocks. I would like to come with you, Ratti ben, but as you see I cannot leave the dang.' However, he extracted a promise that I would visit them every year.

It was time to leave. The old men came and sat around me in a circle. It was then I knew that I really had been brought into the fold because each of those stingy old bastards took a five rupee note from his turban and placed it in my lap. Phagu presented me with a puppy.

Two days later when I had said my farewells to my friends in the home village, to Jaivi and Parma and Lakhma and the others, Rangka took me aside, clasped my hands between his and said, 'To, parivaar hain?' (Are we family then?) To which I replied, 'Ham parivaar to hain.'

I will fulfil my promise to visit my 'family' each year, for as long as I am able, and I know that, on one of those visits, I will find that Phagu has decided that he has had no choice but to sell his flocks. And there will be Coca-Cola, and television, and no more wandering.

Recently I was in Delhi again. Narendra had invited two of our friends to a dinner. In the middle of it he said, 'My dear, I did not want to tell you this before because I knew you would worry. But I also knew you would find out from somewhere. I am telling you now, while Mohan and Suman are here, so they will help me to explain *why* you need not worry. Just before you arrived, there was a bit of a problem at Jodhpur farm. (I already knew that Narendra had been naming names in parliament and my anxiety for his safety had reached absurd proportions.) He continued, 'Seven hundred armed police ended up surrounding my farm as part of a political move to silence me.' My stomach fell to the floor. Mohan ji laughed. 'Robyn ji, if it had been *seven* armed police, *then* you would need to worry! That it was seven hundred is a kind of compliment to him.' Mohan ji himself had spent a couple of years in gaol during the Emergency. If I asked him about that time, he dismissed it as unimportant. It had been the expected outcome of taking a certain position. These people accepted that it was sometimes necessary to risk everything you had, including your life, for what you believed in. You didn't talk about it, it was simply a fact of existence.

And now all three of them, with a kindness and generosity that I have not found in any other place, were explaining things to me, tolerating my ignorance, caring for me in spite of it, allowing me inside the frame.

Until that night I had thought that it was my love for Narendra that connected me to India. He, and the world he created, *was* India to me. But after that dinner I understood that even if Narendra were to disappear from my life I would keep going back, that I would always go back, that part of me, at least, would want to belong there.

Because where I came from life wasn't hard enough, or dangerous enough, to demand greatness of individuals. There, greatness was still possible.

Besides, if the beauty I saw that evening on the rim of the talab
– the blue Aravalli mountains, moonlight on water, the silhouetted
bicycles, the fires of the toy Rabari men – could be broken down
into ugly elements, then the reverse was also true.